Pitt Series in

POLICY AND INSTITUTIONAL STUDIES

DEMOGRAPHIC
CHANGE
and the
AMERICAN FUTURE

R. Scott Fosler
William Alonso
Jack A. Meyer
Rosemary Kern

Published for the

Committee for Economic Development by the

University of Pittsburgh Press

Published by the University of Pittsburgh Press, Pittsburgh, Pa., 15260
Copyright © 1990, University of Pittsburgh Press
All rights reserved
Baker & Taylor International, London
Manufactured in the United States of America

Library of Congress Cataloging-in-Publication Data

Demographic change and the American future / R. Scott Fosler . . . [et
al.].
    p.   cm.—(Pitt series in policy and institutional studies)
    ISBN 0-8229-3638-0.—ISBN 0-8229-5431-1 (pbk.)
    1. Population forecasting—United States—Congresses. 2. Economic
forecasting—United States—Congresses. 3. United States—Economic
conditions—1981–   4. Social prediction—United States—Congresses.
5. Population—Economic aspects—Congresses. 6. Population—Social
aspects—Congresses. I. Fosler, R. Scott. II. Series.
HB3505.D46 1990
304.6'0973—dc20   89-40586
                                                                        CIP

Contents

Foreword

PROJECTED DEMOGRAPHIC trends confronting the United States are likely to require major adjustments in both public and private policies. Changes in age structure, family composition, income distribution, social groups, migration, and rates of growth both within the United States and abroad present a demographic pattern that will affect every major issue on the policy agenda. The Committee for Economic Development (CED), increasingly concerned about the scope and potential force of these changes, commissioned exploratory studies of their implications for policy.

The exploratory studies were prepared in four parts and concentrated on a broad range of economic, social, political, and institutional issues and the mismatches between current policies and the probable effects of projected demographic changes.

CED found the papers to be extremely helpful in organizing its plans for further study. We also found them of such high quality, and discovered that they generated such widespread interest and positive reaction, that we decided they should be published to reach a wider audience. We hope they will be helpful in encouraging more research and thoughtful analysis concerning the policy changes needed to respond effectively to projected demographic changes.

A project of this complexity and magnitude could not have been completed without the assistance of many individuals. In particular, I want to extend special thanks to CED trustees Clifton R. Wharton, Jr., chairman and chief executive officer of TIAA-CREF and Rocco C. Siciliano, former chairman of Ticor, for their skillful leadership of the CED Design Committee on Demographic Trends, and to other trustee members of that committee who worked diligently and most ably in the development of this volume. Appreciation is extended to R. Scott Fosler and Jack A. Meyer, project co-directors, for their significant contributions, to each of the authors mentioned above for their excellent work, and to Carol Alvey, CED administrative assistant, for her perseverance in conducting the processing of this document.

We gratefully acknowledge the Ford Foundation and the Alfred P. Sloan Foundation, whose generous support made this publication possible. The authors would also like to thank the many people who commented on their drafts, including: David D. Arnold, Gary T. Burtless, Daphne T. Greenwood, Sidney L. Jones, Marvin H. Kosters, Bruce K. MacLaury, Thomas E. Mann, Peter A. Morrison, Arnold H. Packer, Michael S. Teitelbaum, Barbara B. Torrey, and Ben J. Wattenberg.

This volume is being made available by CED as a framework for addressing the many concerns relating to projected demographic changes. It does not contain specific recommendations. It differs in that respect from CED policy statements, which do contain recommendations that have been voted on by CED's Research and Policy Committee and that also may contain dissents and reservations. Publication of this volume has been endorsed by the Research and Policy Committee as a fundamental and constructive perspective for ongoing consideration of the implications of demographic changes and is made available so that it may serve that purpose for others as well.

SOL HURWITZ
President
Committee for Economic Development

PART I

Introduction and Overview

Introduction

Demographic trends in the United States portray a population that is aging, having fewer children, becoming more ethnically diverse, living in smaller households, more likely to be unmarried, and residing and working in new geographical patterns.

These trends by now are quite familiar. But what do they really mean? How much validity is there to the old adage: "Demography is destiny"?

Demography certainly plays a powerful role in shaping the social context, but it does not preordain the future. Demographic forces are significant not so much in their own right, but rather in the way they interact with other forces—economic, social, political, technological, and environmental. Nor do the consequences of these interacting forces have to be passively accepted. Action can be taken to prepare for them, and in some instances even to alter them.

Some of the demographic forces affecting the United States are favorable, some are unfavorable, and some are essentially neutral in their impact. But their net direction and momentum add up to major challenges both at home and abroad. They suggest present and future conditions significantly different from those of the past, and sharply at odds with prevailing policies.

In the international sphere, demographic factors will tend to reinforce other trends that are creating a more complex and interdependent world—one increasingly beyond U.S. control, as conventionally defined. In the domestic sphere, the net demographic impact could well cramp our productive capacity and add to social and political tensions. A lot depends on how we prepare for these unfolding developments.

In both the domestic and international spheres, demographic pressures will undoubtedly mount gradually through the end of the century, providing a narrow window of opportunity for appropriate action to prepare for the even greater challenges ahead. For

3

early in the next century, the pressures associated with demographic trends will almost surely accelerate with heightened impact. The gap between demographically associated costs and the capacity to cover them, already evident, is likely to widen further. Without appropriate action, the cumulative stress of this widening "cost-capacity gap" could take a heavy toll.

The purpose of this volume is to examine both the growing stresses and the opportunities for action, and to consider their policy implications. The discipline of demography is used in this exercise in three ways: (1) for analysis—as a source of basic information and diagnosis; (2) for synthesis—as a context and integrating mechanism for understanding the relationship among interdependent forces; and (3) for prediction—as a comparatively reliable means of anticipating future developments. The study does not simply project a series of demographic trends, nor does it focus on demographic factors alone. Rather, its intent is to use demography as a way of better understanding the interaction among numerous forces, and the relationship among the various policies with which they are associated.

The volume is organized in the following manner. The remainder of this section summarizes the demographic trends and the principal lines of argument of the volume. In part II, William Alonso discusses demography from the perspective of one who has dealt broadly with policy concerns. He portrays a world of deep and highly interdependent demographic currents that flow with and through other currents of human activity. The distinctions among these flows are not neat. It is the special task of the demographer to document demographic trends in analytic and statistical language that informs without doing violence to the reality that those trends can only hint at. Alonso undertakes this task for the basic demographic character of the U.S. population, and urges us to approach these and all other demographic analyses with "respectful skepticism."

In part III, Jack A. Meyer and Rosemary Kern consider the economic and social implications of demographic trends. Their central analytic concern is the cost implications for federal social programs of the changing U.S. age structure. However, their purpose in demonstrating the simultaneously alarming but highly uncertain cost impact on American society is to argue the importance of a more systemic and longer-term policy approach to these issues. In particular, they stress the importance of a "life-cycle" perspective on preparing America's workforce—from the newborn to the elderly—for a competitive global economy.

In part IV, I address the political and institutional implications of demographic change. Special attention is given in this part to the implications of global population dynamics. The political and institutional challenge is that the same demographic forces likely to create stress will directly affect the very foundations of the institutions struggling to cope with that stress. But the central question, posed in parts II and III and reinforced in part IV, is not what demographic trends we confront—whether favorable or unfavorable—but how we choose to deal with them.

Since the various parts deal with many of the same demographic trends from different perspectives, there is some overlap in the material covered. An effort has been made to minimize the redundancy, but our principal interest has been to retain the integrity of each piece, to promote the different slants of perspective, and thereby to adhere to the headline caution of this volume that demographic data and projections are imperfect and must be treated with "respectful skepticism."

CHAPTER 1

Implications of
Current Demographic Trends

T HE MAJOR demographic trends affecting the United States have been widely publicized in recent years, and they will be examined in greater detail throughout this volume. But to summarize the discussion, let us highlight them here and attempt to synthesize the wide range of policy implications.

Major Demographic Trends

The U.S. population of 245 million people in 1988 is growing slowly, at a rate of less than 1 percent a year. The fertility rate of 1.8 births in each woman's lifetime is below the replacement level of 2.1. If these trends persist, the American population is projected to level off and begin to decline about the middle of the next century, even allowing for substantial immigration.

People are living longer, and the U.S. population as a whole is aging. In 1985, there were 28.5 million people age 65 and over, or 12 percent of the total population. The elderly population is projected to increase slowly in number and as a proportion of the total population for the next twenty years, reaching an estimated 13 percent in 2000, and 14 percent in 2010.

The dominating age group in the American population continues to be the 77 million people of the baby boom generation born between 1946 and 1964. This group is now fully in their working years, and will continue to dominate the work force until they start to retire. For some, that could begin as early as the year 2000 when the first baby boomers begin to turn 55.

But in 2010, when the baby boom generation starts turning 65, the proportion of elderly people is projected to soar, rising to 17 percent of the total population by 2020, and 21 percent by 2030. During the same period, the working-age population is expected actually to decline.

The United States is also becoming more racially and ethnically diverse. In 1984, blacks and Hispanics accounted for an estimated 19 percent of the total population, a proportion that is projected to rise to 35 percent by 2020. If these trends are sustained, at some time during the next century non-Hispanic whites will join blacks, Hispanics, and Asians as a minority of the total U.S. population.

The composition of American households is also strikingly different from that of the past. Only half of U.S. households in 1984 consisted of married couples, compared with three-quarters in 1950. Single-person households accounted for nearly 25 percent of all households in 1984, up sharply from 10 percent in 1950. Average household size plummeted from 3.7 people in 1960 to 2.7 in 1984.

Important as these domestic trends may be, they reflect the demographic gyrations of only a fraction—4.6 percent—of the world's population, a share that is projected to shrink further. In part because it has only a small share of world population, the United States could be far more significantly affected by global demographic forces in the future.

The world population reached 5 billion people in 1987, up dramatically from 2 billion in 1932. The annual rate of growth in world population has slowed from over 2 percent in the 1960s to 1.7 percent today. But even at the lower rate, the world continues to add 84 million people each year, and is likely to double its population to 10 billion late in the twenty-first century before leveling off.

In about half of the world, the population is growing rapidly, at a rate above 2 percent per year. But in the other half—including the entire industrial world as well as China and most of East Asia—population growth has slowed to less than 1 percent per year. Some countries, such as Germany and Denmark, have actually been losing population.

The world population as a whole is aging, and the number of elderly people in all countries is growing. But the industrial countries are aging far more rapidly than the Third World, and many, such as Germany and Japan, are aging far more rapidly than the United States. Meanwhile, many Third World countries have huge young populations that are beginning to move into their adult years.

Each of these trends has important implications. But even more significant is how they interact with one another and with nondemographic forces.

The Economic and Social Connection

Contrary to popular perceptions, the so-called dependency ratio of predominantly dependent (young and old) to predominantly working-age groups in the United States has been narrowing. In 1960, out of every 100 people, there were 83 between the ages of 18 and 64. That ratio fell to 63 in 1982, and by 2010 is expected to fall further to 58 per 100 persons.

But whether this trend will be translated into tangible financial and economic benefits depends on three other factors: the actual number and per capita support costs of the nonworking population; the size and productivity of the labor force; and the magnitude of other claims placed on the nation's productive resoures. Demographic forces affect each of these factors as well.

Because the number of elderly will rise slowly until 2010, the additional number of Social Security recipients (as distinguished from the level of benefits they receive) is not likely to be a major cost pressure for the next two decades. The more immediate source of increases lies in the rising cost of health and long-term care, especially for the rapidly growing number of people 85 and over who have by far the greatest need for medical and long-term care. This group numbered 2.7 million in 1985, and is projected to nearly double to 4.9 million in 2000, and to reach 6.6 million by 2010.

On balance, the elderly population is substantial, and it will continue growing, but not—for the next 20 years—at a rate that would seem to be unmanageable for a productive workforce.

The key question is how productive that workforce will be. Productivity and economic capacity are affected by numerous factors: the size, skills, and motivation of the work force; saving rates and capital investment; knowledge and technology; entrepreneurial drive; consumer demand; and a host of associated governmental policies. Demography affects several of these factors, especially the size and composition of the labor force.

The working-age population, which grew by only 1 percent per year in the 1950s, accelerated to a 1.8 percent annual growth rate in the 1960s and early 1970s as the baby boom population moved fully into their working years. The steady increase in the percentage of women entering the work force accelerated growth further to 2.5 percent per year by the late 1970s and early 1980s. However, growth in the work force has once again fallen to 1.5 percent per year, because the baby boomers have moved beyond the work entry years, because the number of 18- to 24-year-olds is declining, and because the growth in women's participation has slowed.

Still, as the baby boomers mature, the prime working-age population will increase by 21 million by 1995, when it will account for three-quarters of the total workforce. This could be a boon to productivity, if workers' skills are applicable to new jobs in competitive industries, or if workers upgrade their skills and adjust to new economic circumstances. If, instead, maturing workers become less flexible in adjusting to a rapidly changing economy and work place, or refuse to move in order to obtain better jobs, the aging of the work force could prove to be a drag on productivity.

Meanwhile, the number of younger workers is declining and adding to the labor squeeze in some industries and regions. Not only will the number of younger workers continue to decline through the end of the century, but also that smaller group could contain a higher proportion of poorly prepared workers. Some 57 percent of the net additions to the work force between 1986 and the year 2000 are projected to come from minority groups, including those with the highest proportion of educationally disadvantaged children.

The growing number of educationally disadvantaged children, by some estimates as high as 30 percent of all school-age children, is also associated with changes in family structure. Children from single-parent homes have a higher incidence of school-related problems. The increase in female heads of households is associated with the growing number of children living in poverty, who also are more likely to perform poorly or drop out of school.

The problems of the educationally disadvantaged, therefore, could become a major cost burden. Failure to deal with these problems effectively could result in a future workforce that is not only smaller but less productive, at the same time that the burden of elderly support is growing. Moreover, the higher proportion of disadvantaged children is certain to produce a higher proportion of teenagers and adults who require remedial training, public assistance, or other public programs.

The Global Context

Demographic forces in the international sphere are likely to increase pressures on the United States in several ways.

The work forces of Africa, Asia, and Latin America are projected to grow by some 700 million over the next 20 years, adding an *increment* of workers equal to the *total* workforce of the industrial countries in 1985. This surge of new workers could spur world demand and economic growth, but it could also put additional competitive pressure on the industrial countries.

Failure to provide jobs for these young workers in their homelands could create serious social and political problems, and added pressure for migration, especially to the United States. For example, Mexico will add about 1 million people to its workforce each year during the 1990s. Even if Mexico were to achieve a job growth rate of 3 percent per year, by the year 2000 it would still have 8 million unemployed workers—nearly 20 percent of its labor force.

In the regions of the world still experiencing rapid population growth, economic stagnation and population pressures can combine to aggravate the problems of unemployment, hunger, deterioration of the natural resource base, and social and political unrest. Such conditions pose threats to areas of American strategic interest, especially in Central America and the Middle East.

Among the regions of slow population growth, by contrast, many nations have increased their productivity and narrowed the economic gap with the United States. As a consequence, U.S. economic strength has declined relative to some other countries. Whereas the United States accounted for 40 percent of world Gross National Product (GNP) in 1950, it has about 22 percent of world GNP today. The demographic interaction here involves a simple but important arithmetic proposition: if and as the productivity of nations converges, the relative output of those nations will tend to become more closely aligned with relative population size. And with technology and capital more quickly transferable than ever before, the tendency toward productivity convergence could be pronounced among countries that have passed a threshold of economic capacity. This does not mean that growth in U.S. productivity inevitably must lag behind that of other countries; in fact, there is no reason why it could not grow faster. Many other countries, after all, confront demographic and other challenges far greater than those confronting the United States. But to the extent that other countries can learn from America's technological lead, or otherwise take the technological lead themselves, the United States' per capita economic advantage will be eroded.

Such a change has two important implications. One is that the United States thereby has less of an economic advantage in pursuing its foreign policy interests. It might compensate for this lost advantage in other ways—for example, by increasing its allocation of resources to foreign policy pursuits, by more skillfully using the resources at its command, or by shifting resources from consumption into investment, in order to strengthen its economy.

The second and potentially more far-reaching implication is that no other nation may have the combined population, economic, and political weight to stabilize and provide momentum for the international economic system—the role of the United States for the past half century. It is unlikely that Japan, with half the population of the United States, or West Germany, with half the population of Japan, could amass an economic and political weight that would permit either to exercise world economic leadership alone, even if its productivity surpassed that of the United States. The fact that the populations of both countries are aging more quickly than than of the United States makes that eventuality even less likely. In consequence, unless the international economic system finds a new center of gravity and a new formula for leadership, the likelihood of instability is increased.

The United States' relative decline in its share of the world economy does not necessarily jeopardize its strategic position with respect to the Soviet Union, which has a far smaller economy and whose share of world GNP is also shrinking. Nor are demographic forces likely to alter that strategic relationship. The Western democracies contain 15 percent of the world's population, compared with 8 percent for the Soviet Union and Eastern Europe. And while the population of the USSR is growing somewhat faster than that of the United States, the bulk of that growth is occurring in the Muslim Soviet republics, a fact that gives Kremlin leaders more pause than pleasure. Moreover, the shifting alliances within and between the NATO and Warsaw Pact countries, associated with *perestroika* and the domestic economic and political changes occurring in the Soviet Union and Eastern European countries, should be a reminder that the demographic alignment among nations as a strategic factor is dependent on the strength of political alliances and economic relationships.

But whatever the demographic balance between East and West, far more important will be the shifting demographic weight between North and South.

All of the present industrial countries together—socialist and capitalist—contain less than a quarter of the world's population, a share that is projected to shrink further to 20 percent early in the next century. Demographically, the United States is a small and shrinking national minority, within a shrinking Western minority, within a shrinking industrial (as traditionally defined) minority of the world's population.

The Political and Institutional Connection

These domestic and global trends pose difficult policy choices. In both spheres, the trends tend to increase costs for the United States more than they expand capacities. The widening cost-capacity gap will necessitate political decisions in order to restrain costs, expand capacities, or adjust to the consequent stress.

The outlines of the major policy choices are reflected in the composition of the U.S. federal budget. Between 1980 and 1985, spending for both elderly programs and defense increased substantially, squeezing out other domestic programs. One consequence has been a de facto shift of responsibility for nonentitlement domestic programs to state and local governments. For the past three years, growing concern over the budget deficit has resulted in a curtailment of real growth in defense spending, while programs for the elderly have continued to expand. In 1988, about 29 percent of federal appropriations were allocated to elderly programs, 29 percent to defense and international affairs, and 15 percent to pay the interest on the national debt. The remaining 27 percent included all other programs: support for the poor, grants to state and local government, and all other executive branch agencies.

Programs for the elderly under current benefit levels are projected to absorb a growing proportion of the budget, rising from 30 to 36 percent of the total federal budget by 2010, according to one estimate. There are five options for dealing with the demographically driven expansion of spending on elderly programs (excluding default on interest payments on the debt). These are to reduce spending for defense or other domestic programs; expand the total budget and finance that expansion by tax increases or risk higher deficits; strengthen the economy so that these additional costs can be absorbed without budget cuts or tax increases; reduce benefit levels or tighten eligibility requirements for elderly programs; or some combination of the above.

Each of these choices has serious implications for the well-being of individuals and for national security. It should be stressed that the tradeoff is not necessarily between spending for the elderly and for everything else; the point is that the demographics of aging will drive the budget and force the choice.

Demographic forces are not only posing difficult policy choices. They are also affecting the structure of political institutions that are responsible for making those decisions. Some demographic forces are altering the political arithmetic: in particular, the proportion of elderly and minority-group voters is increasing. But these and other factors are also affecting the political culture of the United States, for example, by increasing age consciousness with respect to spending on programs for the old and young. Tension between the generations could also have an ethnic and racial dimension; by 1995, only 8.5 percent of the 65 and over population will be black, while 17 percent of children under five will be black. In addition, increasing demographic diversity in general appears to be reinforcing the inclination for people to identify with narrower personal and group interests at the expense of broader common goals. Changes in family structure could also have important political ramifications, in part because the family is a training ground for social and political behavior and a paradigm for other institutions.

The 1990s—A Window of Opportunity

The policy choices posed by demographic changes in the immediate future, challenging though they may be, are relatively easy ones compared to those the United States will confront early in the next century, when the large baby boom generation begins to retire. Beginning in 2010, the cost of programs for the elderly is expected to soar, rising by one estimate to 50 percent of the federal budget by 2030.

Twenty years from now, the United States' position in the world could be dramatically changed. As additional countries learn to apply the technology of the industrial world, populous regions of the Third World can be expected to increase their overall weight in international affairs. For the United States to continue to exercise its accustomed international role will likely require a far higher commitment of resources to foreign affairs and economic investment, precisely at the time when the cost of supporting its elderly population soars.

An equally important question is whether a progressively aging U.S. population, confronted with increasingly vigorous and technically skilled populations abroad, will engage that world or draw steadily back into itself, expressing a preference for consumption and relative comfort and security over investment.

It is on this point more than any other that the demographic window of opportunity of the 1990s poses a major choice. If the United States cannot deal with the relatively mild political choices it confronts in the last decade of this century, when the bulk of its population will be in their most vigorous and productive years, how will it deal with the far more formidable challenges in the early part of the next century when the number and proportion of its elderly population rises dramatically, while its working-age population stabilizes or actually shrinks?

The Policy Response

The trends summarized above, and others discussed in greater detail in this volume, portray a world that is changing far more quickly and profoundly than most Americans recognize. In fact, they reflect dramatic changes that have already occurred, but have yet to be fully appreciated. Many of these changes are incompatible with existing policies and with traditional approaches to policymaking. The question is whether Americans will act to turn these forces to their best advantage or simply be swept along with them. From a demographic perspective, there are three kinds of adjustment in policy that can be made.

ACCOUNTING FOR INTERDEPENDENCE

First, there is a need to integrate policies that deal with interdependent forces. For example, the long-term viability of the Social Security system depends not just on the marginal adjustment of payroll tax and benefit formulas or on ways of accounting for Social Security "surpluses," but more fundamentally on changing dependency ratios, immigration, worker productivity, the education of disadvantaged children, demographic trends and economic policies in other countries, and the political cohesion among American generations. And yet, if these factors are treated at all, our policy debates and institutions treat each of them largely as independent and isolated issues, and certainly outside the context of the Social Security debate.

The integration of policy also has an important geographical dimension that is frequently ignored. The dynamics of population are no respectors of political boundaries. Important economic and social decisions are made in the context of regions that are smaller than the nation, yet are broader than local political jurisdictions and frequently cut across state lines. People travel, resettle, and do business among subnational regions throughout the world. Consequently, for many purposes national political institutions are too far removed to provide the detail of attention required in specific regions and localities, and yet too narrow in their geographical coverage to account for the flows over national boundaries.

For most of this century, the United States has exercised predominant power in the world, and the federal government has exercised predominant political power within the United States. This convergence of power in Washington has obscured the extent to which demographic and other forces have moved beyond the reach of the nation's capital, both in subnational and international directions. Political institutions will need to develop the capacity to deal effectively with problems at the world, national, and subnational levels.

LIFE-CYCLE PLANNING

Second, there is a need to restore a sense of appropriate timing to policy thinking and action. Policy decisions are driven (or impeded) by the political dynamics of crisis and by election and budget cycles. The demographic perspective, by contrast, focuses on a time horizon that is more in keeping with the important forces that affect people's lives, and with the collective life of the society as a whole.

Consider that a child who entered the first grade in 1988 will graduate from high school in the year 2000. We know from extensive research that that child's ability to learn, find employment, and become a productive member of society already has been strongly determined by social, economic, and ethnic characteristics. Consequently, the generation of new workers who will determine American competitiveness after the turn of the century, and will begin paying for the baby boomers' retirement in 2010, has already started to be trained. Meanwhile, the medical payments those children will make as adults to keep the retired baby boomers healthy and cared for is being determined right now by the diet, exercise patterns, work habits, and environment of the 21- to 41-year-old age group.

A life-cycle perspective would have us ask what can be done at each stage of life to facilitate healthy, productive, and independent lives for individuals and impose the least cost on society as a whole. This would mean, for example, assuring proper prenatal care for pregnant women, and high-quality preschool education for educationally disadvantaged three- and four-year-olds. By one estimate, every dollar spent on such programs will save $4.75 in future costs of unemployment, drug rehabilitation, and incarceration. Assuring a workforce capable of supporting an expanding elderly population means high-quality elementary and secondary education for all children, reducing school dropout rates, and promoting educational attainment that will lead to higher education or productive employment.

Life-cycle planning would also recognize productivity during the working years as the key to providing adequate support for the elderly without placing an undue burden on workers. The personal saving of workers during their productive years, moreover, will also determine their degree of dependence when they retire. Preventive health care during the working years would not only restrain medical costs and enhance productivity, but would also minimize the need for health care when workers retire.

Finally, the life-cycle approach would recognize that the key to facilitating healthy, satisfying, and independent lives for the elderly begins with the degree to which the elderly are capable of caring for themselves. The longer the elderly stay employed, and the longer they remain financially self-supporting, the more likely they are to stay healthy and emotionally independent. Providing meaningful and emotionally nourishing activity in retirement is not only desirable in itself, but also important to maintaining good health and thereby minimizing costs for medical and long-term care.

TARGETING POINTS OF STRESS AND OPPORTUNITY

A third need is to target more precisely critical points of stress that require policy attention so as to avoid problems, and key points of opportunity where minimal investments can be leveraged into high yields of return. The demographic perspective can help in this exercise as well.

Key points of stress *already* in evidence include the following:

- Rising health care costs for the rapidly increasing old elderly (over 85);
- A shrinking and inadequately prepared pool of young workers;
- A chronically unemployed or underemployed underclass;
- A mismatch between increasingly global economic and environmental interdependence and the fragmented political jurisdiction of nation-states.

Future stress points that can be readily anticipated include:

- The rising number of educationally disadvantaged children who could further swell the ranks of the underclass and debilitate the workforce;
- The mismatch between subnational political jurisdictions and the new patterns of urban and regional development;
- A surge of young workers entering the labor force in the Third World, including many with little prospect of employment;

- The rising economic, military, and political power of populous countries in the Third World;

- The skyrocketing projected number and proportion of elderly people after the year 2010;

- The rapid increase in the proportion of elderly populations among our principal allies and trading partners, especially Japan and Germany.

Not all of the demographic changes to be anticipated cause stress. Some create *opportunities* that can be leveraged into significant benefits, if appropriate action is taken soon enough. These include:

- Slower population growth in many countries that could lessen pressure on natural resources and facilities;

- Declining pupil enrollments in some regions that might permit more resources to be concentrated on fewer students;

- A declining number of workforce entrants that could mean more job opportunities, less unemployment, higher wages, and greater likelihood that employers will seek to remedy the deficiencies of those who have been educationally disadvantaged;

- A more mature and experienced workforce that, with appropriate skill upgrading and flexibility in employment, could lead to higher productivity;

- A particularly high-leverage opportunity in extending the years of productive employment for older workers; this could have the quadruple advantage of easing labor shortages, increasing the tax base, reducing Social Security costs, and sustaining the personal activity and independence of older Americans.

Part of the challenge in dealing with these trends, however, is that they do not occur in isolation, but in combination, and interact with other forces. Nor is the responsibility for taking action to deal with these sources of stress and opportunity highly focused; rather, responsibility falls across a range of major institutions and groups:

- *Decision makers who determine U.S. foreign policy* will confront stark choices with respect to the cost of pursuing U.S. strategic objectives, and of exercising leadership to improve the ability of the international system to cope with the new realities of global interdependence.

- *The federal government* will in turn have to make difficult choices in allocating resources among defense and international affairs, elderly and other entitlement programs, and investment in future economic capacity.

- *State and local governments* will bear an increasing responsibility for government services, including the need to adjust to widely diverse regional demographic profiles.

- *The workforce* will continue to be reconstituted by such demographic forces as aging, changing gender roles, new family structures, and immigration.

- *Educational institutions* will not only bear responsibility for understanding and instructing people about these changes, but also have to adapt to fluctuating student enrollments and other demographic changes.

- *The civic culture* will be challenged to synthesize the diverse goals and values of assertive individuals and groups into a cohesive social agenda and code of behavior.

- *The personal responsibility and adaptation of individuals* will be required in numerous ways, both private and public, as individuals forge new patterns of relationships more attuned to the changing social realities.

It should be underscored that the demographic trends presented here do not constitute the destiny of the United States. But, taken together, they suggest a challenging context in which America must act to determine its own destiny.

PART II

Demography and the U.S. Population

Introduction

Demography may or may not be destiny, but it has certainly become fashionable. *Two decades ago the emergence of the rock and acid culture, rising crime rates, and the Vietnam War protests were attributed to the demographic bulk, and hence the power, of the then young baby boomers. In recent years demographic topics have been everywhere: the baby boom's progress through the labor force and housing; the aging of the population; the baby bust; the feminizing of the labor force and of poverty; growing numbers of illegitimate births; the stunning increase in childless households; the effects of changes in the composition of the labor force on productivity and the United States' competitive position in international markets; the marriage chances of women; immigrants legal and illegal, and refugees; the rural renaissance; white flight; urban gentrification; black suburbanization; migration to the Sun Belt; and, most recently, muted fear that death may return, after seemingly being domesticated, in the form of an AIDS pandemic.*

These are important matters, worthy of concern. A specialized network of print and electronic publications has emerged to meet the information and marketing needs of business and of the welfare state. But demographic statistics have become, in their own way, the equivalent of beautiful people: they are often the subject of sensationalism, of exaggeration, of speculation, of half truths. Television, the daily press, and intellectual journals routinely carry items about them. Information, opinion, moral judgments, predictions, and plain snake oil are all jumbled together.

The remainder of part II will address aspects of the interrelations of demography and policy. Chapters 2 and 3 will try to provide some perspective on the welter of demographic facts and half truths. Chapter 2 argues that the main demographic aspects of American society, from illegal immigration to the decline of the traditional family, far from being a random collection of arresting but independent phenomena, are in fact diverse facets manifesting our socioeconomic structure, and are related one to another and cannot be treated independently. Chapter 3 discusses some of the technical and intellectual limits of demography as a tool for understanding and for prediction, and urges respectful skepticism in the face of the apparent quantitative rigor of this discipline, especially for the diagnosis of problems and the formulation of policies.

Chapter 4 displays and discusses the principal population projections made recently by the U.S. Bureau of the Census, trying to summarize the key differences and common threads among these alternatives, and looks closely at alternative projections of the age distribution. It also explores the geographic variation that hides under the umbrella of national trends and averages, with emphasis on the experience within metropolitan areas and in nonmetropolitan areas, and on the diversity among regions of the United States.

CHAPTER 2

The Connectedness and
the Limits of Demography

Too often demographic issues are treated in isolation when in fact they are related. For instance, in recent years there has been much concern about the long-term solvency of the Social Security system and the burden this may place on those of working age in the future. In parallel, there has also been much concern about the number of asylum seekers, refugees, and illegal immigrants entering the United States. Yet the discussions of these two issues have been conducted, as it were, in separate rooms. In the Social Security debate, the population projections almost universally assumed that the level of immigration would hold to the legal limit of 450,000 per year. Yet it was clear that many more people were entering the country each year, and that this trend would likely continue into the future. Whatever other consequences this additional immigration might have, since immigrants (legal or illegal) tend to be young, it plainly would increase the future ratio of working-age population to the elderly, and thus reduce the old-age dependency burden. Yet this link was seldom made, and the discussions of Social Security and immigration reform went their independent ways.

This is not to suggest that unrestricted immigration is the solution to the problems of Social Security. Rather, it illustrates the interconnectedness of the major demographic issues in industrialized countries such as the United States. These demographic issues are deeply interwoven (result and cause) with the very structure and dynamics of national life, and with the place of the United States in the world. The links between old-age security and immigration, for instance, go well beyond the arithmetic of the future ratio of workers to old people. They are intrinsic to a prosperous advanced industrial society, where people are long-lived and have few children, where it is accepted that there is a social obligation to provide for the economic well-being of the elderly, and where the national prosperity creates certain labor shortages and serves as a magnet for migrants from less-advanced countries.[1]

23

Every important aspect of the U.S. demographic situation is linked to every other, including the divorce rate and low fertility, the growth of the labor force, illegal immigration and refugees, the Social Security situation, and the extraordinary rate of illegitimate births among blacks. Equally, these demographic factors are intimately related to the evolution of our economic and social system, in matters such as the savings rate, the modernization of the South, the shift to a service economy, the gentrification of central cities, and the rate of advancement of employees within organizations. Finally, they are also closely related to the economic and geopolitical position of the United States in the world at large, in such terms as the emerging world division of labor, U.S.-Soviet geopolitical competition, and technological advances in agriculture and medicine.

The purpose of this chapter is to suggest the nature of this connectivity and the pervasiveness of demography. It will not try to be exhaustive; rather, it will present some organizing ideas and illustrative relations.

Integration and Development

The economic development of modern nations is most commonly associated with two aspects of rationality: that of science and its applications, and that of economic processes, whether imposed by central planning or by the discipline of the market. A third aspect of rationality is also necessary for development, namely, that of integration.

The concept of integration refers to the capacity for productive interaction among the elements of a national or international system. It most obviously includes the facilitation of exchanges across time and space, through improved transportation and communications, through technologies to preserve perishables, and through institutional developments such as efficient financial and futures markets, and systems of currency, measurement, and laws. Integration also implies reducing the inefficiencies caused by making distinctions without a difference: if a person can do a job, it is inefficient to deny it because of sex or color, just as it would be inefficient to treat identical sacks of wheat differently according to who grew them.

In this straightforward sense, we can see that many of the social and economic developments of American society are elements of a continuing (though still incomplete) process of integration. These developments include the civil rights movement, the diminishing difference in occupations between men and women, the convergence of incomes among the nation's regions, or the year-round availability of most fruits and vegetables.

But integration is not only domestic. The growing integration of the world economy has meant a new level of competitiveness, new meanings of comparative advantage, and new modes of economic specialization for countries and regions within them. Between the older industrialized countries and those of the Third World, a set of newly industrializing countries is emerging and changing the face of world trade in manufactured products. This is transforming the world geography of economic specialization, and leads to the oxymoron of the "industrialized" countries entering something often called a postindustrial phase or becoming service economies.

There is wide debate as to what this worldwide specialization of labor means. In the United States, employment in goods production (agriculture and manufacturing) has declined steadily for decades relative to employment in the service sector. On the other hand, total product of these goods-producing sectors has continued to grow in absolute terms. Thus the degree of America's economic specialization looks different if looked at from a labor or value-added point of view. But in either case the trend is clear: the American economy is moving toward service industries as part of international specialization.

Important demographic consequences follow from such integration in its national and international dimensions.

Fertility, the Family, and the Economy of Advanced Countries

A good starting point is the stunning fact that not one of the industrialized countries has today a rate of reproduction sufficient to replace its population.[2] The statistic that most effectively conveys this situation is the Total Fertility Rate (TFR). This is the total number of children which a hypothetical average statistical woman would have if she went through life having children at exactly the fertility prevailing at various ages. The rate of 2.1 is a key one, the one at which the woman would reproduce herself: one boy, one girl, and an allowance for early death. Below that value in the absence of immigration, the population would decline in the long run; above, it would grow.

The United States' TFR has oscillated around 1.8 by no more than .08 since the early 1970s. This seems low by some criteria, and is less than half the rate of 3.69 that prevailed in the heyday of the baby boom (1955–59). And it does not seem, at least at first, too different from the "middle" rate of 1.9 which the Bureau of the Census uses for the projections which will be reviewed in a later section of this chapter. But the figures in table 1, below, make it clear that the current U.S. rate is high by comparison to the range prevailing in most industrialized countries. As of the early 1980s, the only industrialized countries with higher rates were those with two-society nations (Israel, with its Jewish and Arab populations, the Soviet Union, with its Europeans and Asians), the very distant white British Commonwealth countries (which track along with some lag), and some southern European countries (such as Portugal, Spain, and Yugoslavia) for which the 1983 figures are a snapshot in the middle of a very rapid fall.

The consequences of low fertility are worrying many in the developed countries, and in some of these (such as France and West Germany) they have begun to play an important role in national politics.

TABLE 1
Total Fertility Rates (TFR) of Various
Industrialized Countries and Regions,
1983

United States	1.79
Northern Europe[a]	1.38–1.76
Southern Europe[b]	1.53–1.98
Western Europe[c]	1.33–1.79
Central Europe[d]	1.32–1.56
Commonwealth nations[e]	1.67–1.93
Japan	1.80
Soviet Union	2.37
Israel	3.14

Source: Adapted from Jean Bourgeois-Pichat, "The Unprecedented Shortage of Births in Europe," Below-Replacement Fertility in Industrial Societies, supplement to Population and Development Review 12 (1986), 3–25.

a. Includes Denmark, Finland, Norway, Sweden, England, and Wales; excludes Iceland and both Irelands.
b. Includes Greece, Italy, Portugal, Spain, and Yugoslavia.
c. Includes Austria, Belgium, France, West Germany, the Netherlands, and Switzerland.
d. Includes Austria, Denmark, West Germany, and north-central Italy.
e. Includes Australia, Canada, and New Zealand.

In the United States these issues have yet to achieve comparable prominence, although there are some beginnings.[3] These consequences are, or are said to be, far-ranging. They include an increasing burden of dependent elderly, lowered economic growth and military power, interethnic rivalry, loss of *élan vital,* etc. And accordingly several of these countries have adopted a variety of pronatalist policies ranging from moral exhortation to baby bonuses and linking the level of pension payments to the elderly to the number of children they had when young.

But why is there such a strong negative association between economic development and fertility? Various authors emphasize different factors, but there is substantial agreement that the association is structural. The factors commonly cited include, for instance, the fact that support of the elderly has been socialized in modern welfare states, so that people need not look to their own children for support in their old age (as is the case in developing countries). This makes children less attractive as a long-term investment. At the same time, in modern societies children not only do not work around the farm or otherwise become productive assets early on (as they do in most less-developed countries) but indeed become increasingly costly as the standards and expectations of their housing, clothing, medical care, and particularly education continue to rise.

In addition to such direct costs, the opportunity costs of bearing and raising children are much greater for women in societies in which they have an option of paid employment than they are in societies where the only choice for women is lifelong economic dependence—first on fathers and later on husbands—and motherhood and unpaid work in the home. Thus, as social and economic development increasingly integrate women into the market economy, it affords more options to their lives; quite reasonably, then, more women will choose to have fewer children or none at all.

Matters of social justice or feminist politics aside, these alternatives to traditional female roles require two conditions: that economic opportunities for women exist, and that they be accessible. Or, put another way, that there be an effective market demand for their labor. The modern developments in the advanced economies has expanded this effective demand in two ways. First, as employment in advanced societies has shifted from goods production to services, it has greatly expanded the proportion of jobs in what have traditionally been women's occupations—nursing, teaching, sales, and secretarial work.

Second, however slowly, the logic of modernization moves toward eliminating distinctions without a difference, so that more women are finding their way into occupations from which they were previously effectively barred, and wage discrimination is diminishing. And the movement feeds upon itself, because as women achieve increasing economic independence, they also achieve greater political power against social and economic discrimination.

The growing economic independence of women also represents growing economic independence for men. When only the man had access to paid employment, in the family the unpaid work of the woman and the paid work of the man were complementary, and their economic dependence was mutual. As they become more independent economically, the marital bond loses the strength of this element. Marriage is more often postponed, and divorce becomes more frequent. Adults of both sexes spend more of their lives unmarried, and indeed in America today, an average white woman can expect to spend most of her adult years without a husband (before marriage, between marriages, and as a widow). This too feeds upon itself, because for a woman the prospect of having to depend on herself for so much of her life naturally increases her struggle for economic self-sufficiency.

Thus low fertility and a decline of the traditional family appear to be an integral aspect of modern societies, at least as far as we know them. This is because economic development and international specialization foster the growth of the service economy and the integration of women into the paid labor force.

Race and the Underclass

The United States, more than any other developed country, is characterized by a substantial underclass. Its membership embraces whites, Hispanics, and members of other minorities. But it is among blacks that this tragedy is most significant at a national scale, and these comments will be confined to members of this group. Apparently without remedy, since this is what defines an underclass, they are poor, largely unemployed and seemingly unemployable, in poor health, drug-ridden, frequently criminal, and the frequent victims of violence. They live in unstable families and bear most of their children out of wedlock.

It may seem ironic that the black underclass has become most visible precisely in the era in which the logic of modernization and the need for national regional and racial integration has produced the civil rights movement and led to substantial economic advances for a large portion of the black population. Yet the process that has brought about this visibility was sadly predictable.

The United States came into being as a society split along racial and regional lines, and much of our history has involved overcoming these beginnings. When, a generation ago, the black population began to become more economically and politically integrated into the general fabric of U.S. society, the general understanding and the rhetoric of the time would have it that all American blacks would move forward in unison. But this is not what happened. Rather, those among the black population who were best situated were able to make the most of the new opportunities. As this expanding black middle class became increasingly joined to the larger system, the links between it and those blacks who were not making it became increasingly weaker. This situation is parallel to that in developing countries during the takeoff period of economic growth, where the growth occurs unevenly among localities and social groups, generally favoring those who are already better off, so that income inequality increases as development gets under way.

The demographic behavior of U.S. blacks varies sharply between economic classes. Middle-class blacks have stable husband-wife unions, very low fertility, and probably the lowest rate of illegitimacy of any major group in America. Life expectancy is comparable to the national average. Poor blacks, on the other hand, have unstable unions and a preponderance of female-headed households. Fertility is relatively high, concentrated in younger women, and the majority of children are born out of wedlock.

This is not the place to try to explain these patterns in detail, to allocate blame, or to advocate solutions. The intent here is only to point to this bifurcation of black experience and behavior according to class. Even so, one must be careful of implicit interpretations of these facts. For instance, the labor force participation of black women has always been high, driven by economic necessity, while the participation rate of white women is only just catching up. Or, for another instance, much concern is commonly expressed about the rate of illegitimacy and the extreme youth of so many black mothers. But it must be noted that the age-specific fertility rates of black teenagers have not been rising. What has been dropping, apparently, is the frequency of marriage after impregnation. Further, it is worth noting that the rate of illegitimacy for Sweden as a whole nearly matches the rate for American blacks: this by itself should stand as warning against simplistic interpretations.

In short, the continued development of American economy and society has resulted in the integration of a substantial portion of the black population. This population behaves demographically like the white middle class, only more so in terms of the traditional pattern of stable marriages and more so in terms of the new low fertility. On the other hand, the integration of the black middle class has only served to highlight the failure to integrate economically an increasingly isolated black lower class.

As a result of this failure of integration, on average poor blacks behave demographically (and otherwise) in ways that are generally seen as detrimental both to society and to their own and their children's prospects for improvement. The problem of the underclass is undoubtedly one of the most serious ones in the nation, and probably fundamentally tragic. But it is primarily manifested in structural aspects of lack of integration. When the unemployment rate of black male youth is on the order of 50 percent, a pregnant black teenager about to gain a small dependent will, quite rationally, be slow to marry when the father is likely to be another dependent.

The Elderly as a Burden

Statistically, the demographic basis of the growing burden of old-age economic dependency is simply the result of two demographic facts: the prolongation of life among U.S. citizens and the decline in births. Both of these are the result of economic development. The burden itself, however, owes as much to social constructions as to the arithmetic of demography.

Life expectancy has risen steadily in modern times. Initially, this statistical prolongation of expected life derived more from reductions in infant mortality, and at first effectively acted to improve the efficiency of fertility: the number of births negated by death in infancy was dramatically reduced, thereby effectively increasing the number of adults produced by a given number of births. But infant mortality now stands at extraordinarily low levels, so that little of the increase in life expectancy derives from its reduction. The continued increase in life expectancy now relies more heavily on reduced mortality at higher ages, so that a 60-year-old has a better chance to make it to 90 than his grandfather did.

Why this long-term increase in life expectancy? There is surprisingly little firm knowledge about this. The modern rise in life expectancy in the West, dating to the eighteenth century, seems to result (in unknown proportions) from better nutrition, biological adaptation between human and microbial populations, and improvements in public health. Science and direct medical intervention seem to have played a surprisingly small role. At any rate, this extension of longevity once consisted largely in the preservation of children into adulthood rather than the preservation of the elderly beyond it.

In more recent years, the extension of human life has become less a statistical artifact based on preserving lives that had just started, and more what it seems to be in its common meaning: the chances that an adult will live longer. This may mean in some cases only the prolongation of life for a few months or weeks by extraordinary and extraordinarily expensive feats of medicine. But, to an unknown degree and in spite of fashionable fears, it is the result of a more sound environment and better lifelong nutrition. Whatever the causes, there is no question that more people now reach what used to be regarded as decrepit old age in vigorous possession of most of their faculties. The "problem" of an aging population thus arises from this fortunate extension of human life (although some heroic extensions of life go beyond sense or sensibility), and for most it constitutes a problem only because of some of its economic consequences.

Of course, the proportion of the elderly depends as much on how "old" and "young" are defined as on the actual number of people of various ages in the population. The ratio of old-age dependency is conventionally taken to be that of working-age population (20 to 64 years old) to those over 65 years of age. It is often argued, on the other hand, that the continued use of age 65 as the break point is a social convention that needs to be reexamined. This particular age, adopted from precedents in Bismarck's construction of the welfare state in Germany, was most firmly established in the United States by the 1930s Social Security legislation. However, in the 1930s life expectancy at birth was 60 years, whereas it has by now risen to 75 years, so that it may be presumed that the health and energy of many people over 65 is such that they would be willing to continue working instead of retiring. And indeed, recent legislation has advanced the age of forced retirement for many occupations beyond the traditional limit; on the other hand, the proportion of men taking early voluntary retirement has risen sharply in recent years. Thus, while the social redefinition of "old age" is a clear path to reducing the future burden of old-age dependency, it will require a considerable and complex effort to modify legislation and other public and private policies and, perhaps most important, people's attitudes.

The other major societal or economic problem presented by the growing numbers of old people is that of medical policy. Old people are naturally more prone to infirmities than young people, and will use more medical help if they can get it—and they usually can to one degree or another in modern societies. For the elderly, this use of medical support is higher per year of life than for younger adults. Further, some of the medically transacted prolongations of life are achieved at extraordinary expense for very small gains of time, and it is often doubtful whether the added months or years are worth living. Although different sources report them variously, the medical costs attending the last weeks of life represent an extraordinarily high proportion of the nation's health expenditures. This problem, already large, will continue to grow, posing increasingly difficult economic, social, legal, and ethical questions.

In brief, the burden of an elderly population arises in an advanced society because of intrinsic tendencies toward low fertility and longevity, from the transfer of social responsibility from the family to the state, and from the definitional conventions of this bureaucratized responsibility.

Immigration

The emergence of the world economy has resulted in an evolving geographic division of labor, as the comparative advantage in various forms of production has shifted between the advanced industrial societies and less-developed nations. This has set up a complex interchange of commodities, capital, technology, and labor, dictated as much by internal political considerations as by purely economic ones. The shifts in comparative advantage, particularly in labor-intensive industries, toward certain developing countries has led the advanced countries to try diverse strategies to adapt to the painful structural changes this has implied for their economies.

In Northern Europe this has taken the form of various combinations of importing labor and protectionism. In the prosperous 1950s and 1960s, these countries relied primarily on imported (and supposedly temporary) workers, but when economic difficulties and chronic high unemployment began to develop in the early 1970s, these governments shifted to trade restrictions and subsidies. Unemployment rates are declining and labor shortages are reemerging in the late 1980s, but it is certain that Northern Europe will not again resort to importation of labor primarily because of the social and cultural dilemmas that the earlier wave of immigrants has posed for those relatively homogeneous societies. As Max Frisch put it: "We called for labor and human beings came."

Japan has carried out quite a different strategy. Because Japan is a highly homogeneous and self-conscious society (often to the point of racism), when its extraordinary economic growth brought rising wages and labor shortages, it responded by exporting capital and technology, dispersing physical production to Taiwan, Korea, Singapore, Latin America, and even Europe and the United States. It has consistently rejected immigration of any sort.

The experience of the United States in these exchanges of labor, capital, and technology has been complex and to a large extent ambiguous. It has flirted with protectionism, while sending some of its production offshore or to low-wage regions within the country. Some domestic labor needs were filled in the two decades following World War II by domestic migrants, primarily rural blacks displaced by the belated modernization of the economy of the American South. A considerable portion of these labor needs have also been filled by the extraordinary rise in female labor force participation and by the coming of age of the baby boom generation. But these domestic sources of labor force growth are now largely played out.

Foreign immigration has been substantial, but not officially viewed as a form of economic immigration. The vast majority of entrants into the country have come as relatives of U.S. residents or as refugees. The numbers officially admitted as economic migrants have been relatively small and concentrated in skilled occupations. Of course, there has been an illegal economic immigration that has been undoubtedly large, although its precise magnitude is not known. This migration has been both the result of the availability of vast supplies of surplus labor among the United States' less-developed neighbors, and of what, for practical purposes, has been the recruitment of such workers by certain U.S. industries such as agriculture, apparel, and various service industries. The Immigration Reform and Control Act of 1986 is in the early stages of implementation, trying to regularize a portion of these immigrants and to expel the rest, for the first time threatening sanctions against employers of illegal immigrants. The industries affected are either asking for dispensation, expanded programs of temporary foreign workers, protection from foreign competition, or threatening to go abroad.

The demand for cheap immigrant labor cannot be explained simply by a shortage of domestic labor resulting from demographic factors: the rate of unemployment in the United States, although improving, is still higher than it was during most of the 1960s, and it is still tragically high for minorities and for the young. There is no simple overall explanation for this situation, but the fact is that the domestic unemployed for the most part do not want the jobs being filled by foreigners at low wages, be they in agriculture, apparel, domestic service, or in the menial tasks of restaurants and hotels, and thus do not constitute an effective alternative supply.

The response of the United States to the shifting patterns of comparative advantage in the world economy has been therefore mixed, involving restrictive trade policies and subsidies, exports of capital and technology, and importation of labor. There are, of course, ambiguities and contradictions in these responses that are certain to continue to evolve as a result of market forces and intended and unintended policy. Moreover, the question of immigration is rendered more complex by the large and diverse streams of family reunification and politically based migration (largely from Asia and the Caribbean Basin) which, whatever the logic of their provenance, represent a vast infusion not only of labor but also of technical and entrepreneurial skills.

In all, economic immigration is a product of the economic and demographic divergences between the United States and its less-developed neighbors. In a more complex way, political immigration is the result of the United States' preeminent geopolitical position. Both types of immigration have become demographically important in several ways. First, immigration is becoming an increasingly important source of population growth as domestic fertility declines. Second, it acts as a moderating influence on the ratio of old-age dependency. Third, because migrants tend to be concentrated geographically, this influx contributes to the variation in demographic trajectory of various parts of the country. And finally, the composition of immigration is a powerful contributor to the demographic characteristics of various ethnic groups in this country and to their role in American society.

This discussion has sought to illustrate, on the one hand, the pervasiveness of demographic aspects in the evolution of our socioeconomic system; and, on the other hand, how much the demographic situation emerges from the fact that the United States is a very prosperous modern state with a preeminent world role. The various facets of the demographic situation are interconnected, from low fertility and divorce to age-dependency and immigration. Appropriate policy, whether responding to demographic trends or aimed at influencing them, must recognize the structural dimensions of the issues.

The Limits of Demography:
The Numbers Are Not as Clean as They Seem

One cannot hope to sort demographic issues into neat formulations that state unambiguously what the facts and problems are, that include reliable projections, and that provide clear-cut guides to policy. Demographic data, seemingly quantitative and objective, often convey a misleading illusion of precision and certainty. It is indeed reasonably good—at least by comparison to, say, economic data and forecasts. But in fact, as is true of any portrait of a complex matter, demographic statistics are artifacts, stick figures attempting to represent fluid multidimensional realities. Demographic information is flawed, projections uncertain, and choices and implications can be seen only through a glass darkly. The stories that demographers tell about the past, about possible futures, and the choices among them, are always wrong to some degree, and always simplified.

There are two reasons for this, social and technical. On the social side, demographic issues, for many and complex reasons, have always attracted a great deal of passion and advocacy. In the past century, for instance, advocates of one or another view (usually millenarian) have used demographic data to advance their cause (usually by pointing with alarm). These include Malthusians worried about overpopulation; nationalists concerned about military might; Social Darwinists, eugenicists, and now sociobiologists concerned about the quality of life and seeking to control reproduction, immigration, and in some cases (Hitler being the prime example) survival; Keynesians (including Keynes himself) worried about the macro-economics of low fertility; social engineers from ministers in the court of Louis XIV to current U.S. Social Security planners; moralists worried about the family and heavenly laws; Marxists who on the basis of the labor theory of value deny Malthusian doomsday predictions and denounce them as decoys to distract attention from the issue of the distribution of power and resources between rich and poor countries; and so forth.

On the technical side, the seeming straightforwardness of demographic data and reasoning may be deceptive. What seems plain and clear often is not. A few illustrations will make the point.

a. The numbers may be crooked or cooked to one degree or another (although this is rare in this country) or they may be unreliable because one cannot count well the uncountable. For instance, illegal immigrants and the homeless are intrinsically difficult to count; the statistics about the "poor" are necessarily arbitrary, and inclusion or exclusion does not take much account of differences in local cost of living, availability of noncash services, and other circumstances.

b. The numbers are the product of particular operational definitions that may not correspond to the common-sense meaning of their labels. For instance, statements are sometimes made about the growth of the "urban" population, calling to mind agglomeration in big cities; but the population classified as "urban" is that living in places of 2,500 or more inhabitants, and thus may live in a small town; indeed, nearly 40 percent of the nonmetropolitan population in 1980 was classified as urban. Conversely, 40 percent of the nation's rural population lived inside of metropolitan areas (SMSAs).

c. Comparisons over time are often problematic because, as the world may change, a difficult choice arises between holding firm to the definition of a statistic for intertemporal comparability (at the cost of the definition becoming increasingly ill-suited), or of adjusting the definition and losing comparability. This problem arises, for instance, in the case of ethnic groups, industrial categories, metropolitan areas, or household arrangements. To give a striking instance, in 1980 the number of American whites was reduced by over 5 million by one such definitional change.

d. Any projection, unless divinely inspired, works by assuming that certain elements (such as rates, proportions) stay the same, and that these constants anchor the changes in other elements. The projection may be quite exact according to these assumptions, but since there are almost infinite choices as to what to hold constant and what to allow to change, and each choice provides different answers, exactness does not guarantee correctness. Moreover, as noted under (c), there are often qualitative changes over time, and these are particularly difficult to anticipate. Thus, in some cases, even if projections prove correct, the categories used may become obsolete or at least misleading in their apparent meaning. For instance, we may expect continued changes in the concept of old age, racial and ethnic identity, illegitimacy, immigrants, families and households, geographic areas, among other concepts and categories.

In short, demography seems straightforward but is not. The information is not technically as clean as it seems, and much of it is filtered through a variety of preconceptions and advocacies. Thus, contrary to appearances, most demographic facts cannot be taken at face value, and may mislead. And this is all the more so for projections, such as those presented in the next section, which are sober and are algebraically correct, given the suppositions. This is because the formal metrics of demography (counts of births, deaths, and migrants; urbanization rates; age and race specifics; and so on) permit consistent algebraic operations to a degree unmatched in the social sciences. Projections thus may seem as solid as good carpentry, but they are only as good as the assumptions that go into them.

Using Demography: Respectful Skepticism

It is important to be aware of these limitations if one is to use demography intelligently in the identification of problems and in the search for solutions. The apparent solidity of demographic information is manipulated by polemicists, deludes the technocrat into misplaced specificity, and awes the lay person.

But this awareness of limitations must not be carried too far. Demographic facts and implications may be less certain than they seem, but this does not make them less important. It only means that these issues must be approached more flexibly, with an awareness that over time the diagnosis and the prescription will likely need to be revised. What is needed is a mix of respectful skepticism for the facts, informed concern for the issues, and a sense of history.

Demographic projections are essential to an understanding of social issues and to the establishment of policies. They are often wrong. During the Depression, when U.S. birth rates were falling, projections promised a leveling off and even a decline in the American population. They did not anticipate the baby boom. During the 1960s, conversely, projections conjured up visions of very rapid growth, with the population doubling within a half century. As fertility has declined, projections have declined as well, although more slowly, as though demographers were not quite believing what was happening: census projections continued to use as their "middle" assumption a total fertility rate of 2.1 (the replacement level) long after the actual rate had been 15 percent lower for a number of years. The projections discussed in the next section use 1.9 as the "middle" fertility, a figure slightly (but importantly) higher than the level that has now prevailed in the United States for several years. They may be right, but a strong argument can be made that in the long term the U.S. fertility rate may continue to decline. On the other hand, although it seems unlikely, no one can rule out entirely a second baby boom, mostly because the reasons for the last one are not well understood.

Skepticism is thus warranted as to the validity of any projection. But there cannot be any doubt that whatever actually happens to fertility will be extraordinarily important, whether or not it was foreseen. Moreover, fertility will interact with whatever happens to mortality and to immigration.

Beyond the stick-figure representation of the world in numbers, moreover, there is the elusive complexity of the real world, which one must try to grasp, however imperfectly. For instance, the precise number of immigrants may matter less than the fact that immigration now consists overwhelmingly of Asians and Latin Americans, people who do not fit easily in the black-white division that has dominated American society since the beginning of the nation; this influx of peoples of diverse ethnic and racial backgrounds will likely redefine the meaning and role of ethnicity in America. Projections, sometimes cited, that by a certain date the Hispanic population will be larger than the black population are very much to be doubted. The very notion that there is such a thing as a "Hispanic" population is a recent but possibly self-fulfilling invention. We are, to be sure, witnessing the social construction of its reality, but it is not clear what shape it will take. Note, for instance, that even in states like New York, where the genetic endowment of the Hispanic population includes a substantial African component, less than 5 percent of Hispanics consider themselves black. Who is Hispanic and who is black is not a fact of nature but of social construction. In short, the numbers tell less than half the story, even when they are correct. Their meaning matters more.

A Sense of History and a Sense of the Future

The next section will discuss a number of population projections extending to the year 2050. This may seem an unimaginably distant horizon, but it is not. Consider the following:

- A child who entered kindergarten in 1987 will graduate from high school in the year 2000.
- His young parents signing a 30-year mortgage will finish paying it off just short of the year 2020.
- A youth graduating from college will retire at 65 in the year 2030.

■ The child in kindergarten will still have (on average) about a decade to live in the year 2050.

We have difficulty with these far horizons, and the range of uncertainty is great, but they are quite real and almost at hand. Many of the people who will be around in 2050 are our children and grandchildren; and indeed many who are 30 years old today will also be around then.

This scope of time is historical. In 2050 America's role in the world will be different. Technology will be different. The economy will be different. Poetry, entertainment, the nature of work, families, and generational relations will be different. It will be another time in history.

This long-term perspective must also look backward for history's uncertain lessons. Many of today's demographic issues are close repetitions of our historic past. Today's raging debates over bilingualism in the United States echo the fears from the turn of the century of the threat posed to democracy in a Protestant America by a flood of new immigrants. The current fears of depopulation echo those of the 1930s. The rhythm of the waves of low-income immigrants in the late nineteenth and early twentieth centuries had a profound influence on the structure of the U.S. economy and its development, and surely today's waves of immigration will have a similar impact. Moreover, as the economy changed in the past, so did the role of the family, gender, race, and ethnicity, and political responses and cultural adaptations evolved accordingly. History may not repeat itself, but a sense of history is necessary to begin to make a guess at the social significance of quantitative demographic changes.

CHAPTER 3

How Many People?
Population Projections

IT IS easy to generate projections that are exact according to a certain set of assumptions; the difficulty lies in making the right assumptions. Therefore, many professional demographers advocate generating a broad variety of projections, each specifying the assumptions behind it, and letting the "client" use his or her own judgment in choosing among them. While there is a certain amount of sense in this approach, it presents two very real difficulties. First, the number of possible projections rises explosively with the permutation of assumptions. For instance, the Bureau of the Census projections to be reviewed here consider only three possibilities for each of three variables (high, medium, and low rates for fertility, mortality, and immigration), but even these few variations manage to produce 30 different projections, which is more than the ordinary mind can hold. The second difficulty is subtler and stems from the fact that it is very hard to know the assumptions that have been made implicitly and unknowingly. For instance, a given rate of immigration will have very different long-term demographic consequences if it consists mostly of mature male workers rather than mostly young women and children. In the latter case, the migrants will contribute many more descendants.

Some Generalizations

Although each of the projections considered in the following pages is quite straightforward, the proliferation of demographic projections can be confusing. However, there are a few points that can be grasped through common sense and need not rely on number crunching:

a. Under any probable scenario, the rate of population growth will be slower in the future than in the past. It is quite likely that population growth will level off, or actually begin to decline slightly, in the 2020s.

b. The key variable to the rate of total population growth is fertility. U.S. fertility, although below replacement, is toward the high end of the

40

rates currently prevailing in industrialized societies, and thus a further decrease is quite possible.

c. Immigration is the second most important variable for the growth of total population. Its contribution to age composition is different from that of fertility, since most immigrants are adults.

d. Mortality (or longevity) makes only a marginal difference in population totals, although it makes quite a difference in dependency ratios.

e. With regard to old-age dependency, if fertility is down, in the long run there will be fewer children and more older people relative to working-age people; but as immigration is up, there will be more working-age people relative to old people.

h. As fertility is down, there will be fewer children per working-age adult; this is largely unaffected by the level of immigration.

g. The size of the working-age population will continue to grow, although more slowly than in recent times, until 2010. Thereafter this age group will grow or decline slightly, in an oscillating fashion. But if low fertility prevails during the 1990s, the size of this group will begin to decline sharply about thirty years from now because there will be fewer children to grow into this age group.

The Bureau of the Census Projections: Assumptions

The projections to be examined here have been prepared by the U.S. Bureau of the Census.[1] The various projections use alternative (low, middle, and high) assumptions about fertility, mortality, and immigration, and these permutations (together with one zero-immigration scenario) yield 30 alternative projections, of which only the most relevant will be discussed here. The specific assumptions are shown in table 2.

In its discussion, the census report stresses what it calls the Mid-

TABLE 2
Assumptions of Census Projections

	Low	Middle	High
Ultimate lifetime births per woman (TFR)[a]	1.6	1.9	2.3
Mortality (life expectancy at birth in 2080)	85.9	81.0	77.4
Yearly net immigration (thousands)	250	450	750

Source: U.S. Dept. of Commerce, Bureau of the Census, Projection of the Population of the United States by Age, Sex, and Race 1983–2080, Current Population Reports, ser. P-25, no. 952 (Washington, D.C.: GPO, 1984).
   a. TFR = Total fertility rate.

dle Projection (#14), which uses the middle assumptions for births, deaths, and immigration. And indeed, it seems to make general sense to avoid the extremes when peering at the future. But it will be useful to take a brief look at the assumptions before going on, reserving more detailed discussions for later.

FERTILITY

The "middle" Total Fertility Rate (TFR) used in these projections is 1.9, below the replacement rate of 2.1, but presuming a slight but important increase from the 1.8 rate that has prevailed in the United States for the past decade with only minor fluctuations. Of course, such a rise is quite possible, but not, in my opinion, inherently likelier than a further decline to the "low" rate of 1.6. If one considers the range of TFRs prevailing in industrialized regions of the world, as shown in table 2, it becomes clear that the United States is in the top portion of this range. Thus, in my judgment, for the foreseeable future the American Total Fertility Rate is likely to oscillate between the middle and the low census fertility assumptions.

The "high" rate, 2.3, is above replacement and most unlikely. It is substantially higher than that of any industrialized country for years, and higher than the rate has been in the United States since 1971.

MORTALITY AND LIFE EXPECTANCY

The census projections assume that life expectancy at birth will continue to rise over the coming decades from its present level of 74.7 to 77.4, 81.0, or 85.9 years, corresponding to high, middle, and low mortality. This seems a reasonable range. For comparison, U.S. life expectancy rose by 5.9 years from 1955 to 1985, an increase of .17 years per year. Life expectancy in Sweden, Switzerland, and Japan was already in the 77- to 79-year range by the early 1980s.

IMMIGRATION

The Bureau of the Census assumptions for yearly immigration are 250,000 for low, 450,000 for middle, and 750,000 for high immigration. These figures seem low. For instance, official figures for U.S. net civilian immigration average to 449,000 yearly for the 1975–79 period, and to 682,000 for 1980–84.[2] These figures probably understate the size of the flows primarily because of uncounted illegal immigrants. Thus, judging from recent experience, I find it likely that the yearly rate of net civilian immigration will be higher than the middle estimate, if not as high as the high estimate.

Total Population: The Range of Projections

Figure 1 shows the historical trajectory of the total American population from 1940 to the mid-1980s and a half dozen of the Bureau of the
Census projections of this total to the year 2050. The assumptions of
the various projections, which are designated by number, are shown
in table 3.

The lowest census projection shown in figure 1 (#28 in the bureau's designation) corresponds to low fertility, low life expectancy,
and zero immigration. According to this unlikely scenario, the total
U.S. population would remain essentially stable from 1995 to 2020,
hovering in the range of 248 to 252 million; it would then begin to
decline at an accelerating rate to 209 million in 2050, 192 million in
2060, and 160 million in 2080.

The highest census projection (#9, but not shown in figure 1) is
based on assumptions of high fertility, low mortality, and high immigration. Although the absolute growth of population would be large,
of course, it would take place at a slow and declining yearly rate:
1.15 percent for the balance of this decade, falling to .97 percent by
2000 (comparable to the 1980–85 rate), and to .73 percent by 2050
(comparable to the rate of population growth during the Depression).
These rates are far below that of 1.71 percent during the 1950s. In
terms of total population, however, this slow increase is sizable, the
total mounting to 281 by the year 2000, and to 428 million in 2050.
Thus, in the year 2050, the total population according to this highest
census projection would be more than twice that of the lowest
growth scenario mentioned in the previous paragraph.

The Census Bureau, in its discussion of the alternative paths,
focuses mostly on its "middle" projection (#14, figure 1), with mid-

TABLE 3
Assumptions Underlying Projections Shown in Figures 2–9

Series	Fertility	Mortality	Immigration
#14 (Middle)	Middle	Middle	Middle
#17	Middle	Middle	HIGH
#8	Middle	LOW	HIGH
#13	LOW	Middle	Middle
#16	LOW	Middle	HIGH
#28	LOW	Middle	ZERO

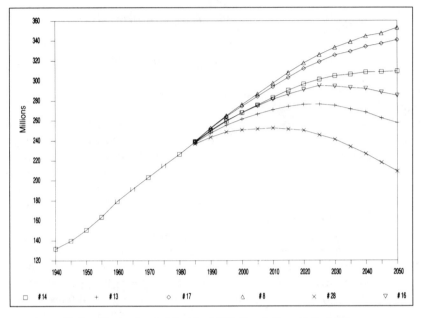

FIGURE 1.   Various Projections of the Total U.S. Population, 1940–2050

Source: U.S. Dept. of Commerce, Bureau of the Census, *Projections of the Population of the United States, by Age, Sex, and Race, 1983–2080,* Current Population Reports, ser. P-25, no. 952 (Washington, D.C.: GPO, 1984).

dle fertility, immigration, and mortality. According to this projection, there would be a very slow, steady growth in total population (268 million persons by the year 2000, 297 million in 2020, and 309 million in 2050).

The bureau's emphasis on this particular projection might seem to imply that it is the most probable. However, for reasons indicated earlier, in my opinion this series overestimates the likely fertility rate and underestimates likely immigration. These two effects, one negative and the other positive on the total, are of course to some degree mutually canceling, and so in the middle term make little difference to total population. Accordingly, the curve for #16, which corresponds to lower fertility and higher immigration, is virtually indistinguishable from the middle projection until the year 2010; after that, however, #16 begins to lag under the middle projection, and shows population decline after 2025. But the more important difference, as will be shown in a later section, lies not so much in these population totals as in the effects of these assumptions on age composition.

The remaining curves in figure 1 are of interest because, whatever the intrinsic probability of any one of them, the differences between them indicate the magnitude of the effect of alternative assumptions.

Recall that the lowest curve in figure 1 (#28) assumes low fertility, middle mortality, and zero immigration. The next curve up (#13) differs from it only by assuming the middle level of immigration (450,000), so that the vertical distance between the two curves is a measure of the impact of immigration at this level. The next curve up (#16) is for low fertility (1.6) and high immigration (750,000), and its vertical distance above #13 shows the effect of the additional 300,000 immigrants per year.

The Middle Projection (#14) differs from the second curve below it (#13) only in assuming a middle (1.9) rather than a low level of fertility, and the increasing divergence between these two curves makes evident how crucial is the assumption about fertility. Recall also that the Middle Projection even lies above the curve for low fertility and *high* immigration (#16): that is to say, the difference arising from a fertility rate at 1.6 as opposed to 1.9 is greater than the difference arising from a rate of immigration at 450,000 or 750,000.

The curve (#17) above the Middle Projection (#14) differs from it only by the level of immigration, and is correspondingly higher. It is worth noting that the difference between these two curves is greater than that between #13 and #16, which also differ from each other only in immigration level. This is because immigration and fertility rates interact, and the immigrants in the #14 and #17 pair are assumed to have more children than those in the pair of #13 and #16.

Finally, the top curve (#8) differs from the one immediately below it (#17) by assuming a low level of mortality. The two curves share assumptions of middle fertility and high immigration, but the fact to notice is what a small difference a lower death rate makes to total population.

AGE COMPOSITION

For many purposes the shifting proportions among age groups are more interesting than the alternative projections of total population. Thus, a projection based on low fertility and high immigration (#16) may produce totals similar to those of a projection of middle fertility and medium immigration (#14), but it implies very different proportions of children and elderly in that population.

Each of the census projections thus far discussed implies a complete age distribution and its evolution over time. One could, of course, look through the many pages of tiny print that present these data, but it is very hard to get a sense of what is going on from this sea of numbers. The following pages will offer two types of graphic summaries for some of the most interesting projections. The first is a three-dimensional representation of the age composition through time, from 1940 to alternative futures to 2050. The second is more conventional, showing time series of the proportion of the very young or the old to the population of working age.

IN THREE DIMENSIONS

Figures 2 to 5 are three-dimensional representations of the age composition of the American population, historically from 1940 to 1980, and according to various projections from then to the year 2050. The number of people by age and date is shown on the vertical or Y-axis; the age group by five-year categories is shown on the left horizontal or X-axis; and the date on the right horizontal or Z-axis. On the surface of the graph, the lines that run parallel to the X-axis show the age distribution at any given date; the lines that run parallel to the Z-axis show the number of people in that age category from 1940 to 2050. Cohorts or generations can be traced as ridges or valleys proceeding diagonally from left to right. The patterns are striking, but rich and complex, so that here I will only point out some of the features.

In any of these three-dimensional graphs, if one looks at the X-axis for 1940, running horizontally to the left, one can see the drop in the number of people with increasing age, which is typical of most societies. But, at the extreme left, one can see that there were fewer young children than teenagers. This is because economic hardship produced a sharp drop in births during the Depression of the 1930s. This decline in births of the Depression produces a valley on the population surface that continues into the present and into the future, eroded by time and death, until the year 2030, when the last of those born during the time of Hoover and Roosevelt become centenarians and disappear from the statistical picture.

The valley of the Depression is followed just to the right by the massive ridge of the baby boom that followed World War II. This ridge dominates the demographic landscape. The baby bust that followed is the far-side downhill of this ridge, creating a new valley, a smaller generation born mostly in the 1970s. In the perspective of the graph, the bottom of the valley is hidden by the baby boom ridge, but just beyond it can be seen a smaller ridge, the echo of the baby boom that is taking place now, when births are rising in spite of low average fertility because there are so many baby boomers in the reproductive years. A second and more diffuse echo will take place about 2010.

The increasing number of elderly can be seen by the gentle rise in those curves on the surface that run parallel to the Z-axis near the front of the graph. The general rise is owing mostly to the historic and projected rise in life expectancy, and its ups and downs are largely the result of far earlier baby booms and busts.

These general characteristics are shared by figures 2 through 5. Figure 2 represents the Middle Projection (#14) and can serve as a benchmark for the others. Note that toward the back corner of the graph, toward the mid–twenty-first century, as a result of a fertility rate slightly below replacement, the number of children settles into a very gentle downward slope. The total population will still be growing at this time (see figure 1), and the growing proportion of elderly can be gauged by the growing massiveness of the bulging surface toward the right front (older people, later periods).

Figure 3 shows the equivalent surface for the assumptions of middle mortality, high immigration, and low fertility (#16). The historic part of the surface, from 1940 to the mid-1980s, is of course identical; the differences occur after that. Figure 1 showed that the total population of this projection is increasingly lower than that of the Middle Projection after 2005, and that a gradual decline in total population begins in the 2020s. Within this, there are two principal differences. First, there is a much sharper drop in the number of children and younger people because of lower fertility. This can be seen most clearly in the much more rapid drop of the surface as it moves toward the back corner. Second, there are slightly more older people, because new people in the population are grown immigrants rather than babies, and immigrants age along with their coevals in the native population. More subtly, the ridges and valleys of the population are somewhat less marked because the age distribution of immigrants when they arrive is not affected by baby booms or busts.

Figure 4 (corresponding to series #17) makes the same assumptions as the Middle Projection of figure 2 except for a high level of immigration. Of course, total population is higher. But the number of children in the later periods is also substantially higher because it includes the children and grandchildren of immigrants. And the

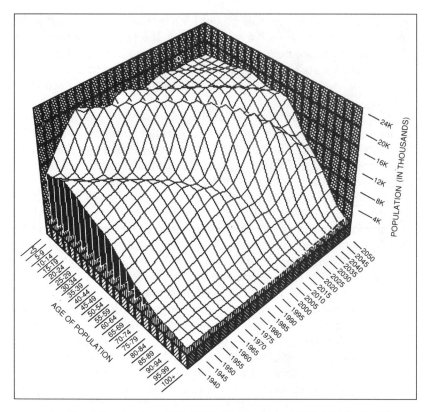

FIGURE 2.   Population by Age, 1940–2050. Middle Series (#14): Middle Fertility, Mortality, and Immigration

Source: U.S. Dept. of Commerce, Bureau of the Census, *Projections of the Population of the United States, by Age, Sex, and Race, 1983–2080,* Current Population Reports, ser. P-25, no. 952 (Washington, D.C.: GPO, 1984).

number of working-age adults is also substantially higher. Thus, the ratio of children to adults is similar, but the share of older people in the population is smaller, and so, as we shall see, the ratio of old-age dependency is lower.

Figure 5 represents series #13, which departs from the Middle Projection of figure 2 only by assuming low fertility, assuming the middle options for immigration and mortality. The main difference from figure 2 other than lower population totals is, of course, the very sharp decline in the number of children and a lagging decline

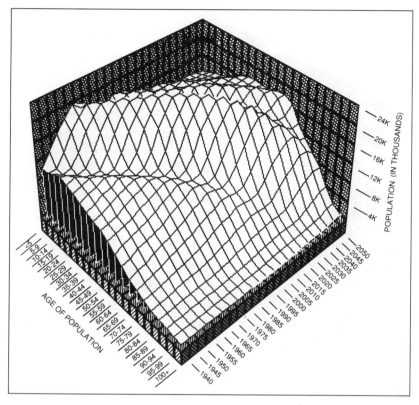

FIGURE 3. Population by Age, 1940–2050. Series #16: LOW Fertility, Middle Mortality, HIGH Immigration

Source: U.S. Dept. of Commerce, Bureau of the Census, *Projections of the Population of the United States, by Age, Sex, and Race, 1983–2080,* Current Population Reports, ser. P-25, no. 952 (Washington, D.C.: GPO, 1984).

among older ages. In all, it amounts to a lower child dependency and a very high old-age dependency in the future.

IN TWO DIMENSIONS

The three-dimensional images of figures 1 through 5 are rich in information, but selected aspects of this information can be seen more clearly in conventional two-dimensional time-series graphs.

It is a commonplace that the number and proportion of the elderly is rising and will continue to rise in every industrial society,

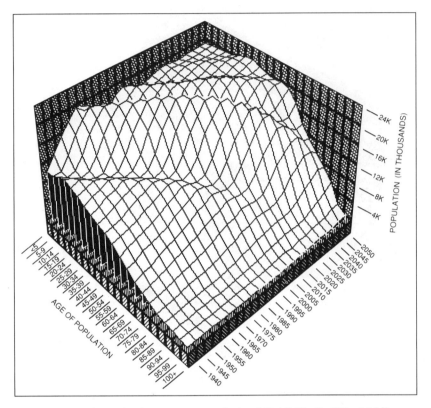

FIGURE 4. Population by Age, 1940–2050. Series #17: Middle Fertility, Middle Mortality, HIGH Immigration

Source: U.S. Dept. of Commerce, Bureau of the Census, *Projections of the Population of the United States, by Age, Sex, and Race, 1983–2080*, Current Population Reports, ser. P-25, no. 952 (Washington, D.C.: GPO, 1984).

including the United States. This is the result both of increased longevity and of lower fertility. Figure 6 shows the striking past and future growth in the number of older Americans according to the bureau's Middle Projection (#14). From 1940 to 1980 the number of Americans 65 years old and older rose from 9 million to 25.5 million. Regardless of what projection is used, this number will continue to grow. The growth will accelerate around 2010 (when the baby boom reaches this age), reaching 66.7 million in 2035, according to the Middle Projection. After this time the increase will slow as the current baby bust children reach this age, the total being less than a

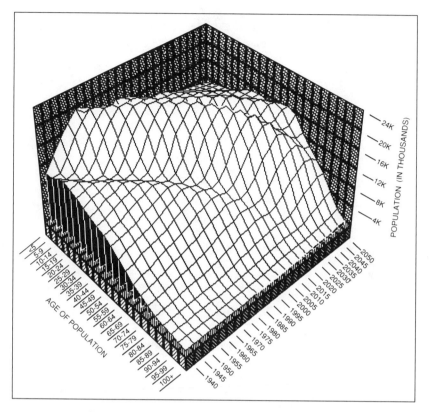

FIGURE 5. Population by Age, 1940–2050. Series #13: LOW Fertility, Middle Mortality, Middle Immigration

Source: U.S. Dept. of Commerce, Bureau of the Census, *Projections of the Population of the United States, by Age, Sex, and Race, 1983–2080,* Current Population Reports, ser. P-25, no. 952 (Washington, D.C.: GPO, 1984).

million greater (67.4 million) in 2050. These numbers will not be affected by fertility, since those 65 and over in 2050 were born in 1985 or earlier. Higher or lower immigration would raise or lower these numbers only marginally. The mortality assumption does matter for this segment of the population, so that under the low mortality assumption (#5) there would be 10.3 million or 15 percent more people in 2050; and under the high mortality assumption (#23) there would be 8.0 million or 12 percent fewer. Or put another way, the number of those over 65 by mid-century would be 31 percent higher

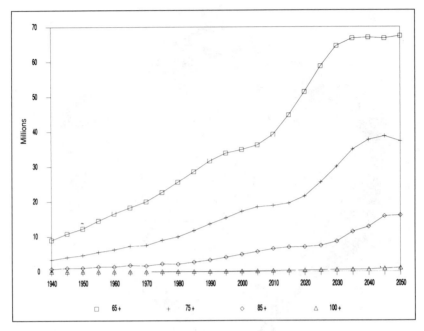

FIGURE 6. Elderly Population by Age, 1940–1950. Middle Series (#14): Middle Fertility, Mortality, and Immigration

Source: U.S. Dept. of Commerce, Bureau of the Census, *Projections of the Population of the United States, by Age, Sex, and Race, 1983–2080*, Current Population Reports, ser. P-25, no. 952 (Washington, D.C.: GPO, 1984).

according to the low mortality projection than according to the high mortality projection.

As important as the total number of people over 65, figure 6 shows the even more rapid increase of those sometimes called the old-old. Among the over-65 population in the United States, the share of those over 75 is 39 percent today, and by the middle of next century this share will rise by half, to nearly 60 percent. The share of those over 85 is 9 percent today, and will nearly triple to 24 percent. Put another way, as a share of the total population the share of those over 75 will more than triple, from under 4 to 12 percent; the share of those over 85 will quintuple, from 1 to 5 percent. These numbers derive from the Middle Projection; other projections would have them otherwise, but not by much. The social and economic consequences of these age shifts will be enormous.

Figure 7 affords some idea of the differences among the scenarios of various projections, by showing the dependency ratio of people 65 and over to the working-age population (20 to 64 years old). The worst scenarios, in terms of higher dependency ratios, are those for low fertility (#13, #16) and low mortality (#8). In the former, low fertility depresses the replenishment of the population of working age; and in the latter, of course, low mortality increases the number of man-years per elderly person.

Conversely, the lowest dependency ratio among those considered in figure 7 corresponds to a high-immigration, middle-fertility scenario (#17). Immigration replenishes the labor force faster than it adds to the aged. The interaction with fertility may be judged by comparing the curve for #17 with that for #16, which considers the

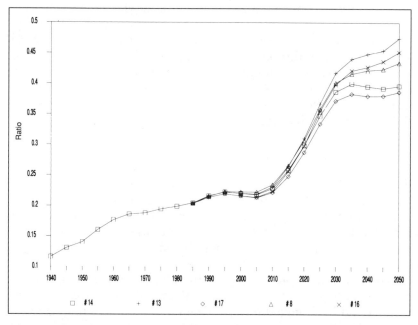

FIGURE 7. Various Projections of the Old-Age Dependency Ratio, 1940–2050 (ratio of persons 65 and older to persons 20–64 years old)

Source: U.S. Dept. of Commerce, Bureau of the Census, *Projections of the Population of the United States, by Age, Sex, and Race, 1983–2080,* Current Population Reports, ser. P-25, no. 952 (Washington, D.C.: GPO, 1984).

combination of high immigration and low fertility. The curve for #16 is intermediate between that for the Middle Projection (#14) and that for #13, which assumes low fertility and middle immigration. In other words, for the purpose of the old-age dependency ratio, high immigration substitutes for about half of the effect of lower fertility.

Thus, the ratio of old-age dependency in the United States is affected not only by the numerator (the number of old people) but also by the denominator (the population of working age). Figure 8 shows that the size of the 20–64 age group varies dramatically over time, depending on one's assumptions. For the year 2050, for instance, the projections shown range from a low of 141 million (#13: low fertility, middle mortality and immigration) to 35 percent more, or 190 million (#8: middle fertility, high immigration, low mortality). It is, however, the pattern of the differing projections that is interesting, rather than the specific numbers. This pattern has two aspects. First, with slight variations, all these projections of the 20–64 age group continue to grow smartly (although not as fast as in recent years, when the baby boomers were coming of age) to a peak about the year 2010, when growth slows down markedly and becomes negative for many of these series. Second, fertility and immigration are the crucial variables, and mortality is relatively unimportant. The highest two curves in figure 8, which correspond to #8 and #17, track very closely together, the difference between them being the difference in mortality. Both of these assume middle fertility and high immigration. The third lowest curve in 2050 corresponds to the Middle Projection (#14), and the distance to the next curve up (#17) is the result of the difference in the immigration assumption (450,000 versus 750,000 yearly). The difference (19 million) is not trivial, but potentially more important is the conjecture that after 2010, while this age group would be just about stable in either case, it would be growing slightly if immigration were high, while it would tend to decline in the case of low immigration. For some purposes, whether the population is growing or shrinking is more important than the absolute level.

The two lowest projections for the 20–64 age group in figure 8 correspond to assumptions of low fertility, with the lower (#13) assuming middle immigration and the higher (#16) high immigration. (The difference between these two, stemming from the immigration assumption, is about the same as that between the Middle Projection and #17, which also differ only in their assumptions about immigration.) The significant point is that low fertility would lead to a sharp

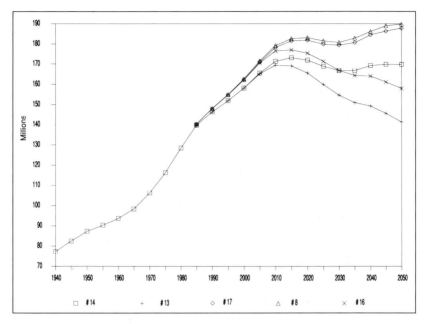

FIGURE 8. Various Projections of the Working-Age Population, 1940–2040 (persons 20–64 years old)

Source: U.S. Dept. of Commerce, Bureau of the Census, *Projections of the Population of the United States, by Age, Sex, and Race, 1983–2080,* Current Population Reports, ser. P-25, no. 952 (Washington, D.C.: GPO, 1984).

decline in the population of working age beginning about 2010, and that this decline will be sharper if immigration is low.

Yet, although they are closely related, the size of this demographic age group (20–64) must not be confused with the labor force. For instance, although over the past two decades the U.S. labor force has to some degree grown because more have entered the age group, the primary factor has been the greater participation of women, while a declining participation of men over 50 and of young people has had the opposite effect.

Finally, figure 9 shows the child-dependency ratio; that is, the ratio of people under 20 to those between 20 and 64. Because of low fertility, the burden of the child-dependency ratio will decline, the more so for lower fertility assumptions (#13 and #16). It is worth noting that because of the baby boom the ratio reached .76 in 1965; it

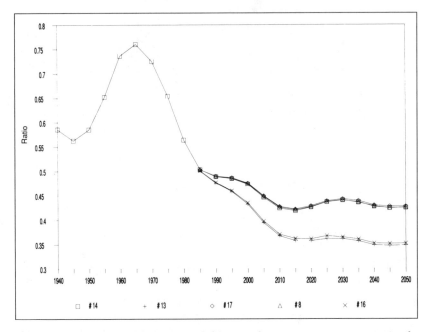

FIGURE 9.   Various Projections of the Child-Dependency Ratio, 1940–2050 (ratio of persons 0–19 years to persons 20–64 years old)

Source: U.S. Dept. of Commerce, Bureau of the Census, *Projections of the Population of the United States, by Age, Sex, and Race, 1983–2080,* Current Population Reports, ser. P-25, no. 952 (Washington, D.C.: GPO, 1984).

now stands at .50. Depending on what happens to fertility, it will continue to decline until the decade 2010–20, and then stabilize at an oscillating level around .43 in the case of middle fertility, or of .36 for low fertility. Putting it another way, for every three children in the United States there were four adults at the time of the baby boom, and there are six adults today; in the future there will be between seven and nine adults for every three children. (By contrast to old-age dependency, however, child dependency is essentially unaffected by immigration.)

CHAPTER 4

Migration and Geographic Distribution

THE HUMAN geography of the United States is in constant flux. Changes in population distribution are driven, in large part, by migratory flows. Some of these flows are of long standing, but there have been surprising developments in the recent past. Less familiar, but an equally important factor in the geographic differentiation of demographic growth is the great spatial variation in vital rates, particularly fertility. This chapter will address both issues.

Migration in General

The pattern of migration in the United States is extremely complex and defies ready summary, let alone simple explanations. The migratory patterns are different for men and women, for young and old, for whites, blacks, and Hispanics, and for any other subdivision of the population for which we have information. Moreover, there are nearly infinite ways of defining the geographic categories for organizing the data, and different categorizations will often show different, and even contradictory, patterns.

Nonetheless, a few forms of migration have traditionally received the most attention, and these serve to organize this discussion. These are urban-rural migration, suburbanization and other intrametropolitan movements, interregional movements, immigration from abroad, and the migration of special groups, such as the aged.

American Urbanization: The Long View

Migration from rural areas to cities has for centuries been a hallmark of development in Europe and North America. This migration accelerated with the agricultural revolution, which intensified the use of capital and land as substitutes for labor in agriculture, and with the industrial revolution, which concentrated economic activity in cities.

In the United States this rural-to-urban flow has taken many forms. In the second half of the nineteenth century it was a two-way flux, as both the cities and the frontier attracted migrants from the established rural areas. Moreover, the massive European immigration of the late nineteenth and early twentieth centuries, although crossing national borders, was essentially the migration of rural populations to urban destinations. As legislation cut off the European influx in the 1920s, it was replaced by a domestic source of migrants in one of the most extraordinary population movements in history: this was the transformation of the black American population, in the space of little more than two generations, from one that was rural and concentrated in one region (the South) to one that was far more urban (85 percent) than the white population (71 percent), and nationally distributed (47 percent outside the South).

The urbanization of the U.S. black population was effectively completed by the late 1960s, and no other significant domestic pool of migrants remained. Yet, in the past twenty years the pattern of rural-to-urban migration has been refreshed to some ill-measured extent by foreign immigrants and refugees from the Caribbean, Latin America, and Asia. For instance, the Hispanic population, like the black population, is already much more highly urbanized than the white population.

The Migration Turnaround and the
New Geography of City and Country

In the mid-1970s a contradictory and utterly surprising pattern of population movement became gradually apparent: the number of migrants from metropolitan areas into nonmetropolitan areas exceeded that flowing the other way, seemingly reversing the immemorial urbanizing trend. This "migration turnaround" captured the imagination of academics, the press, and the public. Its discovery coincided with the Watergate scandal and the first oil shock, and memories from the late 1960s were still fresh of the assassinations of public figures, of burning cities and the civil rights movement, and of the bitter ambiguities of the Vietnam War. The supposed turnaround was hailed by many as evidence of a sea change in the attitudes of a significant proportion of the U.S. population, as a rejection of the urban rat race and artificiality, and as a return to the older values associated with rural areas and small towns. This, of course, is a very traditional theme that runs deep and resonates in our culture. However, the reality was more mundane and, as we shall see, the turn-around phenomenon proved fleeting.

The turnaround consisted of two parts, one more real than the other. The real part was that, for the first time since such statistics have been kept, small towns and rural areas remote from urban centers on the whole attracted more immigrants than large metropolitan areas. The more illusory aspect to this trend resulted from the fact that the geographic reality of urban areas had exceeded the boundaries of their censal definitions.

Let us start with the second point. The magnitude and direction of the reported migration turnaround depended, of course, on where the boundary was drawn between the city and the country. In practice this meant the boundary drawn by the U.S. Bureau of the Census (and OMB) for metropolitan areas. Skipping over details, the definition of the metropolitan area starts from a rather small minimum (50,000) central urban population size, and extends out to include adjacent counties that meet a variety of criteria, which include how many people commute to the central area. There were 261 such areas defined in 1986, and some of these metropolises were well under 100,000 in population. In all, less than one-tenth of the area of metropolitan areas was urbanized, and two-fifths of the nation's rural population lived within the censal boundaries of metropolitan areas. Conversely, the census classifies as "urban" places of 2,500 or more inhabitants, many of which are small towns; indeed, nearly 40 percent of the nonmetropolitan population in 1980 was classified as urban. It should be clear that the censal categories of "metropolitan" and "nonmetropolitan" fit only loosely the ordinary person's concept of "big city with suburbs" and "rural areas and small towns." Thus the migration turnaround cannot be taken simply at face value.

The migration turnaround appears to have been the result of several factors. Something like half of the phenomenon seem to have resulted from the extension of the suburbanization of homes and economic activities beyond the censal boundaries of metropolitan areas: the counties adjacent to metropolitan areas were growing fastest. The great suburbanization of the 1950s and 1960s had carried to the periphery of the metropolitan area not only residences and retail stores, but also manufacturing, wholesale, offices, and business services. This provided a base in the 1970s upon which, with continued improvement of transportation and communications, the functional urban area could spread to great distances: people could live ever further out and still commute to the metropolitan periphery, while many economic enterprises could be similarly dispersed and still maintain their necessary linkages, in some cases drawing their workers from even more distant areas, so that in some cases the urban field extended 100 miles out from the original metropolitan center. To be sure, this extended urbanization was not compact, and many rural and nonmetropolitan activities were interspersed, especially in the outer reaches. Metropolitan development as such will be discussed further in the next section, but this suffices to explain why the migration turnaround was to some extent a statistical artifact: the definition of metropolitan areas had not caught up with the emerging urban structure.

But some aspects of the turnaround were real as well, because many counties distant from metropolitan areas were receiving migrants for the first time in modern times. This responded not so much to any change in American sensibilities as to a set of factors of long standing. First, for the same reasons that much U.S. manufacturing was going offshore, much of it was also dispersing domestically, first to the suburbs, then to smaller urban areas, and then to rural areas. Second, there was rapid growth in the resort industry, which attracted people to less-populated areas. Third, and related to the last item, a substantial number of older people, thanks to Social Security and private pensions, were able to leave the metropolitan areas in which they had been working to go back to the towns where they grew up or, more often, to retirement areas attractive for their amenities. Fourth, it was a period of expansion of employment in resource development and environmental preservation, and this takes place for the most part in nonmetropolitan areas. Fifth, to an undetermined extent, in those recession years (as in the Great Depression) the trend may have included earlier migrants to metropolitan areas returning home to rural areas, where it is easier to manage on scarce funds and where friends and relatives can be of help.

At any rate, by the early 1980s, the turnaround had turned around again. Figure 10 shows the net flows among metropolitan central cities, metropolitan suburbs (as defined by the census), and nonmetropolitan areas, and immigrants from abroad for 1975–76 and for 1983–84. Whereas in 1975–76 there had been 395,000 net migrants from metropolitan to nonmetropolitan areas (278,000 from the central city and 117,000 from the suburbs), by 1983–84 there was a net flow of 351,000 from nonmetropolitan to metropolitan areas. It should be understood that "net migrants" are not real people but the arithmetic difference between those going one way and those going the other. Metropolitan and nonmetropolitan areas exchange about 3 million people in each direction each year, for a total of about 6 million migrants. The net migration, in either direction, is only about 5 percent of this total.

A few other points are worth mentioning on metropolitan migration:

a. Race mattered. The migration turnaround of the 1970s was a white phenomenon. Although there was a shift in black migration, for every 100 blacks who left metropolitan areas, 142 entered them.
b. There are twice as many people in metropolitan areas as in nonmetropolitan areas. Thus, even during the period of the migration turnaround, since the migration streams in either direction are nearly equal, the *rate* of outmigration was higher for nonmetropolitan than for metropolitan areas.
c. In either year, the net migration was very small as a rate: 300,000 persons represents only .002 percent of the metropolitan population and .004 percent of the nonmetropolitan. Moreover, because of the prevalence of return migration, the yearly rate exaggerates the cumulative rate: even if the direction were sustained, a yearly rate of 300,000 would translate to a cumulative rate of only 100,000 or less.
d. In both years, even the official census statistics show that nearly 900,000 migrants from abroad entered metropolitan areas, and over 200,000 entered nonmetropolitan areas (see figure 10). Not all of these are foreign-born, however; these figures include Americans who had been living abroad, both civilian and military. No figures are available for migration in the other direction, those leaving the United States to live abroad, but the number is unquestionably much lower.

In all, then, the following conclusions may be offered:

a. The migration turnaround of the 1970s, although interesting, is obviously too small and inconstant a phenomenon to be significant on the national scale, although it may be important to certain small receiving areas such as retirement or mining towns.
b. On the other hand, it should be clear that domestic rural-to-urban migration can no longer be a source of demographic metropolitan growth.
c. Far more important to the demographic growth of both metropolitan and nonmetropolitan areas has been the decline of fertility and migration from abroad.
d. The geographic spread of the urban field of metropolitan areas has weakened our ability to interpret the statistics because metropolitan and nonmetropolitan areas are in reality (if not in the censal definitions) overlapping rather than mutually exclusive categories.

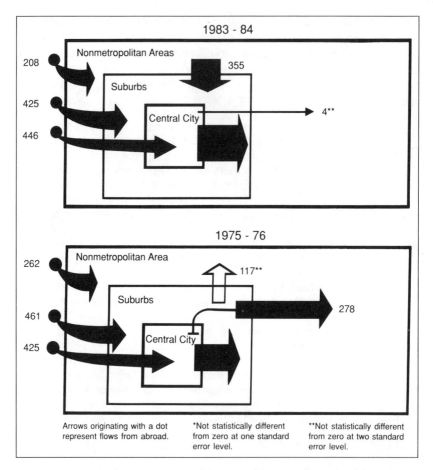

FIGURE 10.   Net Flows Among Central Cities and Suburbs of Metropolitan Areas
and Nonmetropolitan Areas, and Immigrants from Abroad, 1975–1976 and 1983–
1984

Source: U.S. Dept. of Commerce, Bureau of the Census, Geographical Mobility:
March 1983 to March 1984, Current Population Reports, ser. P-20, no. 407 (Washington, D.C.: GPO, 1986).

A NOTE ON METROPOLITAN GOVERNANCE

The geographic boundaries of local governments in the United
States were essentially set in the eighteenth and nineteenth centuries,
when urban fields were primarily determined by walking distances
and the population was much smaller. Since then the demographic

size of urban concentrations has continued to grow, as has their geographic spread. Urban fields have expanded even further because of continuing improvements in transportation and communications.

In consequence it has often been proposed that metropolitan governments be created above the local level, so that the sphere of governmental authority more nearly coincides with the actual geographic extension of the functioning urban area. The first such proposals appeared at the end of the nineteenth century, and continue to this day. Many initiatives have been taken over the decades at the local, state, and federal levels, but the results have been meager. Only a handful of institutions resembling general-purpose metropolitan governments have been formed (Dade County, Florida, being an instance), and a great many special-purpose metropolitan authorities dealing with parks, water supply, airports, among other services.

The logical case for metropolitan government continues to be a powerful one, although not without problems ranging from the legal to the political. This is not the place to review these problems, which are on the whole well known, but it is important to point to an additional one brought about by the current extent of metropolitan dispersion.

The mental image that underlies the traditional concept of the American metropolis, and hence metropolitan government, is that of a central city where economic activity is concentrated, surrounded by a ring of suburbs which are mostly residential, and beyond the suburbs a rural area of countryside and small towns. The urbanized area of this idealized metropolis is essentially continuous and compact.

This picture (sometimes called the concentric zone theory) was essentially correct until some 40 years ago, when the second stage of metropolitan dispersion took off. Today this is a very imperfect picture of the metropolis, which extends much further in geographic space. Economic activity is now distributed in a constellation of dispersed clusters (the major one still at the traditional center). Residential areas are relatively continuous in the older portions of this metropolis, but they have also diffused over a large area, and many clusters are surrounded by open space. Only a small fraction of commuters move centripetally from the suburbs to the central cities; many now travel from central city homes to suburban jobs, and the vast majority of commuting trips go from one suburb to another. The growing ease of movement and communication has reduced the friction of space, and the metropolitan elements need no longer be tightly packed. They can now interact across relatively empty spaces, and the distinction is blurred between the country and the city. Each contains the other. Further, the geographic reach of these functional metropolises has become so large that in most cases the functional hinterland of one metropolitan area overlaps with that of another, so that any boundary between them is arbitrary.

Under these new realities of human geography, it would seem more difficult than ever to advance the cause of general-purpose metropolitan government for many metropolitan areas, especially the largest. This is because the essence of a general government is the clear definition of its boundaries (epitomized in the phrase "the law of the land"), and the boundaries are now hopelessly fuzzed, and wherever they are drawn are sure to include vast amounts of territory and a great many people and economic activities that are not functionally integrated with the metropolitan economy. Moreover, as noted, in a majority of cases the hinterlands of neighboring metropolitan areas overlap with each other.

Instead of general-purpose metropolitan governments, then, it would seem that whatever metropolitan regional integration and rationalization that may be achieved will occur through special-purpose units, with perhaps greater reliance on user fees than property or other general taxes in order to discriminate more carefully between those who are served and those who are not.

Changes Within the Traditional Metropolitan Area

THE MIDDLE CLASS AND THE CENTRAL CITY:
URBAN RENEWAL AND GENTRIFICATION

In the 1950s and 1960s, for a variety of reasons good and bad, enormous efforts were made by the federal government and by a host of local governments (mostly those of metropolitan central cities) to attract the middle class back to the central cities, primarily through the Urban Renewal Program. At the time the massive migration generated by the modernization of southern agriculture was depositing poor rural people (mostly black) in the slums of central cities from which earlier migrants had for the most part graduated. At the same time, the expanding white middle class of those prosperous years was moving to the suburbs. This resulted from many factors, including fear of crime and civil disorder, the decline of central city schools, the new housing made accessible by rising incomes, new roads, and new home financing instruments. Suburban shopping centers rose in competition to the traditional downtown, factories moved to the suburbs and beyond, and soon offices and services followed.

The central cities then faced what was termed the "urban crisis." This had more facets than can be discussed here, but in demographic terms the mere factor of scale was important. New immigrants had for decades crowded into old housing at the center, and did so now. The middle class moved outward largely into new housing at the edge of the urban area, while the working class moved outward into their newly vacated dwellings. This was the geographic expression of the filtering process of housing markets. The problem of scale was that whereas earlier the working class and much of the middle class had moved into new quarters within the municipal boundaries, as a result of massive demographic growth the low-income population now just about filled the central cities, while the working class and the middle class moved to suburban jurisdictions. The central cities thus were accumulating poor, expensive population while losing more stable, affluent, "nice," taxpaying population. Moreover, the associated suburbanization of manufacturing, of retail and wholesale establishments, and of offices and services compounded the city's fiscal, employment, and political crisis. Hence the attempt at urban renewal.

The description just completed is, of course, greatly simplified, but accurate in its general outlines. It only remains to add that this period of the 1950s and 1960s was precisely that of the baby boom, and that the physical and institutional form of the suburbs of the exploding metropolis were largely shaped by this factor.[1] Urban renewal programs failed to attract significant numbers of the white middle class back to the cities to a large extent because of the preponderant middle-class preference for the familial life style that produced the baby boom and to which the suburbs were so well suited.

The 1970s and 1980s saw important demographic changes in metropolitan areas. Rural migrants were no longer a significant source of population growth. The age composition of the metropolitan population was much changed, as the bulge of the baby boomers grew older. More important, perhaps, were changes in life style, especially among the white middle class, resulting in a general postponement of marriage, much lower fertility, and more frequent divorces.

As the 1970s proceeded, the leading edge of the baby boom, born in the late 1940s, began to reach the age at which Americans traditionally form households. It had been common for young middle-class adults to spend some time living in apartments in the central city before settling down to marriage, children, and the suburban life. The size of the baby boom cohort greatly swelled the number at this stage. But even more important was the fact that the period between leaving the parental home and having children began to be considerably stretched out. To visualize the consequences of the extension of this larval stage, imagine a stream of people walking past the scene of an accident and each stopping for half a minute to have a look: this will produce a crowd of a certain size. But if, instead, each person stops for a full minute, the size of the crowd will double. Thus, both the size of the baby boom cohort and the delay in childbearing contributed greatly to an increase in demand for central city housing.

To this must be added the demand generated by various groups which, for a variety of reasons, were growing in numbers: the divorced and separated, the economically self-sufficient elderly, and others (such as homosexuals and some career women) for whom singleness and childlessness was more a permanent than a temporary condition.

In all, the potential demand for housing of these various groups coincided with attractive opportunities in central city housing. The convenient location and the amenities were appealing. The relative price of city housing was low because middle-class flight and the exhaustion of rural immigrants had dried up competing sources of demand.[2] Indeed, for these reasons and because of the decline in the birth rate, the population of central cities in most metropolitan areas was declining. And these expanding groups of the middle class (the young, the old, and the more or less permanently single) shared one attribute: they did not have children of school age. For them, bad schools were not a problem and, indeed, provided them with a comparative advantage in the competition for housing.[3]

Such are the demographic sources of the gentrification that has occurred in many sections of metropolitan central cities. The consequences of this vigorous reentry of the middle class into the housing market of the central city are quite diverse, and well beyond the demographic scope of this chapter, but some may be noted:

a. The politics and institutional forms of housing have experienced rapid evolution in the form of rent control, condo-conversion regulation, and the amazing emergence of a previously obscure form of tenure— the condominium—in the past dozen years.

b. Central cities and their federal representative, the U.S. Department of Housing and Urban Development, had fought long and unsuccessfuly

with Urban Renewal and associated initiatives for the rebirth (however
defined) of central cities. Now, a generation later, they found that a
segment of the white middle class was returning to the cities and that
there was a parallel and possibly connected flourishing of offices, convention centers, shops, etc. Two decades ago Urban Renewal played
King Canute against irresistible tides, but the market is now producing
much of what was then sought because the conditions of demand are
now ripe.

c. This "rebirth" of the central cities has not been untroubled. Arguably
(and likely, although not statistically demonstrated), the reentry of a
portion of the middle class into the central city housing market has
made things harder for the other natural constituencies for this housing stock, namely, the poor. Although the gentrifiers may be few, they
use more of the existing housing stock per capita, and gentrification
has in many cases caused considerable displacement not only where it
occurs but by raising prices in nongentrifying sections.[4]

CONTINUING SUBURBANIZATION: RACE AND AGE

It must not be thought that the gentrification of decaying cities
has signaled the end of suburbanization. Figure 10 makes clear that
the movement from the central city to the suburbs remains the largest
of the flows we have been considering. This is largely because the
baby boom generation is so big that, although a good share may
live—at least for some years—in the central city, the majority (of the
whites) will still live in the suburbs. It is worth noting, however, that
new housing construction in the suburbs is no longer exclusively the
traditional freestanding single-family house, but that changes in the
family have produced a much larger demand share of apartments
and condominiums.

It is worth noting that the black middle class has accelerated its
suburbanization. Whereas 64 percent of metropolitan whites live in
the suburbs, only 29 percent of metropolitan blacks are suburban.
But in 1983–84, the most recent year for which there is information,
the net movement of blacks from central cities to suburbs was
231,000, representing 1.6 percent of black central city population
and an increase of 3.8 percent of the black suburban population. By
comparison, the net white migration from central cities to suburbs
was 1,490,000, which represented 3.1 percent of the white central
city population and an increase of only 1.8 percent in the white
suburban population. That is to say, the migration from the central
city to the suburbs now contributes to the growth of the black suburban population at twice the rate than it does for whites; but con-

versely this net migration takes away white central city population at twice the rate of the black. This apparent paradox derives, of course, from the fact that most whites are already in the suburbs, while most blacks still live in the central cities. Perhaps the simplest way to express what is happening is to say that blacks are accelerating their suburbanization, while on balance whites are still leaving the central cities.

One other point is worth noting on suburban demography. Many suburbs had their formative growth in the 1950s and 1960s, when young families moved in and produced the baby boom. In many cases a large portion of the suburban parents (or quite often, the widow) are still in place, but the children have left home. The age composition of these localities is now radically different. In many cases the housing stock is greatly underutilized because only one or two elderly people live in houses designed for large families—this at a time when many young people are having trouble becoming home-owners. All manner of public and private services, from schools and churches to retail shops, have had to adapt themselves to this change, not always successfully. The subject of the aging of the sub-urbs is not dramatic, and so has received relatively little attention, but it undoubtedly presents an interesting set of local and national problems and opportunities.

A final point deserves clarification. In an earlier section I dis-cussed the diffusion of the metropolitan population beyond the lim-its of the censally defined metropolitan area. This phenomenon is of great importance for a great many reasons, but demographically it is both important and not important. It is important demographically for these thinly populated exurban areas and where an influx of metropolitan-oriented people or enterprises looms large. It is not important, however, for the demography of metropolitan areas as a whole because the numbers involved are small relative to the popula-tion of the entire metropolitan area.

Interregional Movements

FROST BELT AND SUN BELT

A few years ago there was much talk, since then muted, about the Sun Belt and the Frost Belt (or Rust Belt) and about the national flow of people southward. Popular explanations centered on the decline of traditional manufacturing industries in the old Industrial Belt which ran from New York to Chicago and coincided roughly with the

Frost Belt, on the rise in value of natural resources (particularly oil and gas) that were concentrated in portions of the Sun Belt such as Texas and Louisiana, and on the attraction of a warm climate. There was indeed talk of a dawning of a new era of sectional strife comparable to the sectionalism of the nineteenth century; the Texas bumper sticker "Let the bastards freeze in the dark" seemed a harbinger.

As is often the case, this discussion was simplistic and plain wrong on many accounts. First, the general form of interregional east-to-west migration was one of long standing, not some sudden reversal: the settlement of our continental nation began in the East and has since been moving west. Second, Frost Belt and Sun Belt were broad labels that hid more differences than they revealed. The Sun Belt, for instance, included California, Texas, Mississippi, and Florida, which are as diverse as four states can be. The Frost Belt included Massachusetts and New Hampshire, Illinois and Ohio, and the Dakotas. Third, surveys of the reasons for migration during this period showed that for the overwhelming majority of movers, as always, economic considerations were primary, with climate and amenities playing a very minor role.

Figure 11 shows the principal net interregional one-year flows for 1975–76, soon after the oil crisis, and for 1983–84, the last year for which detailed information is available.

In 1975–76 the Midwest was the principal net source of interregional migrants nationally, contributing 138,000 to the West and 226,000 to the South. The Northeast sent its migrants to the West (89,000) and to the South (estimated at 115,000, but not statistically significant). The South received immigrants from the Midwest and the Northeast, but sent 140,000 net migrants to the West. The West received net immigrants from the other three regions.

By 1983–84 this situation had changed markedly. There was no statistically significant net movement between the West and any of the other three regions. Indeed, there was no statistically significant net migratory flow among any of the regions except for that from the Midwest to the South.

IMMIGRATION FROM ABROAD

Immigrants from abroad (which include returning U.S. citizens) present an interesting pattern, as shown in figure 11. If one includes in the calculation those small flows that are not statistically significant, the South received a net domestic migration of 201,000 in 1975–76, and of 426,000 in 1983–84; by contrast, its immigration

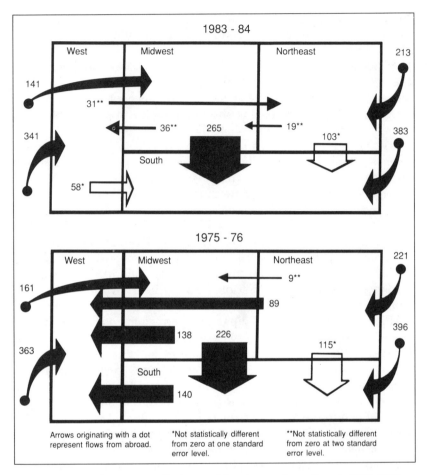

FIGURE 11. Net Flows Among Regions and Immigrants from Abroad, 1975–1976 and 1983–1984

Source: U.S. Dept. of Commerce, Bureau of the Census, *Geographical Mobility: March 1983 to March 2984*, Current Population Reports, ser. P-20, no. 407 (Washington, D.C.: GPO, 1986).

from abroad was nearly 400,000 in both years. The Northeast had a domestic migratory deficit of 213,000 in 1975–76 and of 91,000 in 1983–84; the respective migrations from abroad were 221,000 and 213,000. In these two periods the Midwest had net domestic outmigration of 355,000 and 282,000, while immigrants from abroad numbered 161,000 and 141,000, respectively. The West showed the most dramatic change in net domestic migration, from a surplus of 367,000 to a deficit of 53,000; but immigrants from abroad were 363,000 in 1975–76 and 341,000 in 1983–84.

In short, within the accuracy of the census sample, these broad regions show considerable temporal variability in net domestic migration, but—at least for this period—substantial and relatively stable immigration from abroad.

STATE VARIATIONS WITHIN REGIONS

Aggregate statistics for broad censal regions, it is important to realize, mask many internal differences. Table 4 shows the estimated net migration for the 1980–85 period by regions and states. The net figures by regions for these five-year estimates by the U.S. Census present a somewhat different picture, and one more in accord with the Frost Belt–Sun Belt image, than the 1983–84 figures (also by the U.S. Census) in figure 11. These two sets of estimates are clearly different but not necessarily inconsistent, and I will not try to reconcile them here. Rather, table 4 should be seen as displaying how varied the experiences of different states can be within the large regional aggregates. Within the Northeast, what is happening in northern New England is very different from what is happening in New York and Pennsylvania. In the Midwest all states show net outmigration, but there is a qualitative as well as a quantitative difference between what is happening in Michigan and in North Dakota. In the South, Florida and Texas are vast receivers of domestic and international migrants, but Mississippi is still losing people; Maryland and Virginia include major portions of the northeastern megalopolis. In the West, California has a huge migratory gain, but Oregon and Idaho have net outmigration.

BLACK INTERREGIONAL MIGRATION

The migration of blacks to and from the South is of particular interest. On the one hand, the historic migration of blacks from this region to the nation's cities has been an epochal event in American social and economic history, the echoes of which will resonate for a long time. Blacks left the South by the millions because they were a socially and economically oppressed minority within a backward region. On the other hand, as the result of progress in national economic integration, the South has been modernizing, its per capita income is catching up to the national aver-

TABLE 4
Net Migration in the United States from All Sources, 1980–1985
(in thousands)

Northeast	−327	South (cont.)	
Connecticut	−6	District of Columbia	−27
Maine	8	Florida	1,437
Massachusetts	−28	Georgia	273
New Hampshire	45	Kentucky	−52
New Jersey	39	Louisiana	29
New York	−183	Maryland	25
Pennsylvania	−211	Mississippi	−22
Rhode Island	4	North Carolina	188
Vermont	5	Oklahoma	137
		Tennessee	38
Midwest	−1,772	Texas	1,202
Illinois	−320	Virginia	161
Indiana	−179	West Virginia	−53
Iowa	−122		
Kansas	−11	West	2,192
Michigan	−496	Alaska	69
Minnesota	−62	Arizona	308
Missouri	−31	California	1,429
Nebraska	−28	Colorado	164
North Dakota	−3	Hawaii	19
Ohio	−401	Idaho	−2
South Dakota	−15	Montana	—
Wisconsin	−104	Nevada	94
		New Mexico	52
South	3,435	Oregon	−45
Alabama	−4	Utah	17
Arkansas	6	Washington	86
Delaware	5	Wyoming	2

Source: Adapted from U.S. Dept. of Commerce, Bureau of the Census, *Statistical Abstract of the United States, 1987* (Washington, D.C.: GPO, 1986), table 27.
Note: The four regions can be subdivided as follows: Northeast = New England and the Middle Atlantic region; Midwest = East North-Central and West North-Central regions; South = South Atlantic, East South-Central, and West South-Central regions; West = Mountain and Pacific regions.

age, and it is sprouting national and international metropolises, such as Miami and Atlanta.

Sometime in the last twenty years the migration of blacks from the South to the rest of the county reversed itself, and the South has become a net importer rather than exporter of black people. In the year 1983–84, for instance, 152,000 blacks moved to the South from other regions, whereas only 136,000 left the South. The net migration into the South that year was thus only 16,000, or about .1 percent of the southern black population. Of the black migrants leaving the South, 36 percent moved into the central cities of other regions, 52 percent into metropolitan suburbs, and 11 percent into nonmetropolitan areas. Of the black migrants to the South, 40 percent moved into the central cities and 37 percent to the suburbs of metropolitan areas, while 22 percent moved into nonmetropolitan areas. On the overall matter of "urbanization," it is interesting to note that only 5 percent of blacks leaving the South left metropolitan for nonmetropolitan areas, while 21 percent left southern nonmetropolitan areas for metropolitan areas in other regions. In this sense the black migration *from* the South is still an urbanizing process. Interestingly, of blacks moving *to* the South fully 23 percent moved from metropolitan to nonmetropolitan areas, and only 11 percent moved from nonmetropolitan areas elsewhere to metropolitan areas in the South. In this sense, black migration to the South appears to be a reruralization pattern.

In all, the regional reversal of black migration is a significant fact in American history, and testifies to the growing maturity of the nation in terms of its economic regional integration. But not too much must be made of it: the South is a very large and diverse area that includes Washington, D.C., and its suburbs, Mississippi, and Florida, and in the absence of detailed geographic information it is hard to interpret the realities represented by such gross figures.

Geographic Variation in Fertility and Age Distribution

There is extraordinary variation in the distribution of fertility and age among regions of the United States. We tend to forget this both when we look at a national statistic such as the birth rate, and when we attribute the variety of local demographic differences exclusively to migration.

While the national birth rate hovers at 16 percent, the birth rates of Massachusetts and Connecticut stand below 13 percent, while that of Utah is more than twice as high, on a par with some developing countries. Even in the absence of migration, this variation in birth rates results in a sharp variation among states in age distribution and dependency ratios, as shown in table 5 and figures 12 and 13.

The age distributions in 1980 for Massachusetts and Utah are

TABLE 5

Dependency Ratios in 1980 and Changes That Would Occur in the Working-Age Population of Selected States in the Absence of Migration

	Dependency Ratios, 1980		Changes in Working-Age Population with No Migration (%)	
	Young	Old	1980–1990	1990–2000
Massachusetts	.52	.72	12.7	3.6
Pennsylvania	.68	.76	9.9	3.4
Florida	.50	1.12	7.0	3.5
Utah	.80	.41	22.1	24.4
Texas	.61	.64	17.0	10.4

Source: U.S. Dept. of Commerce, Bureau of the Census, *Statistical Abstract of the United States, 1987* (Washington, D.C.: GPO, 1986).
Note: Young = population 0–19 years of age over population 20–64. Old = population 65 years and older over population 20–64. Working-age population = 20–64 years old.

shown in figure 12 (which also shows the distribution for Florida, to be discussed later). The industrialized eastern states are characterized by low fertility, Massachusetts—in spite of its Catholic heritage— having a very low fertility rate, comparable to that of West Germany, one-third below replacement. Utah, as the center of Mormon culture, has a very high birth rate, and this cultural influence extends to its neighboring states. Examine figure 12. Because of its high birth rate, the share of Utah's population under five years of age was 121 percent higher than that of Massachusetts, while Massachusetts's share of old people was two-thirds higher than Utah's. Looking at it another way, the 1980 median age in Utah was 24.2 while that of Massachusetts was 31.2. Similarly, as shown in table 5, the Utah youth-dependency ratio was .80, while that of Massachusetts was only .52; conversely, the age-dependency ratio was .72 in Massachusetts, but only .41 in Utah.

Utah and Massachusetts represent the extremes of state fertility rates in the United States, but several other states also present distinctive patterns. Elements of Florida's complex history, for instance, are partially expressed in the age distribution of its population: it has been sort of a southern state, a retirement mecca for northerners, and a resort area, and in the past generation has become a haven for Latin American immigrants and a hemispheric trading center. Its role as a mecca for the elderly is still evident in its median age of 34.7, 11 percent higher than that of Massachusetts and 43 percent higher than that of Utah; but this also reflects the low levels of fertility among its

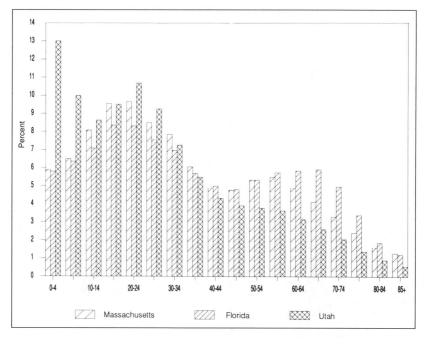

FIGURE 12.   Age Distribution in Massachusetts, Florida, and Utah, 1980

Source: U.S. Dept. of Commerce, Bureau of the Census, *Projections of the Population of the United States, by Age, Sex, and Race, 1983–2080,* Current Population Reports, ser. P-25, no. 952 (Washington, D.C.: GPO, 1984).

Cuban immigrants. If one looks closely at figure 12, one can see that Florida's 1980 age distribution has two peaks. One is at ages 15–19, which corresponds to baby boom births in 1960–65; the other is at ages 65–69, and is related to Florida's role as a retirement center. These two are U.S. phenomena, and somewhere in the distribution, had one the means to analyze them, are the effects of the various waves of Caribbean Basin migrants of the past decades.

Figure 13 shows the age distributions of two states, Pennsylvania and Texas, which, while they have their particularities, may represent the Frost Belt and the Sun Belt without being at the extremes. Notice that the share of young people is markedly sharper in Texas. This responds to two factors: first, fertility has traditionally been higher in the Sun Belt; second, migrants tend to be young, and therefore fertile, so that areas of in-migration tend to have a birth multiplier.

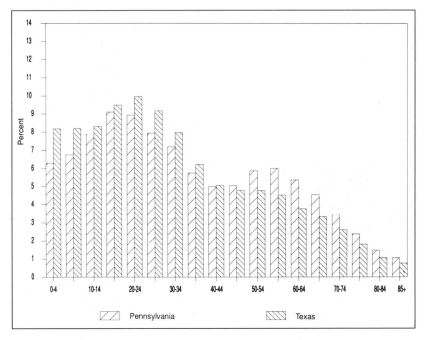

FIGURE 13.   Age Distribution in Pennsylvania and Texas, 1980

Source: U.S. Dept. of Commerce, Bureau of the Census, *Projections of the Population of the United States, by Age, Sex, and Race, 1983–2080,* Current Population Reports, ser. P-25, no. 952 (Washington, D.C.: GPO, 1984).

The differences in the 1980 age distributions of Texas and Pennsylvania as shown in figure 13 are quite visible. While they may not seem remarkable, they are significant, and the implications of their apparently slight differences are quite meaningful. The median age of Pennsylvania is 10 percent higher than that of Texas. The youth- and old-dependency ratios of Texas (see table 5) are both slightly lower than those of Pennsylvania. This would seem to place Texas in a more favorable demographic position than Pennsylvania. But, referring again to table 5, look at the growth of the working-age population, or labor supply.[5] In the 1980–90 decade, if there had been no domestic or international migration, Texas's labor supply would have grown by 17 percent because in Texas there are that many more young people ready to enter the labor force than there are old people ready to leave it. Thus, were there no more migrants to Texas from domestic or foreign sources, that state would have had to generate jobs at a yearly growth rate of 1.5 percent to accommodate its internal growth in labor supply. By comparison, Pennsylvania would have needed to grow at only about two-thirds that rate, or about .8 percent. But it is in the next decade, the 1990s, that the strong local demographic differences would emerge. Pennsylvania's working-age population would increase only by 3.4 percent in the decade, while that of Texas would grow by 10.4 percent, nearly three times as much. Of course, unless the longstanding migration patterns that now prevail are reversed (see table 4), Texas's labor force will increase by much more than 10 percent because it is a large net recipient both of domestic and international migrants, while Pennsylvania's labor force will actually shrink.

An explanatory addendum may be useful when considering the effects of geographic variations in fertility over time. In the period of relatively low fertility associated with the Great Depression, there was a marked difference between low- and high-fertility states. The national increase in the birth rate during the baby boom was not evenly distributed: while all the states showed increases in births, the low-fertility states increased in population more sharply than the high-fertility ones. Conversely, the decline in fertility since then has been sharpest in the traditionally low-fertility states, and the national geography of fertility has become again highly differentiated. Consequently, the peaks and valleys of the age distribution are and will continue to be much more marked in the older industrialized states, and thus their demographic characteristics will become more varied over time.

PART III

Economic and Social Implications of
Demographic Change

Introduction

The purpose of part III is to explore the economic and social implications of some of the major demographic changes now occurring
in the United States. It is designed to develop a framework for
organizing and probing the implications of long-term demographic
trends. It will try to draw out the main issues that will face our
society as a result of these developments, and it will suggest the
types of policy responses in both the public and private sectors
that could help our society adjust to them.

The objective of this section, along with the rest of this volume,
is to lay the groundwork for more detailed exploration and policy
analysis in the future. We will present an assortment of key issues
that jump out of the demographic trends and try to organize them
in ways that relate them to some basic themes and to basic social
and economic goals. In other words, this is not just a recitation of
issues, but rather an effort to relate issues to each other and to a
coherent policy framework.

We will stop short of making specific, detailed policy recommendations; such recommendations will emerge from the next
phase of CED's project on demographic trends. We will develop a
general picture of the kinds of public policy reforms and private-
sector initiatives that could respond to the challenges imposed by
demographic changes. The goal is to provide the reader with both
an understanding of the problems that may arise if we follow a
do-nothing approach and to suggest the general types of responses
and innovations that would be necessary to head off these problems. What we are presenting here are explanations of demographic trends, a notion of what social problems these trends would
cause in a strictly business-as-usual environment, and a set of general options (as opposed to detailed blueprints) for addressing the
challenges posed by expected demographic change.

Part III focuses on three major demographic trends—the aging
of the U.S. population, the changing composition of households

and family structure, and patterns of immigration. Its basic theme is that we can and should be imaginative in shaping and adjusting to demographic trends rather than taking them as inevitable and concentrating simply on how to cope with them. It stresses the desirability of a proactive rather than a reactive stance toward demographic change. Demographic trends can be viewed either as imposing a sentence on our society or as challenges that prompt us to be more creative and innovative in our social policy designs and the management of our social institutions, as well as more productive in our economic performance.

While there are certain imperatives associated with long-term demographic trends, we can take many steps to influence the actual magnitude of such trends, and we can do even more to adapt to them. Hugh Heclo put it this way: "Demography is not destiny."

Part III will emphasize casting a wary, cautious glance at the notion of "dependency ratios." The age-dependency ratio, for example, relates the size of the population deemed dependent for reasons of old age to the corresponding size of the so-called independent working-age population. To begin with, these terms are too often taken literally to mean the ratio of those over working age (that is, 65 and over) to those of working age (20–64 years old). The unstated implication is that people 65 and over are incapable of work or financial independence, and must be taken care of, while people 20–64 are, ipso facto, independent and capable of supporting themselves and others.

Both of these premises are misleading. Many senior citizens are active and independent, just as numerous working-age adults are, in fact, dependent. Moreover, there are many ways that we can foster independence among both groups, thereby conserving resources for people who truly cannot be self-sufficient as a result of illness, disability, and the frailty that eventually accompanies old age.

We will stress the theme that the effective dependency ratio can be lowered through a variety of measures designed to make as many people as possible educated, healthy, employed, productive, and in charge of their own activities of daily living.

Conceptual Framework

In part III, we will focus on human behavior over the life cycle. The emphasis will be on fostering behavior that encourages youth

to prepare properly for an interesting work career and to participate in the mainstream of our social life, that encourages adults to
be self-sufficient and socially responsible, and to provide for their
retirement needs to the extent possible through savings, insurance,
and other means, and that encourages senior citizens to remain
active and independent where possible.

Our framework for analysis blends demographic trends and social goals. These goals include improving our standard of living,
reducing poverty, achieving economic independence and self-
sufficiency, giving fully adequate support to those who cannot
work, and striving for international tranquility and progress. We
explore how demographics will affect these social goals, and how
we can adjust to demographic trends so as to foster them.

There is a strong emphasis in our analysis on the individual's
personal responsibility throughout the life cycle. But our conceptual framework also stresses the role of employers in helping people maintain healthy life styles and put aside enough resources to
protect against the expenses of old age and the risk of illness and
disability. And this framework also acknowledges an important
role for government in assisting those, who, despite their best efforts, have inadequate resources to assure them a decent living
standard.

We will examine the question of how, in the face of expected
demographic trends, we can reform private institutions and provide incentives for sensible private behavior in order to assure a
flow of resources to tomorrow's elderly that will be adequate to
meet their needs. Similarly, we explore public-sector reforms that
will target limited resources more appropriately to needs and de-
liver social services in a more efficient and cost-effective manner.

The above goals can be addressed first through policies targeted to children. Beginning with efforts to reduce infant mortality
and facilitate the health and development of preschool-age youth
and extending through efforts to reduce school dropout rates and
raise basic skills and academic achievement, a successful approach to helping youth is an investment in the future. By making
tomorrow's workers more able to qualify for work and compete in
an increasingly international market, successful interventions in
the early years can offset the danger of future dependency. Thus,
we will briefly discuss general approaches to improving the
health, education, social attitudes, and knowledge of the world of
work among youth.

The effective dependency ratio will also be influenced by people's behavior during their working years. Personal saving during these years, for example, will help prepare people for outlays during retirement when earnings typically decline. The United States has one of the lowest rates of saving of any industrialized nation. This paucity of private saving is made worse by the relentless budget deficits of the federal government. These dual trends jeopardize private investment and threaten the modernization and expansion of facilities and the technological innovation that we need to generate sustainable economic growth and new jobs.

Another important aspect of behavior during the working years that can potentially reduce dependency involves maintaining a healthy life style. Good exercise and proper diet, along with not smoking and avoiding drug abuse, can make people active and productive who would otherwise be ill and unable to work. Proper prevention techniques, such as periodic screening for hypertension and cardiovascular disease, can avert disabling conditions and keep people healthier and active.

Education and health, of course, are crucial to the productivity of the work force, and the greater this productivity, the more able will be a working-age population of a given size to support those who cannot work. In addition, however, productivity will also be affected by such factors as investment in plant and equipment, outlays for research and development, and other factors. Our framework emphasizes incentives both to encourage those able to work to find work and to enhance the productivity of those who are working. The more the economic pie grows, the more we will be able to afford the slice that goes to those unable to contribute to growth.

In a similar vein, efforts to reduce poverty through work readiness and family solidarity will yield more workers and less dependents. Demographic trends toward the breakup of families, coupled with the stubborn incidence of long-term welfare dependency among a portion of the poor, threaten to remove a whole segment of potential workers from the mainstream of economic activity and add them to the dependent category. This in turn puts pressure on others to pull more than their own weight.

Another important factor in assuring a stable relationship between supporters and those being supported involves the integration of immigrants into our economic base. Alarm bells warning of temporary labor bottlenecks, arising from a smaller cohort of those entering the labor market, can be responded to effectively through immigration, provided that those entering the United States are able to participate in economic activity and be independent. Achieving this economic independence among immigrants, however, poses formidable challenges discussed in the final section.

Our framework also focuses on incentives to work, particularly for those from low-income households and for older workers. Labor force participation rates for welfare recipients are relatively low, and in part this results from the system of work disincentives built into our welfare system. And, there has been a steady decline in labor market activity among men in their early retirement and preretirement years. These trends shift people who could be in the denominator of the dependency ratio into the numerator, exacerbating the long-term upward trend in this ratio associated with the aging of the population.

Finally, we will briefly review a range of policies and practices regarding our treatment of the elderly that could be improved to foster independent living. To the extent that we can provide the social support networks and financial mechanisms to enable senior citizens to live at home or in the community rather than in an institution, we will be furthering two goals at once: we will economize on resources, permitting us to target aid to those who have little control over their situations, and we will improve the enjoyment and quality of life for older people who almost always prefer independent living.

CHAPTER 5

The Aging of the Population

IN 1987 THERE were 243.4 million Americans, and 29.8 million, or about 12 percent, were 65 years of age or older. An estimated 12.2 million people, or a little less than 5 percent of the population, were 75 and over, and about 2.9 million, or just over 1 percent, were at least 85 years old.[1]

By the year 2030 the Census Bureau projects about 305 million people in the United States, and the average age will have risen to about 41 years from a level of about 32 today. The population 65 years and over will have soared from 12 percent of the total to an estimated 21.6 percent, and about 3 percent of the elderly will be 85 years of age or older, triple the proportion in that category today. It is also interesting to note that the Census Bureau projects 492,000 centenarians in 2030, as compared to only 37,000 people who were at least 100 years old in 1985. Looking out a little further (which becomes a little speculative), we see that in 2050 there will be some 16 million people 85 years old or older and about a million centenarians. Percentages aside, the sheer number of additional elderly persons will force some adjustments in our economic and social life; clearly, many more people will require personal assistance and social services in the middle of the next century.

In contrast to this sharp growth in the elderly population, the number of working-age people is leveling off. According to the middle series of the Census Bureau projections, the population age 18–64 is expected to grow by only 0.8 percent a year from 1990 to 2010, and then to fall by 0.3 percent a year between 2010 and 2030, from 179.2 million to 174.4 million.[2]

Census Bureau projections also show a ratio of people 65 and over to those in their so-called working years of 33.4 percent in 2030, compared to 20.5 percent in 1985. Stated in reverse, the ratio of working-age to elderly people is projected to drop from about five to one to about three to one between 1985 and 2030. Of course, this trend may actually understate the downward trend in the ratio of workers to nonworkers if the trend toward increased early retirement among men in their late fifties and early sixties, to be discussed later, continues.

A major issue emerging from the growing burden on working-age people is how the adaptation to new circumstances will be divided between younger and older people. The challenge is to avoid bitterness and a sense of unfairness on the part of either group that would emerge from a strategy of adjustment that placed all the adjustment pains on one group. One way to help mitigate this bitterness is to adopt policy changes that recognize the increasing wealth and income of those who will be old in the future, while shielding those who are quite old and not so well off today. Another way is to adopt policy measures that are progressively financed within any given age cohort.

A good example of a policy step that recognized the need to protect current retirees while making some changes for the future was the decision in 1983 to change the age of eligibility for Social Security benefits. The age at which people can retire with full benefits will rise under current law in stages from 65 to 67, but this change will not begin for almost two decades. A good example of the preference for progressive financing would be a decision to tax Social Security benefits more fully than we now do rather than freeze cost-of-living increases in benefits, if we decide that Social Security must contribute more to deficit reduction or to financing new social initiatives than it already does.

Given the magnitude of the decline in the number of working-age people that must support retirees, our society is going to have to face these choices. We are going to need to find ways to finance the current level of benefits (and to share the burden of the bill equitably) or else revise the benefit structure. In other words, we will have to "cut our cloth to fit our pattern," and the pattern will be one of dwindling revenues relative to obligations as we move into the next century.

In the next section we explore expected trends in Social Security, Medicare, and other government programs in light of demographic trends, then discuss the implications for private-sector commitments to the retirement years of workers. These two sections will analyze the likely trends in public- and private-sector programs oriented to retirees and will trace out the broad contours of policy steps that address these trends. Subsequent sections will highlight some of the variables that might attenuate the pressure on the working-age population and modify some of the expected effects on public- and private-sector programs. The factors discussed are in line with those developed in the conceptual framework (for example, increasing labor force participation, reducing unemployment, raising productivity, and reforming social programs).

The Effect of a Changing Age Structure on Public-Sector Expenditures

This section explores the implications of the changing structure of our population for an array of government programs. We focus mainly on retirement programs here, since they are most affected by the aging of our population.

The Social Security system consists of three programs financed through separate trust funds. The Old Age and Survivors Insurance (OASI) program pays benefits to retired workers, their dependents, and survivors, and paid an estimated $209 billion in benefits in FY 1989. The Disability Insurance (DI) program pays benefits at a rate of about $20.4 billion. Together, these programs pay benefits to an estimated 39 million people.[3]

SOCIAL SECURITY

The Hospital Insurance (HI) trust fund covers Part A of Medicare. In FY 1989 we estimated that about 29.4 million elderly and 3.2 million disabled people were covered by Medicare, and outlays were roughly $96 billion for the program as a whole, of which about $53 billion is related to hospital benefits.[4]

The Social Security program is strongly affected by demographic trends, especially as those trends interact with the impact of the maturation of the program. In the first few decades of the program's experience, retirees drawing benefits had not contributed over an entire lifetime, and this tended to make the ratio of benefits received to contributions very favorable. For many years the payroll tax was quite low, but it has been rising sharply over the past two decades and in 1990 stands at 15.52 percent of payroll (including 2.9 percent for Medicare), as compared to only 2 percent at the beginning of the program.

Thus, people retiring when the program was not yet fully mature witnessed an excellent yield on their invested tax dollars. Moreover, demographic factors did not put much pressure on the system in the past, as the older population was growing at a pace that the working-age population could absorb.

The important point for our analysis is that all of these favorable factors are now turning around. The program is reaching full maturity; tax rate increases are slowing down (one occurred in 1990 under prior legislation, but then rates are scheduled to remain flat for the indefinite future); the older population is growing more rapidly at the same time as growth in the working-age population is slowing down.

The Social Security Amendments of 1983 were designed to address the expected long-term shortfall in revenues arising from demographic factors, as well as shorter-term problems associated mainly with the nation's poor economic performance. The 1983 compromise was about an even mixture of changes in taxes and benefits. Scheduled tax rate increases were accelerated, a portion of benefits was taxed for the first time above certain income thresholds, and the normal retirement age was scheduled to begin rising in increments in the early part of the next century. The new law also delayed cost-of-living adjustments by six months and expanded coverage of the system to include new federal employees and all employees of non-profit organizations.

Two conclusions about the 1983 legislation seem warranted. First, there is a general consensus that the law averted the impending short-term crisis in Social Security and achieved what might properly be called a delicate balance in the long-term actuarial soundness of the old age and disability funds. This long-term stability hinges crucially on leaving the income thresholds that trigger taxation fixed in nominal terms, allowing gradually more income to be taxed over time.

Second, the projected soundness of OASDI is highly sensitive to two types of conditions—economic and demographic. Depending upon the actual performance of our economy in the years to come and upon actual trends in mortality and fertility (particularly the former), we could experience almost any outcome over a very wide range. Analysts William Birdsall and John Hankins at the University of Michigan, for example, have projected a variety of scenarios under various assumptions about the U.S. economy, mortality, and fertility. Under one rather polar set of assumptions (poor economic performance coupled with a significant decline in mortality rates), the Social Security trust funds could be projected to be in deep trouble. By contrast, a combination of a buoyant economy and stable mortality rates would mean that OASDI would have a substantial surplus far into the future.[5] Under varying assumptions, this study shows that the ratio of beneficiaries to covered workers could range from 38 percent to 80 percent in the year 2060, and the cost of OASDI as percent of payroll could vary from 11.1 percent to 28.5 percent.

Of course, these are long-range projections; over relatively brief periods, we will not experience such huge changes in the outlook for Social Security. But this long-term volatility suggests that it would be prudent to reassess our course under Social Security every few years, rather than putting the program on automatic pilot and cruising ahead. Under changing economic and demographic conditions, we could drift into troubled waters.

The performance of the economy is important because if productivity and real wages are not growing much, then the inflow to the funds, keyed to nominal wages, is not outpacing the outflow, which will rise in line with price increases as a result of the cost-of-living adjustment. This removes the "wedge" that results from real-wage growth that keeps the actuarial wolf from the trust fund door. In addition, a sluggish economy is usually translated into higher unemployment, and unemployed workers, by definition, do not contribute to the funds when they are not receiving paychecks.

These are not idle concerns. Between 1973 and 1985, annual increases in productivity in the United States averaged only 0.9 percent a year, as compared to 3.0 percent annually over the period 1947–73.[6] Real wages were sluggish and actually declined in some years. Moreover, unemployment was also higher during the later period. If the future performance of the economy conforms more closely to the past decade and a half than to the earlier postwar period, there will indeed be cause for more pessimism and caution about the Social Security fund balances.

Moreover, there has been a consistent tendency to underestimate medical science breakthroughs and consequently to overestimate future mortality rates. After the tremendous decline in mortality in the early postwar years, the gains tapered off for a significant period (the late fifties and the sixties), leading many observers to predict that we had accomplished about all that we could. But another wave of improvement occurred during the seventies and eighties, associated this time with such factors as the reduction in mortality from cardiovascular and cerebrovascular disease.

The actual performance of the economy in the near future and actual fertility and mortality rates will have a major impact on how much of our national output is allocated to Social Security. For example, under the Social Security trustees' intermediate set of assumptions, Social Security would account for 6.2 percent of GNP by the year 2025, compared to 4.7 percent in 1985. But if the trustees' pessimistic assumptions about the economy and demographic trends should be borne out instead, the share of GNP accounted for by Social Security in 2025 would be 7.3 percent, or about 1 percentage point more. The gap between these two sets of assumptions is even greater when one considers the costs of Medicare. This program would absorb 4.2 percent of GNP in 2025 under the intermediate assumptions, but 7.6 percent of GNP under pessimistic assumptions, a figure that is four and half times larger than the proportion of GNP now demanded by Medicare—1.7 percent.

It is important to stress that if the latter scenario occurs (which develops from both "bad" economic news and "good" demographic news), we can fix the trust fund balance without drastic action. But the actions that would have to be taken would be more than marginal and would carry some adverse side effects.

Economist Alicia Munnell has noted that there is virtually no threat during the period from 1990 to 2020. According to her estimates, even under pessimistic assumptions about the economy and mortality, the Social Security system will run surpluses until 2013 and have positive trust balances until 2020. If the economy did more poorly than has been imagined by the most pessimistic assumptions of the Social Security actuaries (a possibility involving a real-wage differential of less than 1 percent, which some other observers consider realistic), revenues would still be adequate to cover benefit commitments, although insufficient to produce substantial surpluses.[7]

According to Munnell, the financial solvency of Social Security after 2020 "hinges crucially on demographic developments being in line with the Social Security trustees' intermediate projections and to a somewhat lesser extent on productivity growth producing an adequate real wage differential." The intermediate assumption about U.S fertility is that it will rise from its current level of about 1.8 to 2.0 by 2005, a path that Munnell finds realistic, although it slightly exceeds recent Census Bureau forecasts.

If the long-run real-wage growth averaged 1.0 percent instead of 1.5 percent (the intermediate assumption of tax trustees), the cost of the Social Security system over the 2020–59 period would be roughly 1.0 percent of taxable payrolls higher, and the cost of the program over the entire 75-year forecasting horizon would be 0.8 percent higher as a percent of payroll (13.7 percent instead of 12.9 percent), or 6 percent of program expenditures over the 75 years.[8]

WILL WE STORE ENOUGH GRAIN?

The federal government will face an enormous temptation to "eat the seed corn" of today's wage and salary earners, leaving them lean and hungry in the "harvest years" of their lives. The year-end balance in the OASI fund stood at $57.5 billion in FY 1987; by 1990 this balance is projected to more than triple to $192.5 billion, and by 1992, it will be 1.61 percent of payroll; but it is projected to go higher, to a peak of 2.68 percent of payroll in 2005–06.[9]

Students of the federal budget process will perhaps recognize in these figures the siren song of new federal spending initiatives, beckoning the Congress and succeeding presidents to finance popular new programs, or extend existing ones, out of the burgeoning surplus. Indeed, the federal deficit today is being held down by this surplus. Since we are going to need the surplus later to pay benefits, we really should be saving it. Instead, this policy is permitting and masking a growing deficit in the rest of the federal ledger even as we congratulate ourselves for bringing down the deficit.

What we will experience here is not unlike the biblical tale of Joseph and the pharaoh in ancient Egypt. Interpreting the troubled pharaoh's disturbing dreams of seven fat cows parading across his line of vision followed by seven lean ones, the clairvoyant Joseph foretold of seven years with overstuffed granaries arising from record harvests, followed by seven lean years of parched earth and withered crops. The humble Joseph catapulted himself from incarcerated slave to deputy pharaoh with the economic equivalent of today's Social Security rescue plan. Fundamentally, it was simple—save and store the surplus! This the Egyptians did, stretching their surplus stocks to cover the seven lean years.

Happily, the cost of our profligacy, should we opt for consuming all our grain, need not be starvation. But it will be higher taxes if young workers today are to receive full benefits. Again, the work of Alicia Munnell tells us that the cost of a restoration of grain stocks would not be catastrophic; but it would be significant. The tax rate hike that would be required if reserves are not accumulated during the 1990 to 2020 "storage" period is roughly 1 percent each on employees and employers, an outcome that Munnell calls "fairly modest," though other observers might express a greater concern.[10] A 2-percentage-point increase in the total payroll tax rate would be about a 13 percent increase in the rate, an outcome that could have significant adverse effects on employment, particularly for lower-wage workers.

Thus, it is important to stress that Social Security is not in any imminent danger of running out of money in the next several years, in contrast with Medicare which *is* in such danger, as described in the next section. Indeed, over the next several years Social Security will begin to bulge with surplus stock. The important lesson for our society is that we must save for our future, by whatever means, rather than transfer this saving into current consumption. What matters is not so much the extent to which we save publicly versus privately (Social Security is public saving), but rather that we save enough to meet our future needs.

The important lesson for policy is that in order to be able to finance the retirement of people who are now in their thirties and forties, the growing surplus in the Social Security trust fund has to be used, in one way or another, to stimulate economic growth in the next three decades. If the burgeoning surplus results in a greater amount of national saving and a corresponding greater amount of productive investment, our capacity to meet retirement needs in the future will be enhanced. The surpluses reflect public saving; we could also build up the equivalent of such surpluses privately. But the basic thrust and appeal of Social Security is that it forces us to put this money aside; we do not allow ourselves the private option of consuming all our grain. The key is to avoid transmitting the surpluses into deficits elsewhere in the public-sector ledger, deficits that become larger than would otherwise occur. If this were to happen, today's baby boomers would surely come up short of wheat at harvest time.

In terms of actual budget operation, a good operational principle would be to set a goal of balancing the federal budget exclusive of Social Security.

FINDING THE RIGHT MIX TO MAINTAIN SUPPORT

As the Social Security system matures, the proportion of benefits "purchased" by the OASI taxes of workers is rising sharply. Stated in reverse, the amount of "excess" benefits that the average retiree receives, over and above lifetime contributions, recedes. This decline in the yield of invested taxes is occurring at different rates for different groups, depending on earnings level, marital status, and gender. For example, low earners will have higher yields than high earners, and married couples will have higher yields than unmarried individuals.

But even the group with the lowest yield, single men in the maximum earnings category, is still projected to receive less than 100 percent of its benefits in 2025. In other words, under realistic assumptions, about 40 years from now even the subgroup with the highest ratio of money in to money out (in absolute dollar terms) will get back only a little more money than it put into Social Security.

Nonetheless, a small marginal return is a lot different from the veritable bonanza that current retirees are reaping, and the politics of Social Security support can be expected to be affected by this change. In other words, as the population's benefits change from being an excellent deal to barely a good deal, support for the system could erode. Moreover, is it even barely a good deal? The true test of this is not whether people will get back more than they put in, but whether dollars *invested* in Social Security will do as well as they would invested in other ways.

Viewed in this way, the Social Security system may be in a bit more trouble than some people might believe. As economist Martin Feldstein has observed, the return received by people who got in on the ground floor of Social Security was far greater than they would have received by putting the same funds in a bank or buying government bonds. But the situation is changing. Feldstein calculates that a 36-year-old worker now has to contribute about $3,000 in employee-employer payroll taxes to earn $9,000 in benefits, in 1985 dollars, at age 66. If the individual invested that same amount in government bonds, he would have $15,000 at the age of 66.[11] According to Feldstein, this means that people born after World War II could enjoy both more consumption while they are working and more income after retirement if Social Security taxes and benefits were lowered somewhat.

But Feldstein argues that these adverse effects of Social Security must be balanced against the desirability of protecting those who would otherwise save too little for their old age and thereby experience poverty and hardship. To accomplish this balance, he would reduce benefit replacement ratios for middle- and upper-income retirees and shore up the incomes of the elderly poor through greater reliance on the Supplementary Security Income (SSI) program.

Another social benefit of a strategy that scales back replacement ratios for higher-income people would be to reduce the alleged dampening effect of Social Security on private savings. There is considerable debate about the magnitude (and even the existence) of such an effect. Indeed, it has been argued that people would undersave if Social Security benefits were reduced. But if there is some truth to Feldstein's contention that the capital stock is made smaller by Social Security because private saving—and therefore investment—is reduced, then the performance of our economy could be enhanced by reducing this drag.

Thus, some of the key choices facing Social Security in the years ahead will include: (1) whether to spend part or all of the growing surplus to meet other short-term social needs, and if so, how to replenish the funds so as to assure adequate retirement incomes for future retirees; (2) whether to reduce benefits somewhat for the higher-income recipients so as to take some pressure off tax rates and avert possible adverse side effects on private saving; and (3) whether to redesign Social Security so as to bring in more revenue from higher-income recipients (for example, by taxing more of their benefits) and recycling the funds to shore up the purchasing power of lower-income elderly people (e.g., by establishing a higher minimum Social Security benefit and/or raising SSI benefits).

MEDICARE

If the situation in Social Security is delicately balanced, but tenuous, the long-term outlook for Medicare is bleak. An impending short-term crisis, viewed as imminent in the early 1980s, was averted by a series of factors including the slowdown in the rate of growth in outlays attributable in part to the prospective payment plan for hospitals initiated by Medicare in 1983. But looking down the road, most experts foresee an exhaustion of the HI trust fund balance unless steps are taken to bring in more revenue or to restructure benefits. David C. Lindeman, an analyst with the Congressional Budget Office (CBO), put it this way:

> A lot of people suppose that the so-called surpluses in the trust fund will be used to get Medicare through whatever time is necessary. I am not sure. I think the magnitude of the Medicare problem in the 1990s is considerable. I think it dwarfs the problem that we had in 1983. . . . The magnitude of the problem in Medicare is so much greater that it is hard to see how the political process is going to grapple with it. Indeed, it must. I have not even mentioned Supplemental Medical Insurance, which is open to hemorrhage in the general revenues.[12]

While there is a window of opportunity in which to work on this problem, it is not open very wide. The balance in the HI trust fund is projected to rise, under CBO's baseline forecast, from $51 billion in FY 1987 to an estimated $87 billion in 1992; by 1995 this balance edges down to $74 billion, but then it begins to plummet, reaching exhaustion in 1999 and changing to a *deficit* of $84 billion in the year 2000.

Of course, such an estimate is based on the extrapolation of growth rates of income and outlays into the future (in this case extrapolating CBO's projected 1991–92 rate of change for the remaining years of the decade). To indicate how volatile the situation is, the projected deficit of $84 billion in 2000 would turn into a surplus of $36 billion if Medicare outlays turn out to be 1 percent a year *less* than the rate of increase built into the baseline forecast. By contrast, the year-end balance in 2000 would be a deficit of $213 billion if annual outlays grow by 1 percent more than the pace incorporated in the baseline forecast, and the exhaustion year would be moved up to 1997.[13]

The projected deficits rise dramatically after the turn of the century. Clearly, deficits of hundreds of billions of dollars in Medicare trust funds will be unacceptable. The prospect of such deficits will force us to make some hard decisions. The main choices would seem to involve using Joseph's "surplus grain" from the OASI fund, taxing the actuarial value of Medicare benefits on a basis that avoids double taxation, raising the payroll tax rate and/or the payroll tax base, and raising premiums under the Medicare program (presumably scaled to income). Congress is currently considering a measure to lift the ceiling on earned income subject to the Medicare portion of the payroll tax. (In 1989 this ceiling was $48,000 per year.) This measure is estimated to raise about $8–9 billion per year when it is fully implemented.

In order to understand an important source of difference between the Social Security and Medicare situations, it is important to note that cost increases for Medicare are driven by a combination of normal inflationary forces and the unique factors leading to an inflation "premium" in the health care sector. Throughout the last two decades, health care price increases have outpaced general inflation, and sharp increases in the quantity of services provided have also played a key role in escalating total health care outlays.

Indeed, in 1988 the United States spent 11.2 percent of its GNP on health care, a higher rate than any other industrial country. Yet an examination of such indicators as life expectancy or infant mortality reveals that the United States is by no means at the head of the pack—several countries have better records than the United States in this regard. Measures of improvements in the quality of life are harder to find, and, to some extent, relatively higher outlays for health care in the United States may have purchased a decline in morbidity even if they have not led to dramatic breakthroughs in mortality. But, some hard questions remain—are we getting our money's worth for the more than half a trillion dollars we spend on health care annually? Are we paying those who provide the care— doctors, hospitals, nursing homes, and so forth—more than necessary to obtain top-quality services?

In recent years both the U.S. government and private employers have been abandoning the traditional cost-based reimbursement systems that had been handing the providers of health services a blank check. Prospective payment, reviewing the use of services with prior authorization, a greater emphasis on health promotion and prevention, greater reliance on alternative delivery systems such as health maintenance organizations (HMOs), and profiles of provider charges and practice patterns, with patients encouraged to use those providers who are not "out of line"—these are some of the major trends in tighter cost management that are rapidly developing in the United States.

Further measures for containing health care costs can attenuate the need to impose some combination of benefit changes and tax increases, and the deceleration of health care outlays would clearly help to reduce the projected deficit. It seems likely, however, that many of the measures that can be taken would produce one-time savings, while those that go beyond prudent purchasing measures to significantly higher out-of-pocket outlays for consumers or explicit rationing of health services would be very unpopular. In any event, it is our judgment that cost management reforms, while important and necessary, will not fully obviate the need for some tough decisions about Medicare.

There will also be pressure on Medicare arising from the aging of the U.S. population and the continued explosion of new technology (for example, an enhanced capacity to conduct successful organ transplants). These forces are likely to put strong pressure on the HI trust fund.

Ultimately, such pressure may lead to a merger of Parts A and B of Medicare, with a much greater reliance on a programwide premium that rises rather significantly with income. It may also lead to a voucher-type payment for the program as a whole that opens it up to more choice and imposes more cost discipline.

CIVIL SERVICE RETIREMENT

The civil service retirement and disability system covers most of the 2.7 million federal workers in the United States. Total outlays for retirement benefits for civilian federal workers in FY 1988 were about $27 billion.

The issue of federal pensions must be seen within the context of the overall system of compensating federal workers. These workers are to be paid according to the principle of "comparability" between public- and private-sector pay. In practice, comparability determinations are based on the professional, administrative, technical, and clerical (PATC) survey, which excludes employee benefits and is based solely on wage and salary comparisons.

The pension system for federal workers is relatively more generous than the typical private-sector pension plan, and the failure to include pensions in setting federal pay is a factor that leads to overcompensating federal workers, all other factors being equal. Federal workers can receive full retirement benefits at age 55 if they have 30 years or more of service, a practice that is highly unusual in the private sector (with the auto industry as an important exception). Benefit levels are based on the employee's highest three salary years and are indexed to the Consumer Price Index; these practices are also not typical of private-sector pension plans. Although companies often do make periodic upward adjustments to correct partially for past inflation, the inflation "recovery rate" is typically less than one-half. In recent years the generosity of the cost-of-living-adjustments (COLAs) for federal retirees has been scaled back somewhat (for example, from semiannual to annual adjustments and less than full COLAs for those retiring before age 62).

It is worth noting that federal employees do contribute 7 percent of wages to their retirement plans; their employing federal agencies contribute a matching 7 percent of payroll, and the remaining funding (about 60 percent of the total) comes from general revenues. Between 1973 and 1983, contributions from all three sources combined grew by 15 percent per year, and benefits grew at 16 percent annually, or 7 percent in real dollars. In real 1983 dollars, average benefit payments per retiree grew by 27 percent over this 1973–83 period.[14]

Employer contributions to the federal civil service retirement system amounted to 29 percent of payroll in 1983; this contrasts with a figure of 20 percent of payroll for that year in the private sector, including both Social Security and private pension plans.[15] If present trends continue, the explicit employer's cost of federal pensions, as a percent of payroll, will approach the full cost of all employee benefits in the private sector, comparably expressed. Moreover, the situation is actually more serious because as an employer the federal government does not practice what it preaches to the private sector—in terms of complying with minimum funding standards set up by the Employees Retirement and Income Security Act (ERISA). If the civil service retirement system were brought in line with ERISA, the explicit cost would rise toward the cost of the system, and the percent of payroll accounted for by federal pensions would rise steeply. Of course, costs not covered by employee contributions must ultimately be paid by government, and less than full funding of retirement commitments systematically understates the cost of government operations and programs.

As time goes on and the federal workforce ages, it is not hard to imagine a rather explosive cost situation developing in the future. Proposals to defuse the ticking time bomb include: (1) reducing the annuities for retirees who stop working for reasons other than disability prior to age 62; (2) limiting the cost-of-living adjustments to some proportion of the increase in the Consumer Price Index, rather than 100 percent; (3) increasing employee and employer contributions to the fund from the current 7 percent level; and (4) changing the base on which benefits are computed from the highest three years to the highest five years. In a longer-term sense, pay reforms might include a broader definition of comparability that includes employee benefits in the determination of federal pay, as well as actually departing from the comparability concept and substituting more market-based pay determinations.

VETERANS' BENEFITS

The federal government spends about $27 billion a year in veterans' benefits and services. This total covers a wide range of programs, from both service-connected and non–service-connected pensions to education, training, housing, and medical benefits. Some of these benefits are related to service-connected injuries and illnesses or related to financial need, while others are provided to all veterans regardless of income or the nature and origin of their disabilities.

In the last few years there has been a bulge in the veteran population in the preretirement years, as the World War II veterans have begun to approach retirement. By the year 2000, two out of three veterans, or an estimated 9 million people, will be 65 and over; indeed, two out of three elderly males will be veterans at that time.[16]

Clearly, we are on the verge of an upsurge in outlays for veterans' services under a business-as-usual model of government benefits.

Because of the increase in longevity and the large size of the cohort of World War II vets, the spending bubble already anticipated in the social insurance system in the early part of the next century is likely to arrive early in the veterans' area.

An important arena for policy decisions related to veterans' benefits involves the VA health care system. This system was designed in large part to assist veterans with service-connected injuries and/or low incomes; but it also serves those illnesses and injuries unrelated to their military service and those of middle- to upper-income status. Many of these veterans have either private insurance if they are nonelderly or are eligible for Medicare. One set of policy reforms designed to hold down federal costs in this area without jeopardizing access to care for veterans would require reimbursement from insurance policies held by veterans for health care unrelated to service-connected disabilities. Higher-income veterans would be able to use VA facilities after they have first used some of their own resources to purchase medical care in the private sector. Additional reforms could involve efforts to encourage a substitution of home care for nursing home care for veterans and greater reliance on community- and state-run nursing homes instead of more costly VA-owned homes for those veterans who require institutional care.

A RISING SHARE OF THE FEDERAL BUDGET FOR THE ELDERLY

The confluence of these trends in Social Security, Medicare, civil service retirement, and veterans' programs portends a sharp increase in the share of the federal budget allocated to senior citizens. According to one careful estimate by Barbara Torrey, the proportion of federal outlays allocated to people 65 and over, which stood at about 30 percent in 1986, will rise gradually to about 36 percent in 2010 and then begin to take off, reaching a level of roughly 50 percent of the budget in 2030.[17] Torrey's estimates are based on the IIB economic assumptions in the 1981 OASDI Trustees' Report and an assumption that improvements in the mortality rate over this period will be half the average annual improvement that occurred between 1900 and 1978.

The expected expansion in federal outlays to accommodate the needs of a swelling elderly population will pose a central challenge to our society. In short, if benefits are to be kept intact more or less as we know them today, how shall we pay the tab? Will national defense outlays be curtailed to make room for the higher spending on seniors? (This is the only portion of the federal budget where comparable dollars can be found.) Will we squeeze spending on youth and adults in the areas of education, training, or unemployment assistance, and if so, at what cost? Will we back the federal government out of other functions such as support for agriculture, transportation, housing, and community development, or can bold new ways be discovered to perform these functions more economically and/or more locally?

Alternatively, shall we maintain these national commitments to defense, youth, and special sectors of the economy and try to finance higher outlays for the elderly through tax increases? Or should the elderly contribute more themselves through higher premiums, cost-sharing, and the greater taxation of their benefits, with their added contributions based on ability to pay? Surely deficit financing on a continuing basis is an unacceptable alternative, so that an unwillingness to scale back and modify other commitments translates more or less directly into a need for either more taxation or higher contributions to the programs by elderly recipients.

If we select the course of taxation, there will be important choices to make regarding the type of taxes that will be necessary to underwrite our commitments. A steady reliance on the payroll tax to finance escalating social insurance outlays has the virtue of maintaining the important link between inflow and outflow that President Roosevelt believed was vital to assuring ongoing political support for social insurance. But the payroll tax is more regressive than the income tax, and it would ride up significantly as a share to total revenues, changing the overall distribution of the tax burden across income groups. Yet we know that reliance on personal and business income taxes brings costs of its own (for example, adverse effects on the incentive to work and invest). The search for an appropriate financing mechanism that is both fair and preserves incentives to work, save, and invest may reopen the debate over consumption taxes.

The Effect of a Changing Age Structure on the Private Sector

The aging of our population will also have important implications for the private sector. Just as the federal government has made commitments to current workers that will have to be honored when they are older, so the private business sector has taken on corresponding obligations to workers to help assure them a decent and affordable retirement. Individual workers are also helping to fund their own retirement, and are increasingly trying to balance obligations to their own future needs with today's obligations to their parents and children. Financing commitments to the four-generation family today poses many difficult choices between current consumption needs and the desire to "invest" in both the future of one's children and in one's ability to maintain an adequate life style in old age.

The main commitments of private employers to retired employees involve company pension plans, related salary reduction programs, and retiree health benefits. Looming on the horizon is the possibility of integrating employer/employee contributions to long-term care insurance into the employee benefit package as well.

The growth of employee benefits in the private sector has mirrored the growth in public-sector social insurance and social welfare systems. Over the past 50 years the United States has seen expansions of benefits in both the public and private sectors, and it is important to view the two systems jointly in order to assess the adequacy of the overall protection system. Comparisons of the United States to other countries, where proportionately more of the social protection system is public, are misleading unless one factors in the insurance that workers obtain from employers against the risks of illness, disability, and old age.

Of course, one major problem is that significant numbers of people in the United States fall between the cracks of the public- and private-sector social insurance systems. Particularly vulnerable here are both the working poor and the unemployed.

PENSION PLANS

A mainstay of the private-sector social protection system are contributions by employers to pension plans and related savings plans with tax-favored status. There were 15 million people receiving an estimated $91 billion in pension benefits from employer-sponsored pension plans in 1983. Among the employed population, an estimated 48 percent received an employer-sponsored pension in 1985 (this includes public- as well as private-sector employees and the self-employed). Coverage had edged downward at that point from a level of 56 percent of those employed in 1979.[18]

Coverage under a private pension program, however, does not assure the receipt of benefits in the future. An estimated 31.3 percent of the private-sector workforce covered by the Employee Retirement and Income Security Act (ERISA) were entitled to future benefits in

1983 (or about half of those with coverage), while this was the case for 56.6 percent of government workers.[19]

Of the 795,000 pension plans at the end of 1984, 554,000 (or 70 percent) were defined contribution plans, while the remaining 240,000 (or 30 percent) were defined benefit plans.[20] Defined contribution plans include money purchase pension plans, target benefit plans, profit-sharing plans, stock bonus plans, and employee stock ownership plans (ESOPs).

It is important to examine the relationship between private-sector coverage and public expenditures. This relationship is complex. First, it seems that the government has invested in reducing its own direct outlays by deferring tax revenue in order to encourage the spread of private pension coverage. For example, the deferral of taxes on contributions to and earnings on employer-sponsored retirement plans cost the federal government an estimated $86.8 billion in revenues in 1987.[21] But the pension coverage encouraged by this foregone revenue will raise retirement incomes, and this will save future outlays in federal public assistance programs available to the elderly, such as Medicaid, SSI, and the Food Stamp program.

Section 415 of the Internal Revenue Code limits on the amounts of employer contributions that may be deferred (currently $102,582 and $30,000 per year for defined benefit and defined contribution plans, respectively) can influence the amount of money put into these plans, and Congress has been clamping down on them in recent years after allowing the limits to rise sharply with inflation in the late 1970s and early 1980s.

While pension coverage is by no means limited to high-wage workers, the array of tax deferrals, as a whole, tends to benefit relatively higher-paid people the most. Left behind in this process are those who are not poor enough to qualify for public assistance, but also cannot afford to set aside money and shelter it from taxation. These people, dubbed the "tweeners" by economist Timothy Smeeding, are not sharing in the benefits of the general improvement in our public/private social protection system for retirement.

One study highlights the already emerging polarization of retirees according to whether they have employer-sponsored pension income on top of Social Security income. Examining data from the Current Population Survey and the Census Bureau, the Employee Benefit Research Institute found that in 1984, 43.1 percent of higher-income elderly households (defined as having incomes at least four times the poverty level) received income from pensions or veterans' payments, compared to only 10.8 percent of those in households whose incomes were below the poverty line and 19.4 percent of those with incomes just above it (that is, less than 125 percent of the poverty level).[22] Another factor that seems to separate the elderly poor from the nonpoor is earnings, as the higher-income group (those with incomes at least four times the federal poverty level) was seven times more likely than the poverty group to have income from earnings (24.9 percent, as compared to 3.5 percent).[23]

What seems to be emerging is a group of elderly who are heavily supplementing Social Security with some combination of benefits arising from past work (in the form of employer pensions) and current earnings—a relatively small proportion of the elderly that works. At the same time, another group of elderly relies heavily on some combination of Social Security and public assistance (SSI, food stamps, Medicaid). Of course, in reality the elderly represent a continuum, not a dichotomy between these two extremes. But the important point is that Social Security and Medicare do not take much account of the significant disparities among the elderly in income from other sources and from wealth (the distribution of which is very skewed). Given that Social Security is likely to be a little wobbly in the long run and that Medicare will be on the ropes in about a decade under business-as-usual assumptions, an argument could be made for either taxing benefits or varying the contribution by beneficiaries to Medicare with their ability to pay. These steps could be coupled with augmenting assistance to low- and moderate-income seniors, particularly for long-term care, which can wipe them out financially.

This, of course, would be a controversial step. Many people understandably believe that any such adjustments, including the taxation of benefits, is a violation of a prior commitment, and are quick to point out that in receiving these benefits, the elderly are simply getting back their own money, as opposed to receiving public assistance. The counterargument here is that sensible proposals to increase the taxation of benefits would not tax money already contributed by beneficiaries in the form of their share of payroll taxes or medical premiums. Such proposals may offer an attractive compromise between means-testing for the receipt of benefits, which would convert social insurance programs into welfare programs, and a business-as-usual approach that may prove untenable as our population ages.

Eventually, we will have to face this issue head-on. Will we continue to add to the tax burden of workers in order to finance benefits with steadily escalating real value, when a significant portion of the beneficiaries are at least as wealthy as, or wealthier than, those paying the taxes? Can we continue to allow the escalation of payroll taxes, which are paid on the first dollar of income by lower-income workers as well as those with substantial earnings, when we exempt the first $600,000 in the value of estates from taxation?

Recent evidence indicates that the elderly are increasing their wealth position relative to the nonelderly. Somewhat surprisingly, this trend does not result only from a growth in home equity. (A majority of the elderly own their own homes, often with no outstanding loans.) It also reflects gains in the value of financial assets during the period prior to the rise in the stock market (late 1970s, early 1980s), when the rest of the population was experiencing declines in the value of financial assets.[24]

RETIREE HEALTH BENEFITS

An estimated 22 percent of workers now retiring have employer-provided health plans covering their retirement years.[25] This proportion is projected to edge up slightly in the future. In actual practice, however, the long-run future of retiree health benefits is likely to hinge on the rules governing prefunding of retiree health care programs and on considerations and expected trends in Medicare.

Retiree health benefits continue the company health plan's coverage for retired workers until they are eligible for Medicare (if they retire before the age of 65) and fill in some of the cost-sharing gaps related to Medicare after age 65.

Contrary to the situation regarding pensions, where many companies find themselves overfunded in today's environment, the typical company health plan provided by the employer is *underfunded*. This underfunding reflects both the absence of an ERISA-type mechanism in the health care area and the tendency in recent years for Medicare to unload more obligations for covering older workers onto private employers (for example, making private employers of workers 65 years of age and older first instead of second payers).

As with pensions, retiree health plans are part of a trend in which a significant portion of retirees has much while another significant portion has little. While about one-fifth of today's retirees have a company-provided health plan continuing their private coverage (often in conjunction with private Medigap insurance policies and always in conjunction with Medicare), another one-fifth of the elderly lack both Medigap policies and Medicaid. Indeed, among those with incomes below $5,000 in 1984, those who need supplemental coverage the most, 28.5 percent lacked both private supplementary coverage and Medicaid; in the $5,000–9,000 income range, the corresponding figure was 29.9 percent.[26]

Retirees rarely have any choice of coverage under a company-provided health plan. Most retiree packages consist of the same coverage that companies offer their active workers, with the employer-paid insurance serving as the second payer after Medicare. In practice, this often means that the company plan covers the copayments and deductibles associated with Medicare benefits, rather than providing limited coverage for needs that Medicare ignores. Since this is also the case with most private supplementary insurance (Medigap), retirees may find themselves covered twice over for Medicare-related cost-sharing, while still vulnerable to large expenses for such items as posthospital recovery care received at home. Some retirees might prefer more "back-end" protection instead of coverage up front for copayments. Yet, in 1986 only 2.5 percent of the nation's nursing home tab was paid for by either Medicare or private insurance.

In the face of growing pressure on retiree health plans coupled with the unmet needs of those suffering from chronic illness and disability, employers could begin to think creatively about how benefits can be redesigned and the outlays for their retirees stretched and used more judiciously. One possibility involves a greater degree of integration between Medicare and company benefits, using the savings achieved from coordinating benefits and carefully reviewing their use for acute care to extend a measure of coverage in areas of ongoing vulnerability.

Under a system of managed care, employers and Medicare might be better able to provide some limited benefits for chronic illness, as care at home or in the community is better coordinated with institutional care. Under a managed care system, with risk-sharing arrangements between the providers of health services and the payers, providers would incur more financial risk for providing unnecessary or inappropriate health services. Thus, they would have an incentive to substitute home for institutional care.

Reducing the Pressure Caused by the Aging of the Population

In this section we analyze several ways that we can ease the burden caused by the changing composition of our population. We examine numerous approaches that hold some promise of helping us adjust to an aging population without cutting social protection or raising taxes. This is not to say that if we take these steps we will not have to scale back benefits or raise taxes, but rather that we may be able to rely less heavily on such approaches.

INCREASE WORK AMONG THE POPULATION THAT CAN WORK

As indicated earlier, the size of the working-age population is beginning to level off just when the size of the elderly group is increasing. This heightens the importance of taking steps to assure that as many people as possible who can work actually do work. In our conceptual framework, this involves a reexamination of the incentives our society offers people who can choose either to work or not to work. We believe that work should be encouraged, but not mandated; we should try to make the "terms of trade" between work and leisure favorable to work, but we also need to recognize that at some points in people's lives there are important and compelling reasons to leave the workforce (such as child-raising responsibilities).

The following key challenges emerge from this concern with encouraging employment:

Creating Enough Jobs to Employ Those Who Want to Work. A prerequisite to fully employing the human resources in our economy is a strong, growing economy itself. There is considerable evidence that economic growth reduces poverty.[27] It is important to pulling in potential workers from the sidelines. Clearly, a growing economy is not sufficient, by itself, to draw in everyone who can and who wants to work; there are people who will be bypassed in even the most buoyant economy for lack of skills, illiteracy, lack of knowledge, and other reasons. But we cannot simply work on augmenting human capital without also paying attention to creating a strong demand for that capital.

Sensible fiscal and monetary policies are critical to the achievement of strong, sustainable economic growth. While an analysis of such policies is beyond our scope here, it can be stated that an effort to get the federal deficit under control is vital to the achievement of long-run economic growth. Although the deficit has fallen in recent years as a share of GNP, it remains unacceptably high, particularly in light of the low savings rate in the United States. Clearly, there is a lot of work left to do in fashioning prudent fiscal policies.

Building More Incentives to Work into Our Welfare System.   We have imposed effective tax rates on lower-income citizens that are much higher than the explicit tax rates in our federal income tax system. Options for improving the incentive to work among low-income households include:

- reducing the penalties on earnings in terms of reduced benefits that are incorporated into the welfare system;

- imposing work requirements on welfare recipients, backed up by support services such as day care and health coverage, as many states are now doing; these two options are discussed further in the next section;

- increasing the minimum wage to make low-wage jobs more attractive compared to welfare (this, of course, may carry some adverse side effects in terms of employment opportunities, and the tradeoff needs to be carefully weighed);

- increasing the generosity of the Earned Income Tax Credit;

- giving Social Security tax relief for low-income workers, as achieved through exempting the first $2,000 in wages from payroll taxation;

- wage subsidies to firms hiring low-skilled workers.

Reducing Disincentives to Work Among Older Workers.   The proportion of men in their preretirement years and early retirement years who are not working at all has increased sharply. For example, the proportion of men age 55–64 who are not working tripled between 1954 and 1984.[28] More recently, the labor force participation rate for older men has stabilized. Options for increasing labor force activity among older workers include:

- examining the provisions of both Social Security and private pensions to ascertain whether they contain incentives favoring early retirement. This analysis could also be extended to the early retirement provisions of the civil service system;

- restructuring and redesigning work to fit the needs of older workers; finding alternatives to the "all-or-nothing" choices that often confront older workers;

- reassessing recent Medicare policies transferring a measure of responsibility for the health care protection of older workers to the private sector;

- exploring more systematic ways of mobilizing the healthy young elderly and other potential volunteers to provide nonmedical help to those who are frail, disabled, or seriously ill.

Encouraging Female Labor Force Participation.   Specific ways of aiding potential women workers include:

- helping to assure adequate day care and flexible work hours;
- establishing sensible maternity leave policies.

Examining Incentives Built into Government Programs to Ascertain Areas Where Work May Be Discouraged.   Measures that could address this problem include:

- reforming unemployment compensation to place more emphasis on retraining;
- reforming disability insurance and related problems so that people do not lose benefits abruptly when they reenter the workforce;
- allowing Social Security recipients who work to retain their full benefits.

IMPROVING THE PRODUCTIVITY OF THE LABOR FORCE

Because the size of the working-age population is leveling off, we need to make a major effort to foster a more productive workforce. Efforts to enhance productivity have been analyzed in more detail in other CED studies.[29] Generally speaking, a sensible strategy will avoid protectionism and quick fixes and focus on measures to help workers adapt to change rather than retard change. Some of the measures that could be included in this analysis are the following:

- increasing domestic private saving in order to stimulate private investment;
- enacting tax and regulatory reforms that foster investment in plant equipment;
- setting up flexible compensation arrangements that give workers a stake in greater company profitability;
- eliminating obsolete work rules;
- fostering adequate investment in research and development;
- reorganizing the work place to give workers more decision making and flexibility;
- reforming employee benefits so as to foster worker mobility;
- extending health insurance coverage and placing more emphasis on a healthy life style and preventing disease and accidents—healthier workers are more productive.

In addition to these steps to make existing workers more productive, we need to examine various ways to make future workers more productive by improving our educational system. Recent CED reports have laid out an extensive set of recommendations for improving our schools.[30] In general, the main areas of reform include:

- establishing an effective system of early childhood education and corresponding efforts to foster the nutrition and development of young children;
- making a major effort to reduce the number of school dropouts;
- establishing performance standards for both students and teachers;
- focusing on improving the literacy and basic skills of youth who graduate from high school;
- augmenting knowledge of the world of work among youth;
- creating incentives for schools to perform well and modernizing school curricula;
- soliciting greater business involvement in improving our schools and job placements for graduates;
- assuring adequate financing arrangements for higher education;
- placing greater emphasis on continuing or midcareer education and retraining among adults.

REDUCING HIGH SCHOOL DROPOUT RATES AND ILLITERACY

We now focus special attention briefly on one key aspect of this problem—reducing the number of school dropouts.

There has been no substantial progress in reducing the United States' overall school dropout rate of about 25 percent since 1965. Measures of the phenomenon often vary because of differences in the definition of *dropout* used among different communities for reporting purposes. One estimate of the number of dropouts at the national level was made by the Bureau of the Census, which defines dropouts as the percent of adults age 18–24 (in 1980) with three years or less of high school. The rate, using this definition, was 23.9 percent. The dropout rate varies considerably among demographic groups, and has been estimated at 27 percent for blacks, and 42 percent for Hispanics.

Dropping out of high school usually means restricted labor force participation in the future. Over one-fourth of male dropouts and nearly one-third of female dropouts surveyed were looking for work. Sixty percent of the males and 33 percent of the females were working full- or part-time, and only a small fraction of these were doing skilled work. In fact, those surveyed reported that waiting on tables was their most frequent type of work.[31]

Many businesses have become involved with secondary education through adopt-a-school programs. Firms participate to varying degrees in improving education programs in targeted schools. Businesses donate money or resources to a designated project that may involve tutoring, career exploration, job placement, or incentive programs such as scholarships or other awards. For example, the Tenneco/Jefferson Davis Business School Partnership in Houston, Texas, offers 100 high school students preemployment training, summer jobs, summer school enrichment courses, community volunteer work, tutoring, counseling, and mentoring. The purpose of the program has been to help prepare students who are likely to drop out of school to assume more productive roles as workers and citizens.

The Primerica Corporation's program with Martin Luther King Junior High School in New York, which was regarded as one of the city's most troubled schools, attempts to keep students in school and to prepare them for employment. Regular program services include a security guard training program administered by Primerica in conjunction with Burns International Security, an internship program for 15 students per year at Primerica, a scholarship program, and a one-day World of Work program administered by a Primerica insurance subsidiary.

Besides adopt-a-school programs, many businesses are involved in industry-labor-education councils in major cities. In New York City, for example, the New York City Partnership program includes corporate executive officers of Fortune 500 corporations, labor leaders, and the chancellor of the public schools. Members have helped provide work experience for New York City students and adult mentors for one-on-one discussions with juniors and seniors.

Businesses involved in curtailing the incidence of dropping out of high school recognize the problem's enormous social and economic costs to the nation. Estimates indicate that high school dropouts cost the economy about $77 billion annually; $71 billion is lost in tax revenue, $3 billion is spent on welfare and unemployment, and another $3 billion is spent for crime prevention.[32]

In addition to the problem of high school dropouts, another hindrance to a productive workforce is illiteracy. There are between 17 and 21 million U.S. adults who are functionally illiterate, for an overall rate of nearly 13 percent. Illiteracy closes the door to many labor force opportunities; moreover, it hampers the necessary adjustments and transitions that workers are often called upon to make in the job market.[33]

Other revealing statistics show startling ineptitude in literacy among the general population. The recent National Assessment of Education Progress test undertaken by the U.S. Department of Education found that among 21–25-year-olds, only about 60 percent of whites, 40 percent of Hispanics, and 25 percent of blacks could locate information in a news article or almanac. Only 25 percent of whites, 7 percent of Hispanics, and 3 percent of blacks could decipher a bus schedule. Moreover, only 44 percent of whites, 20 percent of Hispanics, and 8 percent of blacks could correctly determine the change they were due from a two-item restaurant bill.

This inability to organize and process information is all the more serious at a time when higher educational levels are being required in each job category. According to U.S. Department of Labor rankings of occupations and the skills required for each, there is a direct correlation between the level of skills required and the rate of growth of employment in the occupation. Thus, the fastest-growing jobs require much higher math, language, and reasoning capabilities than the average current job. If trends in capability continue, the U.S. labor force may not be able to meet the basic requirements of many employers in the near future.

We need to be able to compete in an increasingly global economy in which information, technology, and finance are more mobile than ever and many countries have caught up with or have surpassed our level of productivity. By addressing the fundamental causes of our problems instead of fighting the symptoms with palliatives, we are more likely to generate job opportunities for our working-age population, opportunities that help them balance their overlapping responsibilities to children and aging parents. In addition, by learning how to adapt to a changing world, rather than trying to stop change to insulate our workers from adjustments, we can foster mutual interdependence with our trading partners and more harmonious patterns of international relations.

CHAPTER 6

Changes in the Composition of Families

A NUMBER of demographic changes are taking place in the United States that reflect some very deep-rooted changes in the composition of families. The American family as we have known it is still the norm. But the "traditional" family has been becoming somewhat less prevalent in recent years.

Decline in Household Size

The average household size has been shrinking, reflecting several different trends.

INCREASE IN ONE-PARENT FAMILIES

First, the number of one-parent family groups has been growing since 1970. For example, whereas in 1970 there were almost 4 million one-parent families in the United States, by 1980 there were close to 7 million. This trend reflects the increase in the number of divorces, separations, and parents who have never married. The number of women who were divorced nearly tripled from 1970 to 1984, from 1.3 to 3.7 million. While many women remarry, their families are headed by only one parent in the interim. Ninety percent of the one-parent families are maintained by the mother. Another way of stating this trend is that one-parent families accounted for 26 percent of all family groups in 1985, compared to 13 percent in 1970.[1]

DELAYS IN MARRIAGE

The average household is becoming smaller as more people are living alone. This is especially marked among men and women between the ages of 25 and 44, for whom the number living alone increased fivefold between 1960 and 1984. This reflects the trend among Americans to delay marriage.

Among women age 20–24, the proportion who are single and never married has doubled over this same period, from 28.4 percent to 56.9 percent. And while only 10.5 percent of women 25–29 were single in 1960, this proportion was two and a half times larger in 1984 (25.9 percent). But among women in their late thirties, about the same proportion were single in 1984 as in 1960. And for women over 40, a somewhat *smaller* proportion were single in 1984 that in 1960.[2]

The delay in marriage reflects both the higher incidence of men and women living alone in their twenties and early thirties and a sharp rise in the number of unmarried couples living together. About 2 million people fell into this category in the mid-1980s, compared to only a half million in 1970. Thus, the smaller average household size can be attributed to young men and women living on their own or cohabiting prior to, or in lieu of, marriage. But while there have been delays in marriage, there have not been declines in the likelihood of eventually getting married. In fact, by the time they reach their late thirties, women today, on average, are as likely as their counterparts in 1960 to be married. About nine out of ten men and women eventually marry.

DELAYS IN CHILDBEARING

Delays in childbearing parallel delays in marriage. Data show that the birth rate has stayed fairly constant for women in their early twenties—109.9 births per thousand in 1978 to 108.9 births per thousand in 1985. The birth rate has increased slightly for women between 25 and 29. But larger increases in birth rates can be seen among women between 30 and 34 years of age: from 52.3 births per thousand in 1975 to 68.5 in 1985. Thus, women are delaying childbearing. But the proportion of women who have had a child by their late thirties—90 percent—has stayed quite constant over time.

INCREASED LABOR FORCE PARTICIPATION

The trend to delay marriage may be both a cause and effect of the dramatic increase in the number of women doing paid work. Indeed, there are many factors propelling women into the labor force. Between 1970 and 1985, the number of women working increased at an annual rate of 3.3 percent, much more rapidly than the 1.4 percent annual increase among men. By 1988, more than half of all women of working age were in the labor force. Women's share of the labor force increased from 38 to 45 percent between 1970 and 1988.

Labor force participation by women is increasing across all categories of marital and family status. Bureau of Labor Statistics data show that 72.7 percent of women between the ages of 25 and 54 were in the labor force, compared to 33.6 percent in 1947. This rise reflects several developments, including the decline in real male earnings after 1973, which is likely to be one factor encouraging women to work outside the home.

Thus, multiple demographic and economic trends are converging: more women, single or married, without children up to age 35; greater labor force participation by mothers; growth of single-parent households headed by women, which virtually necessitates labor force participation; and a squeeze on real earnings per worker. All of these trends tend to bring more women into the labor market. Of course, attitudes about women working have also changed, and to some extent the rise in female labor force participation is independent of economic and demographic forces.

There are two other subtrends that are noteworthy in the changing composition of families. The first is the growth in the number of elderly living alone, a trend that is notable for its sheer size and the income deficiencies and isolation of many people in this circumstance. The second is the incidence of teenage pregnancy, which is notable not so much for its absolute size as for its part in a syndrome of school dropouts, split families, and long-term welfare dependency. We examine these two elements because each is a barometer of increased dependency and economic and social needs among certain segments of the population.

The Elderly Living Alone

The shrinkage in household size and the changing composition of families reflects more than new patterns of marriage and fertility among younger women. It is also explained by the number of women age 65 and over living alone, which increased threefold from about 2 million to over 6 million during the 1960 to 1984 period. The number of men in that age group living alone doubled during the same period, from about 850,000 to about 1.6 million. Thus, of the 20 million people living alone in 1984, compared with only 7 million in 1960, about 8 million were 65 years of age and older.[3]

This trend among the elderly is significant because this age group is particularly vulnerable to disability and—among widowed, never-married, or divorced women—poverty. When the elderly person is in need of custodial care or assistance with daily activities, the absence of immediate family support in the household translates into a need for support, through Medicare and Medicaid, social service programs, and voluntary groups to provide assistance.

Studies of family caregiving suggest that family members are not abandoning their elderly relatives and, in fact, many family members spend considerable time caring for them. But these studies also show that the family caregiving responsibilities usually fall on one person, often the adult daughter. Some employers have recognized the burden that employees bear in caring for elderly parents. The Travelers Company, for example, found that a substantial number of employees spend a significant amount of time—both after and during working hours—caring for elderly relatives. An employee's responsibility at home inevitably cuts into productivity. Employers may be called on to help employees balance work and caregiving responsibilities, particularly as more women, the traditional caregivers, continue to enter the labor force. Thus, individuals, businesses, and families will need to provide assistance to meet the growing needs of the elderly.

A survey of members of the New York Business Group on Health showed that companies are aware of the effects of such responsibilities on employee productivity. Of the 69 companies responding, about 70 percent reported that lateness and absenteeism were a problem among people providing long-term care to an aged parent. Also, 60 percent of the respondents observed excessive stress and physical complaints among the caregivers.

Some companies have seen it in their interest to help their employees assist their elderly family members. One way is by offering them information on available services in their communities. Con Edison, Mobil, and Ciba-Geigy conducted a series of seminars for their employees on the services that are available to provide respite care. Other companies have given employees time off during work hours to provide care or to be with an elderly parent who is recuperating from a hospital stay.

According to a study by the Conference Board, company support for eldercare is likely to become the new, pioneering benefit of the 1990s.[4] One reason is that corporate officials themselves are likely to encounter the problem of caring for an elderly parent and recognize the need to help employees cope with their own caregiving responsibilities.

The use of health care services and the cost of such services are likely to continue to increase as a result of the sharply rising number of old-old, whose demand for physician, hospital, drug, and nursing home services is high relative to the younger population. For example, while those over 65 account for 12 percent of the population, they account for over 40 percent of total days of hospital care and one-third of hospital discharges. A study of the disabled population in Pennsylvania shows that by the year 2000 there will be a 40 percent increase in the need for residential care and institutions for the disabled in that state, primarily because of an increase in the elderly population.[5] In general, the cost of long-term care in a home or institution will put pressure on public- and private-sector expenditures.

The aging of the population is likely to increase the number of people requiring institutional long-term care. Today about 1.5 million people live in long-term care facilities; this figure is expected to increase by 50 percent to 2.1 million in 2000. Projections based on current trends show the need for over 4 million nursing home beds about 40 years from now.

There is a debate over whether the incidence of disability will increase among the elderly as they live longer. Some suggest that we are on the verge of a breakthrough leading to a cure for Alzheimer's disease; as a result of this and other gains that reduce disability among older people, the elderly of the future will live with less frailty. Others contend, however, that frailty will inevitably *increase* as people age. Moreover, there is a great deal of uncertainty over the number of nursing home beds that will be needed. The projections depend on the degree to which the elderly may continue to use nursing homes or make greater use of new congregate living arrangements that may emerge or find ways to remain at home. Thus, projections of needs and how those needs will be met are not based on clear-cut assumptions.

As the population ages, there will be proportionately fewer young people and proportionately lower expenditures on education and other services targeted to youth. But public expenditures for the elderly are about three times greater per capita than expenditures for youths. Hence, spending on proportionately fewer youths will not yield sufficient resources to finance the needs of the elderly.

POLICY IMPLICATIONS

In the public sector, the increase in the number of the elderly, particularly the frail elderly, will necessitate an increase in expenditures for long-term care, combining both some degree of additional institutional care and expanded home care and related social services. Medicare, Medicaid, and private insurance programs could be redesigned to carve increased home care benefits out of savings from reduced institutionalization. This will not be a "magic bullet," however, as many people will still require institutionalization, and the costs of home care can approach the costs of a nursing home. Yet, costs aside, the quality of life for senior citizens is bound to improve if we can find a way to organize community resources, on a paid and voluntary basis, to help people live at home.

Currently, health care services for the elderly are fragmented. The payment system mirrors this fragmentation, as there is little coordination of acute and long-term care insurance coverage. As private long-term care insurance develops and matures in the future, it can help coordinate and rationalize coverage. Ways should be explored to leverage limited public-sector dollars to encourage greater use of private long-term care insurance. This might include subsidies for premiums, deductibles, and copayments for lower-income people and either a government stop-loss that limits total asset depletion or a system of public reinsurance to cover private insurers for very large losses. To the extent that such subsidies augment private coverage, public outlays under Medicaid (about half of which are now allocated to long-term care) will drop.

Also lacking for the elderly is a system that *manages* the health care that is needed. In the absence of a good case management system, the elderly are understandably confused about the extent of their access to care, the forms that need to be filled out, and the array of overlapping benefits for which they are paying premiums.

Hence, a more integrated system of health care service delivery and financing is needed to respond to the multiplicity of medical and custodial needs required by the elderly. One thrust in this direction involves experiments with social health maintenance organizations (SHMOs) and the growth of life care communities, which begin to bridge the gap between medical and custodial care. To date, these initiatives are quite limited. Another thrust involves the possibility of coordinating employer-based health plans for retirees with Medicare benefits, as noted earlier. This could reduce overlapping coverage, help meet unfilled needs, and save both parties money.

The goal should be an integrated system of payment and delivery of primary, acute, custodial, and long-term care. Enrolling Medicare beneficiaries in HMOs should be considered the first stage of prepayment of care for the elderly, from which subsequent delivery and finance systems will be developed. These will not all look like today's HMOs. But they will address the fragmentation of the health care delivery and payment systems and the lack of proper incentives in the traditional system.

In the private sector, there will be an increased need for voluntary services to provide a social support base for elderly persons, particularly those living alone. A number of organizations have established voluntary programs to assist the elderly. In St. Paul, Minnesota, the Block Nurse program was established in 1982 to draw on the professional and volunteer services of neighbors and family to care for the elderly in their own homes. The program tries to avoid nursing home confinement by coordinating health and social services that make it possible for the frail elderly to remain at home. About 80 men and women have been helped by volunteers in the program. In New Haven, Connecticut, the Southern New England Telephone Company has established a network of volunteers to do telephone reassurance and hospital discharge monitoring. In Houston, Tenneco, Shell, and Exxon participate in Project Heart, an outreach program for older adults in the community. While programs of this nature are not panaceas, they do represent an important and unique contribution that the voluntary sector can make.

Teen Pregnancy

Trends in the number of elderly and the likely expenditures that will be required to meet their medical and related needs dwarf many of the other demographic changes taking place in the United States today. But some trends, while not noticeably reflected in aggregate numbers, are significant nonetheless, not so much for their numerical magnitude, but for their social implications for successive generations. This is particularly true of the persistent problem of teenage pregnancy. This problem is important not because teenage pregnancy is rampant or even crucial to *overall* demographic trends. Rather, teen pregnancy often sets off a cycle of social and economic dependency that cannot be totally solved by economic growth. Moreover, this dependency among young mothers and their children contributes to rather than mitigates the increasing dependency ratios propelled by the growing elderly population.

There is some evidence that the problem is getting worse. Over the past 15 years, teenage pregnancy rates in the United States have risen about 20 percent. This growth has not occurred in most other industrial countries. Since a rising share of teenage pregnancies are terminated by abortion, the birth rate among teenagers is actually a little lower today than in the recent past. But a long-range decline in the teenage birth rate has been offset by a corresponding trend—a sharp increase in the proportion of teenage mothers that are unmarried. While only 14.3 percent of births to women 15–19 years old were out of wedlock in 1955, 55.6 percent were out of wedlock in 1984.[6] In 1984, about one of five births was to an unmarried mother, compared to only 4 percent of all births in 1950.

In 1984, out of 10 million teenage females, about 1 million became pregnant. Of these, 470,000 gave birth. Indeed, by the time they become 20, 19 percent of white girls and 45 percent of black girls have given birth.

The U.S. teenage pregnancy rate of 96 per thousand is much higher than that of any other industrial country. In England, France, and Canada, pregnancy rates are lower than 45 per thousand teenagers, and birth rates average 29 per thousand among teenage girls in these countries. Particularly alarming is that U.S. girls under age 15 are at least five times more likely to give birth than young adolescents in any other developed country for which data are available.

In aggregate, the problem of teenage pregnancy is a mere blip on the demographic charts. But the social and economic implications of teenage pregnancy and single parenthood can affect several generations. A teenage parent is more likely not to have completed high school, and is therefore more likely to be excluded from opportunities in the labor force because of lack of basic skills. Hence, teenage mothers are more likely to become dependent on publicly supported services.

The cycle of deprivation continues as these tendencies are passed on to children of parents who themselves often become dependent. Indeed, from the moment a teenage girl conceives a child, that child's prospects for ultimately achieving self-sufficiency are affected by the environment in which it develops. The absence of intangibles such as a motivation to excel and the absence of tangible necessities like good health care may lead to social problems and public and private expenditures in subsequent years. Thus, there is cause for concern as we look at the bleak prospects of children of the current dependent population.

There are also some hopeful signs. For example, one recent study that tracked teenage mothers and their children over a 17-year period concluded that while the prospects of achieving self-sufficiency and escaping poverty were lower for the children of teen mothers than for other children, many of these youths did overcome the odds. Young mothers, absent fathers, and their children *can* achieve success in the worlds of school and work, and some programs are helping them do it.[7]

We are also encouraged by the early findings of the Summer Training and Education Program (STEP). This program, which is being tested in five cities, tries to increase basic skills and reduce school dropout and teenage pregnancy among girls 14–16 years old by giving poor and underperforming youth remediation, life skills, and work experience during two consecutive and intensive summer programs. Findings from the first three summers suggest that STEP is reducing teenage pregnancy and arresting the "summer loss" phenomenon, whereby the gains that some young people make during the school year dissipate during the summer.[8]

ECONOMIC AND SOCIAL IMPLICATIONS OF TEENAGE PREGNANCY

Businesses often need to train their employees in basic skills before they can meet job requirements. Expenditures for training programs effectively transfer resources from productive investment into activities that businesses and households are already paying for through the taxes that fund primary, secondary, and public higher education. Lost educational opportunities require remedial efforts later, and the cost of offering public education to those unwilling or unable to profit from it can eventually exceed the benefits. Also, as technology advances and its applications become more widespread in daily life, the gap widens between those who can and cannot perform required tasks on the job. Deficiencies in reading comprehension, math, and science, and the lack of computer literacy and knowledge of the world of work are usually severe handicaps in today's job market. The loss of human capital is very significant.

Costs are borne by society also, through government expenditures for food stamps, cash assistance, health insurance, housing allowances, and other cash and in-kind benefits targeted to low-income families. A government safety net *should* exist to help those people who may experience temporary personal dislocations and job loss, and it should provide decent benefits. Moreover, those who are poor by virtue of old age or disability should be assisted. Indeed, many people on public assistance fall into these categories. But many others who are able to be self-sufficient have fallen into the trap of dependency, and the costs are borne by households and businesses through higher taxes.

In 1983, there were about 200,000 teenage mothers receiving cash assistance through Aid to Families with Dependent Children (AFDC), which represents only a small portion of the total AFDC households (about 3.6–3.7 million in 1986). But an increasing proportion of teen mothers are becoming AFDC recipients.[9] In the late 1970s, about 25 percent of all teenage mothers 15–19 years old were recipients. By 1984, about 30 percent were recipients. Those on welfare are more likely to have dropped out of high school and are disproportionately black.

As David Ellwood suggests, women who are young, who have young children and are single when they start to receive benefits, or who have not worked recently before going onto AFDC are more likely to be dependent on AFDC for many years. For example, women who have not worked during the two years before initially receiving AFDC are predicted, on average, to receive benefits for eight years, though not necessarily for a continuous period.[10] Indeed, about two-thirds of teenage mothers eventually spend time on welfare.

Public expenditures for welfare, pure and simple, have not risen in real terms in recent years, as the AFDC caseload has been almost constant, and real AFDC benefits per capita have fallen by about a third since 1970.[11] Nevertheless, teenage mothers and their children account for substantial government outlays for welfare, food stamps, and Medicaid. Teenage pregnancy is part of a pattern of isolation from the economic and social mainstream that triggers expenditures in public systems ranging from child welfare and juvenile justice to health services and public housing. The cost of crime in material and human terms, the cost of drug use, sexually transmitted diseases, incarceration, and alcoholism all divert resources from productive activity and investment into maintenance, caretaking, and corrective activities. Government and employers bear these costs in the form of higher health insurance premiums.

In sum, the social diseases that are bred from dependency have far-reaching consequences in terms of increased spending at all levels of government, higher taxes, and added costs to business. Not only are those who are young and healthy yet dependent unable to help sustain the growing elderly population, but also they are unable to support themselves. Teen pregnancy is a major barrier to adult self-sufficiency. The issue is how this dependency can be redressed and prevented.

In aggregate terms, the proportion of the total non-aged population that is dependent on public assistance is rather small. Of the roughly 32 million people living in poverty, only about 11 million—roughly a third—are receiving AFDC. Many of these recipients are on and off the rolls in a relatively short period (for example, about half the AFDC caseload is on welfare for less than two years). Those who are both persistently poor and on welfare for many years constitute only about 1–2 percent of the total U.S. population. We focus on this group because we think it is a "ticking time bomb." Neglecting the problem can lead to both direct and indirect costs that are disproportionate to the numerical size of the population directly at risk.

A variety of measures have been undertaken to reduce the rate of teen pregnancy and mitigate the resulting dependency. The research on teen pregnancy makes clear that a sense of self-respect, positive views about academic success, and aspirations related to future opportunities are critical to motivating an adolescent to avoid teen pregnancy and dependency generally.

A number of efforts by government, local communities, churches, and families have been undertaken around the country to prevent teen pregnancy. Several such programs have sponsored vocational education to encourage young people to look to the future and to convince them that early parenthood can hamper the fulfillment of aspirations.

PUBLIC-SECTOR EFFORTS

Welfare programs have certainly offered disincentives to work. High implicit tax rates in AFDC, whereby recipients must forego up to a dollar of benefits for every dollar earned, would deter anyone from working. AFDC can be restructured to reduce high implicit tax rates and to foster work through a combination of a requirements for work or schooling and job-readiness assistance such as child care and health insurance coverage.

At the same time, AFDC can be reformed to put a basic floor under benefit levels. If recipients are to be expected to work to fulfill their end of a reciprocal bargain, government should be expected to provide a decent minimum for people who are trying to be self-sufficient or who simply cannot work. Disparities in cash assistance (and therefore Medicaid eligibility as well) are as high as five to one between states with high benefits like California and poorer states like Alabama and Mississippi, where benefit levels are only about one-seventh of the amount established as the federal poverty level.

Public assistance can be and is being reformed to decrease long-term dependency. This is particularly important for teenage parents, since about one-half of all AFDC expenditures are spent on mothers who had their first baby as a teenager.

The Family Support Act of 1988 makes some headway in reforming public assistance by emphasizing education and training, job search assistance, child care support, and health benefits for those enrolled in the program who are making the transition to work. Limited work requirements for two-parent families and enforcement of child support obligations are also part of the reform package. These program components are the main ingredients for the act's basic thrust, the Job Opportunities and Basic Skills Training (JOBS) program. JOBS applies only to a small segment of the AFDC population, however. Another limitation of this legislation is that it does not put a floor under benefit levels.

In recent years, a number of states have established work and training programs, with varied degrees of success. They are based on the notion that the current system is flawed because recipients need not work in return for benefits. But most programs are *not* strict "workfare" models in which AFDC benefits are "worked off"—they involve paid work. And almost all programs provide support services to help recipients meet a work obligation.

Current work and training programs at the state level reflect parallel trends. First, the attitude of government is changing toward favoring work requirements and away from providing welfare as an entitlement without corresponding reciprocal obligations. The second trend is the changing attitudes favoring labor force participation by women in general.

Evaluations of mandatory participation in a work-related activity have shown that most welfare mothers are willing and able to participate in short-term job-related activities. Across a variety of work and training programs, the subsequent employment rate of women who participate is a little higher than among those who do not, earnings of participants are somewhat higher, and the number of those receiving benefits is a little lower.[12] The observed gains from these programs are usually small, but positive, and it will be important to see if they hold up over time.

According to studies by the Manpower Demonstration Research Corporation, those with relatively less education and relatively less work experience benefited relatively more from state programs that focus on job search assistance, short-term training, and placement.[13]

Another approach to ameliorating the effects of teenage pregnancy is to enforce the payment of child support by absent fathers. The chance in the short run that enforced child support can significantly reduce poverty and welfare dependency is not great. But reforms of the child support system would insure greater income to some teen mothers; and over time a strong enforcement system that holds fathers more responsible may reduce the incidence of teenage pregnancy in the first place. Such programs are currently being designed, implemented, and evaluated. As a start, several counties in Wisconsin and New York have instituted payroll withholding of the wages of absent parents, with the proceeds going to custodial parents.

An appropriate welfare system should provide fully adequate short-term assistance for those who are temporarily facing hard times. Cash assistance plus food stamps should permit a decent standard of living during this transitional period, and health coverage should be assured regardless of work and family status. But cash assistance should not be permanent for those who are able to work. After a period such as two or three years, welfare should terminate, with recipients offered a public-sector job at or near the minimum wage.

PRIVATE-SECTOR PROGRAMS

In the private sector, there are a host of programs to prevent and to ameliorate the effects of teen pregnancy. A hospital-based clinic at Presbyterian Hospital in New York, for example, sponsors a program for young men in need of medical services and counseling. In the inner city of Philadelphia, a community health center provides services to 6,000 teens each year including medical care, family planning, counseling, and group sessions on personal hygiene.

Since the late 1970s, more than a thousand programs have been established in the United States to help teenagers who have given birth. They address a multiplicity of problems that plague teen parents by providing a variety of services including counseling about nutrition and parenting, pediatric care, child care, and transportation. These programs have not been widespread enough to diminish the ill effects of teen parenthood. But some have been successful in reducing the incidence of low birth-weight babies and facilitating young mothers' return to school or entry into the job market.[14]

Teenage pregnancy can be prevented and its effects ameliorated only by concerted effort on the part of families and community groups, along with redesigned welfare assistance programs that encourage rather than discourage productive activity among young people.

CHAPTER 7

Immigration

Immigration Patterns

AMONG THE most controversial demographic changes in the United States are those caused by immigration and its impact on the economy and the society. Recent increases in the number of immigrants have reversed the declining trend in the proportion of immigrants in the total U.S. population. In 1910, 14.7 percent of the population was foreign-born, but this dropped to a low of 4.7 percent in 1970. The percentage crept up to 6.2 percent in 1980 and is higher today.

The number of legal immigrants entering the United States was 373,000 in 1970, 531,000 in 1980, and 570,000 in 1985. These figures are much lower than the annual counts of more than a million that were recorded six times between the years 1905 and 1914, when the total U.S. population was much smaller. But recent figures do not account for illegal immigrants, newly arrived immigrants, and newly arrived refugees. If these were included in immigration statistics, the total number of new U.S. residents each year might be as great as it was at the turn of the century, in absolute terms.

But even though immigrants constitute a small proportion of the population (compared to the elderly, who account for 12 percent), immigrants raise more controversy because of perceptions by the indigenous population about their effects on the economy and the society.

What is the impact of immigration on the U.S. population? Since 1965, fertility rates in many of the industrial countries have fallen substantially below the level needed to replace their population in the long run. For example, prior to 1972, fertility rates in the United States were consistently above replacement, but by 1972 they dropped below the level of 2.1 percent needed for replacement. Since that time, U.S. fertility has remained below replacement and is now 1.8 births per lifetime per woman.[1]

Given this relatively flat growth in the indigenous population, immigrants constitute an increasing proportion of population growth. For example, 11 percent of the population growth in the United States between 1955 and 1959 was attributed to immigration. In 1980–85, however, 28 percent of the population growth was accounted for by immigration.

Characteristics of the Immigrant Population

The educational attainment of immigrants varies significantly by country of origin. About 82 percent of immigrants from Africa in 1980–85 had completed high school; from Asia, 73 percent; from India, 89 percent; from Mexico, 21 percent. Among the U.S. indigenous population, 67 percent of the population over age 25 had completed high school.

Factors Contributing to Immigration

There are powerful forces pushing immigration, including the extremely low average age in many countries in our hemisphere (for example, the average age in some countries is 15 years) and the poverty and low potential earnings in those countries. The combination of large youth cohorts and bleak economic prospects makes the United States look very attractive.

The conditions in the home countries that "push" their residents to emigrate are paralleled by conditions in the United States that encourage a strong "pull" from U.S. employers. The cohort of indigenous youth in the United States that will enter the labor market in the remaining years of this century is quite small relative to the numbers of baby boomers already in the labor force. For example, the number of young people between the ages of 20 and 29 will shrink from 41 million in 1980 to 34 million in 2000, and their share of the total population will drop from 18 to 13 percent.

Thus, some employers may face temporary labor bottlenecks, already a reality in some regions of the United States and some occupational subgroups, such as math and science teachers. Food service establishments, for example, which are accustomed to hiring young workers at low wages, may find they must raise wages, invest in labor-saving technology, or compete for older workers. At the same time, there will be limits on employers' ability to increase compensation in response to a growing demand for workers caused by a reduced supply. The potential expansion of immigration will work against too strong an upward shift in wages in certain sectors.

Impact of Immigration on the Economy

Immigration could be viewed not only as a means to offset a substantial labor shortage in the United States, but also as favorably affecting the dependency ratio—if immigrants enter the mainstream of economic life. In 1986 the Council of Economic Advisors suggested that "There is evidence that immigration has increased job opportunities and wage levels for other workers. . . . Immigrants come to this country seeking a better life, and their personal investments and hard work provide economic benefits to themselves and to the country as a whole." Others have suggested a different impact of immigration: "So dubious are the advantages of immigration that one wonders why the governments of industrial countries favor it. . . . One will find few clarifications, but official statements hint that the goals are to fill essential jobs and to stimulate population growth. One suspects that the actual causes are government inertia and pressure by employers to obtain cheap labor."[2]

Indeed, immigrants have made vital contributions to the labor force in both skilled and unskilled jobs. Skilled immigrants have been responsible for many scientific achievements, and the United States benefited tremendously from its "brain gain" in theoretical and applied sciences, research and technology, economics, and a host of other areas.

The immigration of highly skilled people is less controversial than that of unskilled and semiskilled workers. Less-skilled immigrants tend to occupy low-wage jobs. There is considerable debate as to whether immigrants take jobs away from indigenous workers and whether they reduce wage rates. There is less debate over the view that immigrants prevent wages from rising as fast as they otherwise would. In California, there is evidence that illegal aliens may displace low-skilled native workers in some labor markets, but the evidence also shows that native-born Americans move up to better jobs.[3]

The same study by Muller and Espenshade found that in Los Angeles in 1980 there was no statistically significant relationship between black unemployment rates and the concentration of Hispanics in a cross-section of the local labor markets. This study also found that between 1972 and 1980 average wages in low-wage manufacturing industries in Los Angeles increased only about 77 percent as fast as average wages in those same industries nationwide. Mexican immigrants constituted nearly one-half of all production workers in those industries. Thus, according to Muller and Espenshade, there is some evidence that immigrant workers lower the average level of wages in some industries. This, in turn, could increase employment.

Indeed, the aggregate level of unemployment among non-Hispanic California residents did not increase over this period. It is suggested that the jobs taken by Hispanics are to produce goods that are, in most instances, substitutes for foreign imports. A Rand Corporation study comes to the same conclusion and suggests that immigration has provided a boost to the California economy by allowing companies to expand rather than contract in the face of foreign competition.[4] Yet the debate over the economic impact of immigration still includes the view that immigration is a cause of higher unemployment in the short term.[5]

There is also evidence to suggest that an increasing proportion of Hispanics in a metropolitan area has little effect on black family income. For example, in 1980 raising the share of Hispanics in an area from an average of 5 to 7.5 percent produced a decline in average black family income of just $85 a year. In the Southwest, an increase in the proportion of Mexican immigrants in local labor markets raised average local family income slightly.[6]

Immigrants and Public Expenditures

One major concern is the degree to which immigration results in a drain on public services. A report by the Council of Economic Advisors suggests, however, that immigrants often pay more in taxes than they use in services. Illegal immigrants are less likely to use public services, although public hospitals often ignore a patient's immigration status and public schools must enroll illegal immigrants' children.

But in other areas, some immigrants, both legal and illegal, have a difficult time qualifying for welfare programs. Immigrants who received amnesty under the November 1986 Immigration Reform and Control Act are not eligible for any means-tested programs like AFDC. Moreover, many of the Hispanic immigrants are young men without families in the United States and do not meet the categorical eligibility requirements for welfare programs. The Food Stamp program, which normally allows single persons to be eligible, has a special provision that excludes legal aliens. Thus, welfare expenditures for low-income immigrants are tempered by some limits on eligibility.

Social Implications

One of the major concerns among the indigenous U.S. population is the degree to which immigrants will become assimilated in the mainstream of the society. Recent movements for a bilingual society create fear and suspicion, since language barriers are symptoms of more deeply rooted divisions in the society.

Other issues arise in those regions of the nation where immigrants are concentrated. Will indigenous Americans in Texas, for example, want to pay taxes to educate a predominantly minority school-age group? We are already seeing a rising concern about language, as various groups in states with high proportions of Spanish-speaking immigrants initiate campaigns to maintain English as the official language. This raises the question as to whether immigrants will remain an identifiable group or whether they will be assimilated in the first or subsequent generations. Tensions may mount as indigenous disadvantaged groups in the United States perceive, rightly or wrongly, that their jobs and wage opportunities are being threatened by immigrants.

Already, the rapid demographic shifts involving immigrants are having social implications. In California, about a quarter of the 4.2 million public school children are now Hispanic, an eighth are Asian, and over 500,000 in the state do not speak English. Whites are projected to comprise barely one-third of school enrollment within a generation. Interviews with nearly 300 immigrant children in California schools indicate that volatile race relations are a real and pervasive problem for immigrant youth, often leading to fear, abuse, and occasional violence. These race-related problems often isolate immigrants from other students, obstruct the process of learning English, and hinder student achievement.[7]

There are also linkages between two of the demographic changes highlighted thus far: the growing immigrant population and the changing age structure of the population. Growth in the number of elderly persons in states like Texas will be far more substantial for elderly Hispanics and Asians because of the continued immigration into Texas of young adults who will comprise the elderly of the twenty-first century. In fact, the number of Hispanics age 65 and older will increase ninefold over the next 50 years.

In the years ahead, the United States will have to make some basic decisions about the flow of immigrants—legal and illegal—into the country. Considerations of economic conditions, politics, foreign policy, and philosophy will enter into these decisions. Fundamental conflicts between our desire to foster liberty and open shores, on the one hand, and to protect domestic jobs, on the other hand, have governed much of the past debate. To the extent that labor markets may tighten in the future, however, philosophical and economic factors may converge and reinforce an approach that grants immigrants relatively free entry into the United States. This approach, in turn, may intensify the pressure on those in the United States who lack basic skills as they strive to become self-sufficient and achieve an adequate standard of living.

Conclusion

Several important demographic trends are converging in the United States. Some of these trends will eventually be of great magnitude, like the aging of the population. Other demographic phenomena such as the growth in the number of men who are retiring in their late fifties and early sixties, changes in the composition of families, teen pregnancy, and immigration, all deserve attention.

The reason that we focus on some of these trends involving only a small percentage of the U.S. population is that these groups have the potential to affect the dependency ratio significantly. Participation or nonparticipation in the labor force can affect, at the margin at least, the degree to which the working-age population will be able to support the growing elderly population. Certainly, teen pregnancy and early retirement cause a drain on the number of active workers available to support those who cannot work. Immigration can help offset the increasing size of the aged population, to the extent that immigrants contribute productively to the economy.

We have noted the expected shift in the ratio of *working-age* to *retirement-age* people in the coming years. This shift will be significant. In a "do-nothing" or "business-as-usual" environment, this shift will force very difficult public choices between cutting support benefits and raising taxes. And it will put a burden on the business sector and families as well.

This chapter has tried to outline a number of steps that might mitigate the tension and pressure arising from the expected shift in the relative sizes of age groups in the U.S. population. These steps include various ways to enhance labor force participation, measures to increase the productivity of the labor force, and policy reforms that improve the efficiency and effectiveness of social programs.

Further ideas and specific policy recommendations in these areas can help attenuate adverse effects that might occur as a result of these expected demographic trends.

PART IV

Political and Institutional Implications of
Demographic Change

Introduction

Demographic forces have three important political and institutional implications. They affect the cost of meeting social goals; they affect the capacity of society to pay those costs; and they affect the character of political institutions whose function is to set goals and to resolve the tension caused by disparities between costs and capacities. Some favorable demographic trends tend to alleviate costs, increase capacities, or enrich the political culture. Unfavorable trends do the opposite. Many are essentially neutral, or are likely to have a political impact only in combination with other forces.

The net tendency of the demographic trends now affecting the United States is to create political stress in three ways. First, demographic forces are widening the gap between social costs and the capacity to meet society's needs. Second, international trends are likely to exacerbate those in the domestic sphere, and vice versa. And third, the task of resolving the political tensions created by the widening cost-capacity gap will be complicated by the fact that the structures and processes of political institutions themselves will be under stress from many of the same demographic forces.

This is not to suggest that these tendencies are either inevitable or immune to efforts to alter them. It is the general theme of this volume that we need not be the captives of demographic forces. Demographic projections themselves are subject to error, and the impact of demographic forces depends on how they interact with numerous other factors. It is also possible to prepare for them, adjust to them, turn them to best advantage, and even to alter them. The argument here is that there is a high probability that demographic forces will create political tension, and it is all the more important to confront that probability because the institutional foundations we depend upon to resolve political tensions will themselves come under stress.

135

Costs

In the domestic sphere, the principal cost pressures are the increasing number of elderly people driving up pension and medical costs, and the rising number of those persons 85 and over who will incur especially high costs for medical and long-term care. The relatively smaller number of children 18 and under will offer some compensating cost relief, but this will be limited by the rising proportion of educationally disadvantaged children who will require preventive and remedial programs if they are to become productive workers and constructive citizens. The extent to which these demographic forces will actually increase costs depends on political choices, such as how much to pay for Social Security, Medicare, education, and other programs.

In the international sphere, the United States' proportional share of the world's Gross National Product has declined since the Second World War. Yet the United States today is attempting to pursue foreign policy and strategic goals established when it commanded a much higher proportion of world resources and was in a stronger position to influence world events. The United States could choose to compensate for this relative change by committing more resources to international affairs, shifting resources from consumption to investment to strengthen its economic base, or using the resources at its command more skillfully. But these are all policy choices with strong political ramifications.

The nation's reduced economic strength relative to that of some other countries also raises the question of whether the United States or any other power will have the combined population, economic, and military strength to exercise the strong national leadership upon which the international economic system has long depended. Building a new basis for international economic stability is likely to require extra exertion on the part of American leaders; a failure of such leadership could be even more costly.

Costs are variously described as burdens, expenditures, priorities, commitments, obligations, responsibilities, and so on. They may also be characterized as consumption or investment, depending on whether cost outlays are believed to have enduring value. The connotations of these terms are important in the political context, since they reflect varying degrees of enthusiasm on the part of the cost bearer. For example, U.S. leaders used to characterize

the cost of maintaining armed forces in Europe as an "investment" in world peace, whereas today those costs are characterized
as a "burden" in which our allies should share.

Capacities

Demographic trends are affecting the capacities of our nation in
several ways. In recent years the United States labor force has
rapidly increased as the baby boom generation moved into its
working years and a rising proportion of women entered the labor
force. As these two forces abate, future growth in the labor force
will be slower. Whether a maturing baby boom workforce will become more or less productive depends on several factors, including how effectively workers upgrade their work skills and adjust to
an increasingly competitive economy.

Meanwhile, three demographic trends could tend to reduce the
economic capacity of young people entering the workforce: there
will be fewer of them; an increasing proportion of them will come
from social groups with the highest proportion of educationally
disadvantaged children; and changing family structures have
tended to reduce the role of many families in the education and
training of their children. Action can be taken to compensate for
these trends, but all entail political costs. Early childhood intervention and remedial education and training programs, for example, can be effective, but they are expensive. Immigration offers a
means of bringing new, energetic, and often highly trained workers
into the workforce, but immigration entails other costs and encoun-
ters political resistance.

International demographic forces will also affect our nation's
capacities. A rapidly growing world labor force could expand potential markets, but it could also intensify competition. Pressures
on the environment associated with a rising population could diminish the global resource base—the atmosphere, water, the diversity of animal and plant species—or otherwise raise the costs of
protecting and using these resources.

The Cost-Capacity Gap

The squeeze created by these trends in both the international and
the domestic spheres is reflected in the composition of the federal
budget. About 29 percent of the budget is allocated to defense,

and another 29 percent to programs for the elderly. Meanwhile,
chronic budget deficits have generated a national debt that now
requires nearly 15 percent of the budget to service each year.
Demographic forces will continue to drive up the costs of programs for the elderly, thus defining the political choices: reduce
defense, cut other domestic programs, expand the budget by raising taxes or accepting higher deficits, or restrain the costs of elderly programs. None of these options, to say the least, is politically attractive.

In the longer run, the more desirable course is to expand our
capacity to pay for rising social costs. But developing that capacity is likely to require substantial investments that are fiscally and
politically painful. For example, the movement of the baby boom
population into its most productive work years could be a boon to
productivity, but only if business, government, educational institutions, and individuals invest in the training needed to keep pace
with changing needs for work skills.

On the positive side, some demographic trends are favorable,
and with appropriate action could be turned to advantage. For
example, the reduction, or slower growth, in the number of school-
age children could free up considerable resources to strengthen
education. Some measures could go far toward restraining costs
and expanding capacities. For example, raising the retirement age
would ease costs by reducing the number of pension recipients
while increasing the nation's capacity to support Social Security
and other programs for the elderly by keeping taxpaying workers
employed longer.

For approximately the next two decades, demographic forces
are likely to exert slow but steadily increasing pressures to widen
the cost-capacity gap. However, once the baby boom generation
begins to retire, shortly after the turn of the century, the ratio of
workers to elderly people will turn sharply unfavorable. Moreover,
the productivity of that relatively smaller workforce will depend
substantially on how well the large numbers of educationally disadvantaged children currently enrolled in our public schools have
been prepared for employment. In the international sphere, meanwhile, it is likely that the more productive nations of the populous
regions of the Third World will have increased their relative economic, technological, and military capacity, further diminishing
the margin of international influence the United States has en-

joyed in the post–Second World War era, or—said differently—
will increase the cost of maintaining its influence.

Institutional Stress

These trends pose formidable political challenges to the United
States. Difficult choices must be made to resolve tensions that
have already arisen; at the same time, even more difficult choices
must be made to contend with the still greater tensions that will
arise in the future. But perhaps the greatest challenge of all is that
the institutions responsible for dealing with these political challenges are being weakened by many of the same demographic
forces that are widening the cost-capacity gap.

The stress on the structure and process of political institutions
shows up in three types of mismatches.

First, there is a rising tension in the United States between the
increased dispersal of power and the growing interdependence
among people who hold power. Both of these tendencies are associated with historical processes that are widely applauded. The
dispersal of power results in part from greater democratization,
growing affluence, and increasing technological capability, all of
which give more people the freedom and the wherewithal to pursue their own desires. The interdependence among powerholders
is associated with the nation's economic specialization, urbanization, high volumes of commercial activity, and advanced technology that require people to interact harmoniously.

Internationally, power is becoming more widely dispersed
among nations. No single nation or small group of nations exer-
cises decisive influence. Alliances are often strained by economic
disputes, and few international organizations carry much weight.
And yet the nations of the world are more interdependent than
ever before.

Within the United States, power is widely dispersed among voting citizens and highly organized interest groups. Yet American
society is more urban, more specialized, and more interdependent
than it ever has been.

Demographic factors alter the political equation most directly
by changing the relative size of politically influential groups. The
elderly and minority groups, for example, make up a growing proportion of the electorate. Greater access to wealth, technology, and

political legitimacy can also enhance the power of groups that have been cut off from such resources in the past. Equally important, the political culture itself—its ideology, legitimacy, and cohesiveness—is undergoing change due to a combination of demographic and related forces.

The second type of mismatch is more abstract, although it has quite practical consequences. In all nations today, the United States included, familiar categories of analysis and policy action tend to be at odds with increasingly interdependent real-world forces. Viewing the world in terms of economic, social, technological, and environmental divisions, for example, offers useful but only partial descriptions of forces that are increasingly interdependent, and not easily distinguishable in practice. Such distinct conceptual perspectives have had a powerful effect on how governments organize their approaches to policy, differentiating as they do among "economic policy," "environmental policy," "science and technology policy," "social policy," etc. The failure to integrate interdependent policies not only limits their effectiveness but increases the likelihood they will exacerbate problems because of lack of attention to their interrelated nature.

Similarly, familiar demographic categories are enlightening to a point, but tend to obscure important shifts within those categories. Thus, for example, in the United States the "elderly" include not only the frail, sick, and poor of the conventional perception, but also people 65 and older who are robust, healthy, and affluent; substantial income gains for many blacks tend to hide the serious losses suffered by other blacks; and today's "family" is likely to contain unrelated individuals, so it is more accurately described as a "household."

The third important mismatch is geographic. The basic unit of world political organization, the nation-state, seems, as Daniel Bell has noted, to be too small for the big problems of life and too big for small problems. The nation-state is defined principally in terms of the territory over which it claims sovereignty. But national governments are limited in their ability to control information, technology, capital, goods (including drugs), and even people that flow easily across their borders.

Similar geographical incongruities are found in subnational government organization. National demographic trends may not appear at all, or may be greatly exaggerated, at the regional and local levels, and those aberrations may not be acknowledged in national policy. In addition, urban agglomerations have expanded beyond conventional metropolitan boundaries and have confounded traditional concepts of "city-suburb-country" by concentrating employment and retail activity in multiple nodes throughout vast and amorphous urban expanses far from "downtown." These transforming regions, moreover, constitute primary units of economic geography in the new global economy. Southern California and New England, for example, are now in direct competition with other regions of the world as much as with one another. State and local governments in recent years have made great progress in adapting to these regional demographic and economic changes. But the mismatch between political boundaries and economic geography, and the inappropriate distribution of powers and responsibilities at the federal, state, and local levels, seriously impede that progress.

The challenge posed by these mismatches is not insurmountable, but it is formidable. For it entails adapting political institutions to the pressures that are transforming them, just when those institutions are trying to contend with the widening gap between social costs and capacities.

Organization of This Part

In addressing these issues, in this part of the volume I treat demography not just as an important force but also as a common thread and organizing concept to better define the political equation: how are the costs and capacities changing? what are the options for closing the gap between them? and what is the political potential for exercising those options? Numerous studies have been done on various demographic topics that address these issues. Here I will draw on that body of knowledge and link together the pieces that bear on these questions.

The section begins with an assessment of key world population trends in chapter 9. Chapter 10 then considers the changing role of the United States in the context of increasing world interdependence and the nation's international standing. Chapter 11 analyzes the political implications of an aging U.S. population, including the impact of a rising cost burden and changing generational outlook on the U.S. role in the world. Chapter 12 assesses how demographic changes are altering political culture, in part by placing greater emphasis on differences than on common interests. Chapter 13 examines demographic changes at the regional, state, and local levels. Of particular interest here is the potential for more effective governmental action to cope with the new patterns of population settlement and economic geography. Finally, chapter 14 discusses the stress on U.S. institutions and the opportunities posed by these demographic trends.

CHAPTER 8

Global Interdependence

INTERDEPENDENCE among the world's population is increasing principally because of economic and technological changes. The globalization of the economy—in production, marketing, capital flows, and the dissemination of knowledge—has been accelerating. Marked improvements in communication and transportation have facilitated this integration.

The primary demographic implication of these changes is simply that they are affecting so many people so quickly. People throughout the world are being brought into closer and more frequent contact with one another, and their actions—or inaction—are much more likely to affect one another than in times past.

But underlying these dramatic changes is a demographic current that has a momentum of its own: the dynamic of birth, aging, migration, and death on a world scale. That current, to be sure, is affected by economic and technological changes. But its direction is not easily diverted, and its momentum is powerful enough to impact the economic and technological forces, or to join with them in producing other consequences.

World Population Trends

The world's human population did not reach 1 billion until about 1850, then doubled to 2 billion by 1926, and then more than doubled again to 5 billion people in 1987.

Some analysts have characterized this trend as a population explosion. In 1968, Paul Ehrlich's book *The Population Bomb* implanted a powerful image in the American mind of a world jam-packed with people, fulfilling the dire Malthusian prediction of population outpacing food supply.[1] Other analysts, noting the generally declining fertility rates in nearly every country and the slowing rates of population growth in even the faster-growing countries, have claimed more recently that the explosion has fizzled.

143

In reality, neither the "explosion" nor the "fizzle" characterizations appropriately describes what is occurring. Fertility rates generally have been declining in nearly every country, and the rate of total
world population growth has been slowing from its peak of 2.1 percent annually in the late 1960s to 1.7 percent in 1987.[2] Even with
slower rates of growth, however, current world population is already
so large that 84 million people are added to the population each year,
10 million more than the annual additions that were made during the
years of peak growth. United Nations middle-range projections estimate that world population will reach 10 billion people before stabilizing in the twenty-first century, although that would require a further substantial drop in growth rates.[3] (See figure 14.)

Whether one gives greater importance to growing numbers of people or to the slowing rates of growth, the focus on aggregate world

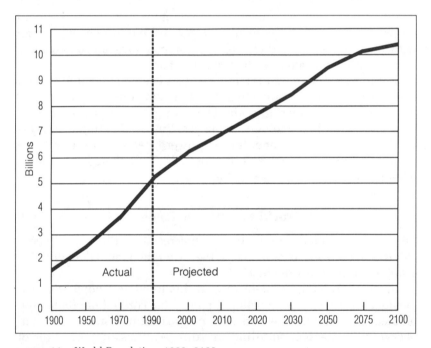

FIGURE 14.   World Population, 1900–2100

Sources: K. C. Zachariah and My T. Vu, *World Population Projections, 1987–1988
Edition* (Baltimore, Md.: Johns Hopkins University Press, 1988); Jane Menker, ed.,
World Population and U.S. Policy (New York: Norton, 1986).

population obscures the widely varying rates of growth from region to region that have significant implications.

Variable Growth Rates Among Nations

The world's population is divided roughly in half between those countries that have slowly growing, stable, or declining populations, and those countries still characterized by high population growth. The slow-growth regions, which are growing at about 1 percent a year or less, include Western Europe, North America, Eastern Europe, the Soviet Union, Australia and New Zealand, and East Asia. The rapid-growth regions, which are growing at about 2 percent a year or more, include Southeast Asia, Latin America, the Indian subcontinent, the Middle East, and Africa. The slow-growth regions, with a total 1986 population of 2.3 billion, are currently adding about 19 million people to the world each year. By contrast, the rapid-growth regions, with a 1986 population of 2.6 billion, are adding 65 million people every year. (See table 6.)

Equally important, the pattern of population change in some of the faster-growing countries does not appear to be conforming to the historical pattern of the slower-growing countries.

In 1945, demographer Frank Notestein developed a theory of demographic transition that postulated three stages. In the first stage, premodern societies are characterized by slow population growth because both death rates and birth rates are high. In the second stage, economically developing societies are characterized by rapid population growth because death rates fall due to improved living conditions and medical innovations, while birth rates remain high in keeping with the social custom of having many children. In the third stage, population growth is slow, stable, or negative, because birth rates fall to levels approximately equal to the lower death rates. The lower birth rates generally are attributable to the desire for smaller families (children are perceived less as an economic asset and more as an economic burden), lower infant mortality rates, which reduce the need to have many children in order to guarantee the survival of the number desired, and more effective birth control.

According to the Notestein model, countries move from a condition of relative population stability, through a transition period of rapid population growth associated with economic development, and return to a condition of stability, albeit at a higher level of

TABLE 6
Projected Population Growth Rates Among Nations: Annual Averages, 1986–2000
(in percent)

Above 3 percent		1–2 percent (cont.)	
Kenya	3.9	Australia	1.9
Saudi Arabia	3.8	Ireland	1.0
Tanzania	3.4	Hong Kong	1.0
Nigeria	3.3		
Pakistan	3.0	0–1 percent	
		Cuba	0.8
2–3 percent		Canada	0.7
Algeria	2.9	USSR	0.7
Bolivia	2.6	United States	0.6
Vietnam	2.4	Japan	0.5
Philippines	2.3	France	0.4
South Africa	2.3	Spain	0.4
Mexico	2.1	Italy	0.1
		United Kingdom	0.1
1–2 percent		East Germany	0.0
		Sweden	0.0
Brazil	1.9		
India	1.8	Less than 0 percent	
Indonesia	1.8		
Thailand	1.6	Austria	−0.1
China	1.4	Belgium	−0.1
Chile	1.2	Denmark	−0.1
Korea, Republic of	1.2	Hungary	−0.1
Argentina	1.1	West Germany	−0.3

Source: World Bank, World Development Report 1988, table 27.

population. This conceptualization repudiates the Malthusian formulation that did not allow for the possibility that people would modify their childbearing habits to reduce population growth, but assumed that continued high fertility rates would inevitably strain the capacity of environmental and social systems to sustain larger populations and thus lead to starvation, war, disease, and other forms of "natural" population control. The Notestein formulation was based on the observation of changing population patterns in Western European countries, virtually all of which had successfully industrialized and enjoyed sustained economic growth by 1945.

While the Notestein model explains demographic changes for much of the world's population, it does not appear to explain what is occurring in other parts of the world.[4] For while approximately half of the world's population appears to have made, or is making, the transition through high population growth accompanied by economic development to a new level of population stability, the other half of the world's population has not. For the latter half, there is every indication that rapid population growth is continuing and, equally important, is continuing at rates that exceed economic growth.

Lester R. Brown and Jodi L. Jacobson have referred to the condition of the Third World nations caught in the middle stage of transition as the "demographic trap."[5] Economic growth in these countries has been slow to negative and, most important, has been outpaced by population growth. Death rates have fallen because of improvements in prevention and treatment of disease. But because economic growth apparently has not been substantial enough to alter traditional childbearing habits, fertility rates have not fallen quickly enough to substantially reduce birth rates.

Some of the rapid-growth countries, such as India and Zaire, are increasing their per capita income and thus have not fallen into the demographic trap. And some countries in the rapid-growth regions, such as Argentina, Cuba, and Uruguay in Latin America, have much lower rates of population growth that would appear to place them closer to the third stage of demographic transition. Some of the rapid-growth countries, such as Thailand and Indonesia, have had good family planning programs which may help curb population growth and keep it from outpacing economic advances. For many of the others, however, falling per capita income and continued rapid population growth appear to be reinforcing one another in an ominous downward spiral.

Changing Age Composition Among Nations

Differences in age structure can be as important as variations in growth rates. As the overall fertility of world population falls and the growth rate declines, the world population in general will continue to age, with several results.

The number and proportion of elderly people is already high by historic standards throughout the world. In the industrial countries, between 10 and 15 percent of the population is 65 or over. Most other industrial countries are aging much more rapidly than the American population. For example, by 2010, the elderly population is projected to equal 26 percent of the labor force in the United States, while it is projected to be 40 percent in both Japan and Germany (compared to 15 and 29 percent, respectively, in 1986).[6]

Aging has also increased the number of elderly people in the less-affluent countries. But the far more dramatic development has been the explosive growth in the younger age groups in the Third World, where some 40 percent of the population is under the age of 15, compared to about 20 percent in the United States and Europe.[7] Within the next generation, 3 billion young people will be entering their reproductive years in the Third World.

Economic Implications

Thomas Malthus established the intellectual benchmark for the population debate by predicting in the late eighteenth century that population growth would outpace the world's resource capacity. Since then, there have been numerous refutations and reformulations of the Malthusian proposition.[8]

In 1986 the National Research Council of the U.S. National Academy of Sciences attempted to synthesize existing knowledge on the relationship between population growth and economic development.[9] It concluded that in general "slower economic growth would be beneficial to economic development for most of the developing world," but added that this conclusion was more a matter of judgment than a conclusion based on quantitative proof.[10] In essence, the council's assessment supports the view that population growth can affect economic development, but that other factors are also involved and are likely to be more important. Rapid population growth does not necessarily prevent economic development, even if it may inhibit it; nor will slower population growth necessarily promote economic development. The key in both cases is institutional capacity: the ability of social, economic, and political institutions to adapt to the consequences of population change, and turn them to economic advantage.[11]

Between 1950 and 1973, the world economy grew at an average rate of 5 percent per year. Virtually every country, whatever its economic condition or rate of population growth, participated in this worldwide expansion.[12] Since 1973, however, world economic growth has fallen to under 3 percent per year. With world population increasing annually at roughly 2 percent, real per capita income growth fell from just over 3 percent per year in the two decades prior to 1973 to barely 1 percent since 1973.

The slowdown or decline in per capita economic growth, in part attributable to the failure to slow population growth sufficiently, has led to massive borrowing, as many countries have attempted to sustain the standards of living to which their citizens have become accustomed. Many Third World countries now face the combined problems of sluggish national and international economic growth, continued population growth, and the burden of spending nearly all their export earnings on the repayment of debt.

The magnitude of these pressures bodes ill for economic growth in debt-ridden countries and increases the likelihood of substantial losses by U.S. lenders. For example, between 1980 and 1986, the Latin American countries' combined Gross Domestic Product increased by 8.1 percent, with steady growth between 1984 and 1986 more than making up the losses suffered in the recessions of the early 1980s. However, because of high population growth, the Latin American countries sustained a 6.2 percent drop in real per capita Gross Domestic Product over the six-year period. Meanwhile, the total external debt for Latin American nations in 1986 was $382 billion, up from $368 billion in 1985 and $231 billion in 1982.[13]

The demographic trends of the industrial world could have a quite different economic impact. In those countries, the labor force is likely to grow far more slowly, which could have the beneficial effect of easing unemployment, but could also create labor shortages and pressure for higher wages. By 1988, employers in regions of high economic growth in the United States were already feeling this effect, finding it difficult to fill skilled jobs and paying wages substantially above the minimum wage for low-skilled workers. Similarly, the impact on consumer demand could be mixed. On the one hand, the growth in the number of consumers will slow, the more so as the trend toward lower household size and a higher rate of household formation plays itself out. On the other hand, the concentration of the adult working-age population in their middle years of high earnings and high consumption could increase demand and shift demand toward more highly differentiated and higher-valued goods and services.

The recent phenomenon of population decline in some of the industrial countries raises a whole new series of economic issues. West Germany, for example, because it is losing population, can now have zero growth in its GNP, or even a slight decline in economic output, and still see its per capita GNP increase. Immigration from East Germany due to the loosening of border controls may result in short-term surges of population, but it is not likely to affect significantly the long-term trends toward population decline in the German nation as a whole.

Differences in population growth rates and age structures among countries can also have an economic impact. Over the next 20 years, Third World countries are projected to increase their workforce by some 600 to 700 million workers. That addition to their labor force alone will exceed the total workforce of all the industrial countries combined in 1985.[14] These new workers constitute a potential stimulus to worldwide production and consumer demand. The recent history of emerging industrialized countries suggests that the growing cadre of Third World workers will become effective producers before they become avid consumers; thus they will challenge U.S. production more than they will be likely to buy U.S. products. They will also challenge the industrial world not only with cheap labor, but also with a growing cadre of scientists and technicians. Meanwhile, failure to absorb this massive influx of workers into productive jobs could create an enormous drag on economic development in Third World countries, leading to defaults on international loans and mounting pressure for migration to the more industrialized countries.

Differences in age structure may also affect the capital flows among nations, not only between industrial and less-affluent countries, but among industrial countries themselves. Japan and Germany, for example, may have an incentive to export capital to the United States or other industrial countries as they seek investments to support their more rapidly increasing retired populations. On the other hand, the need for aging countries to support larger numbers of retirees with fewer workers could result in their using greater quantities of their own capital as a substitute for labor.

Environmental Implications

The relationship between population change and economic development is closely associated with the relationship between population and its environmental impact.

The 1972 publication *The Limits to Growth*, sponsored by the Club of Rome, predicted that "if the present growth trends in world population, industrialization, pollution, food production, and resource depletion continue unchanged, the limits to growth on this planet will be reached sometime within the next one hundred years. The most probable result will be a rather sudden and uncontrollable decline in both population and industrial capacity."[15] A similar theme was sounded in *The Global 2000 Report to the President of the United States* in 1980.[16]

The principal criticism of the limits-to-growth argument is that it fails to account for adaptations in behavior that could alter these dire predictions. In particular, it is argued that the market mechanism, if permitted to work, would both dampen demand for limited and more costly resources and prompt innovation in the development of new resources. Julian Simon's *The Ultimate Resource* (1981), for example, argued that human ingenuity could overcome the predicted Malthusian squeeze on resources.[17]

Still, the debate continues. Serious people claim that the human species is already "consuming its capital" by causing irreversible damage to the atmosphere, to the most productive farmland, to water resources, and to the diversity of organisms. Serious concern and unanswered questions have tended to focus on the impact of air pollution on the destruction of the ozone layer in the stratosphere, the impact of acid rain on forests in the temperate zone, the depletion of soil, and the loss of biodiversity through the extinction of organisms as a consequence of clearing rain forests. Harvard biologist E. O. Wilson, for example, foresees "the greatest extinction since the end of the age of dinosaurs" as a consequence of the logging and mining of forests in the tropics that will eliminate countless species of plants and animals.[18] There is also concern over the potential synergistic effects of human behavior generally on the quality and vitality of the earth's biosphere. One study, for example, claims to have found a complex relationship between human population growth, the increase in plant-eating animals, increased methane production, and ozone depletion in the atmosphere.[19]

Environmental harm is caused not so much by sheer numbers of people as by damaging behavior associated with producing, using, and disposing of materials. The wealthier countries generally have had the largest impact on natural resources, although they have also made progress in developing more environmentally sound practices in certain instances. While the environmental impact of Third World countries may be lower on a per capita basis, negative practices associated with both economic deprivation and economic growth can nonetheless be significant, the more so given the large and growing populations in Third World countries. In parts of the Third World, when population growth increases the demand for wood fuel in excess of sustainable supply, forests are often depleted. The reduction of tree cover, in turn, leads to soil erosion and land degradation. Excessive grazing by livestock beyond the sustainable yield of cropland causes herdsmen to feed their animals forest foliage, thereby damaging the tree cover even further. Inadequate protective vegetation permits water and wind erosion of the soil. The consequence of all of these forces is desertification, defined as "a sustained decline in the biological productivity of land."[20]

Environmental degradation is a problem of global dimensions in several respects. Most obviously, the damage caused by one country can have an impact on others. But there are also important economic and financial linkages. The clearing of tropical forests in the Third World is motivated in part to satisfy foreign demand or to meet debt payments in industrial countries. Specific projects are frequently financed by international agencies, such as the World Bank, the Inter-American Development Bank, and the European Coal and Steel Community.[21]

A 1987 report by the Rand Corporation on ozone depletion highlighted the international policy dilemma in dealing with potential damage to the global environment. The report observed,

> Emission of chlorofluorocarbons and related chemicals to the atmosphere may promote the chemical reactions that reduce the concentration of stratospheric ozone and contribute to global warming (the "greenhouse effect"). Depletion of stratospheric ozone could increase the quantity of ultraviolet radiation penetrating to the earth's surface, which could have significant adverse consequences for human, animal, and plant life.[22]

Normal market mechanisms may not respond to such externalities, the report continues, because "there are believed to be substantial lags between production and emission of potential ozone depleting chemicals, and between emissions and effects on ozone concentrations." This poses a critical issue: "By the time it becomes clear whether ozone depletion is an important threat to global welfare, it may be too late to prevent serious adverse consequence."[23] A report released by the National Aeronautics and Space Administration in 1988 concluded that ozone depletion resulting from the release of chlorofluorocarbons had proceeded more rapidly than previously believed, and by 1989, a general consensus had developed that the situation did in fact pose a serious threat to the earth's atmosphere.[24] The contribution of population increase to this threat is straightforward: without substantial changes in patterns of production, consumption, and disposal of wastes, a rapidly increasing population must be assumed to accelerate atmospheric damage.

Nutrition and Health

While many countries have learned to feed themselves and still export food, others are losing the race between population and agricultural growth. Some, like India and Indonesia, are now agricultural exporters, even though the number of hungry people in their populations continues to rise.[25] The paradox of world agriculture is that national governments continue to subsidize farmers heavily to produce surpluses for which there is no market, while an estimated half billion people are hungry because they cannot afford to purchase those subsidized surpluses.

The United Nations World Food Council and its parent body, the United Nations Food and Agriculture Organization, estimate that the number of hungry people in the world grew between 1970 and 1980 by some 1.5 million people a year to a total of 475 million. However, as economic growth slowed in the early 1980s, the number of hungry people increased by nearly 8 million a year, reaching an estimated half billion in 1985.[26] A 1986 World Bank study estimated the number in 1980 to be between 340 million and 720 million, and growing.[27]

Progress has been made in the past half century in mobilizing world resources to alleviate starvation and malnutrition. An estimated 4 million children have been saved in the past five years through immunization and oral rehydration therapy. Nonetheless, frequent infection and widespread undernourishment are estimated to be responsible for the deaths of 14 million children annually.[28] Efforts to help the undernourished are frustrated by chronic economic problems in many of the poorer countries that require austerity measures such as cutbacks in services to the poor, sick, and undernourished.[29]

Meanwhile, the growth in per capita world agricultural output has been slowing. World grain production expanded by 3 percent per year before 1973, but has slowed to 2.3 percent since then. Per capita grain output has fallen to a 0.4 percent annual increase.[30]

Political and Social Stress

There is no persuasive evidence that population growth, or even high concentrations of population, in and of themselves necessarily create political or social stress. But in many Third World countries, the growing numbers of people competing for finite or shrinking resources cannot help but generate social and political tensions. Large numbers of young people are overwhelming educational institutions and flooding labor markets that are already plagued by high unemployment and underemployment. The number of people living in cities in the developing countries has increased from 100 million in 1920 to 1 billion today, and is projected to increase by another 750 million by the end of the century, creating enormous pressure on urban services.[31] Some urban agglomerations in the Third World are growing to unprecedented proportions: by the year 2000, Mexico City is expected to reach 30 million, Shanghai 25 million, and Bombay and Jakarta 17 million people each.[32]

Such pressures appear to be adding to social and political stress in countries that are strategically important to the United States. For example, political analyst Sergio Díaz-Briquets believes that population growth has exacerbated Central America's problems by adding pressure to labor markets, increasing the pressure on the land, taxing the government's ability to provide social services, and planting seeds of discord among an already struggling population.[33]

Similar problems are confronting Egypt. With a population of 50 million, Egypt is adding 1.2 million people per year, but losing ground in its ability to feed itself. In 1960 it grew over 80 percent of the grain it consumed; in 1986 it had to import over half of its grain consumption.[34]

Mexico's exploding young adult population could further dampen real wages, which have already fallen by more than 20 percent during the 1980s. This could further skew an already lopsided distribution of income in which 41 percent of total income is claimed by 10 percent of the population, while 3 percent of total income is distributed among the poorest 20 percent of Mexicans. These pressures could also make it difficult for Mexico to cope with its huge foreign debt ($102 billion in 1986) and to raise the capital required for economic growth.[35]

International Migration

A combination of the forces described above is creating pressure for increased international migration, by both pushing people out of Third World countries and attracting them into the industrialized countries.

High population growth combined with sluggish or negative economic growth drives people out of struggling countries in search of employment. The explosion of the young adult population adds a double presssure because the new entrants saturate the workforce and because young adults are prime candidates for emigration.[36] They are more mobile and more adventurous, have more to gain and less to lose by leaving, and have the greatest difficulty finding employment at home.

Pressures to emigrate will be especially intense in the United States' immediate neighbors to the south. By the year 2000, the countries of the Caribbean Basin are projected to have a combined population of 250 million, close to the 266 million population projected for the United States in the same year.[37] Here again, economic conditions in Mexico account for a substantial part of the pressure.

To keep unemployment from worsening, Mexico would have had to create 900,000 jobs per year during the late 1980s, and will have to create 1 million jobs per year in the 1990s. In comparative terms, Mexico will have to find new jobs at a level one-half that of the United States even though its economy is one-twentieth the size of the United States'. Even if it were to achieve an extraordinarily high job growth rate of 3 percent annually, Mexico's unemployment rate would still be 8 million, or nearly 20 percent of its labor force, by the year 2000. An estimated 9 million people would still be underemployed.[38]

At the same time that conditions in Third World countries will push people out, demographic trends in the industrial countries are working to attract them. The young adult population in many industrial countries will decline both in absolute terms and as a proportion of the labor force. Consequently, the already vast wage differential between the industrial and the poorer Third World countries could increase—even if the real wage rates in both decline due to worldwide competitive forces—if they decline more steeply in the Third World. Meanwhile, a siphon effect develops whereby immigrants stimulate additional immigration from their home countries. Immigrants who have already entered the industrial countries facilitate the migration of their compatriots and family members by providing information and a familiar home in the host country. In addition, some immigrants return to their native countries with firsthand experience as to the benefits of a higher standard of living abroad and personal testimony to the fact that emigration is both possible and rewarding.

There will also be strong incentives within industrial countries to encourage immigration, whatever official policy may be. Employers will be eager to find low-wage, energetic workers. Agricultural producers in the United States, for example, complain that the tighter restrictions on immigration are depriving them of the labor they need to harvest crops, and the garment industry claims that their inability to hire foreign labor will result in the loss of business to producers abroad.

Immigration pressure on the United States will be all the greater because of the disinclination of other industrial countries to accept outsiders. The United States has been a beacon for immigrants throughout its history, despite a variable historical record in opening its borders to different types of immigrants, and considers the welcoming of the world's dispossessed as part of its national heritage and character.

Japan and Western Europe, by contrast, have a totally contrary tradition and inclination. Japan retains its historical tradition of racial exclusivity, and treats its relatively small population of immigrants as permanent outsiders, few of whom obtain Japanese citizenship. The practice in several Northern European countries in recent decades of luring foreign "guest workers" to fill labor shortages during the boom years of the 1950s and 1960s is regarded by many in those countries as a mistake, despite its economic benefits. Millions of the guest workers stayed during recessions, and many of them and their children now consider the "host" countries to be their permanent homes. The second generation faces an especially difficult future. The children of Turkish workers in Germany, for example, feel neither Turkish nor German. They tend to speak German poorly and are not welcomed in German institutions, but neither do they feel a close kinship with the homeland of their parents or face bright prospects of returning to a country they do not know and where unemployment is already high.

Institutional Implications

The conventional concern about the expanding world population has tended to focus on the consequences of total population growth on the world's natural resource base and economic development. Now there are some new dimensions in the equation: increasing global interdependence, extremely slow growth and population decline in many countries, and the changing age structure within and among countries. Each of these dimensions underscores the necessity for all nations to adapt their domestic policies or work collectively to account for critical issues of concern to all.

National and international economic policy instruments must be developed that can take account of global economic interdependence. But even achieving balanced economic growth in the industrial world, as daunting a challenge as that may be, will not be sufficient to address the problems associated with growing world interdependence. Economic development has proved to be elusive for many poorer countries, even under conditions of world economic growth. Moreover, modest economic growth will not prevent backsliding if it fails to outpace population growth. And this—falling per capita income despite overall national economic growth—has been the prevailing experience for much of the Third World for the past decade or longer. Some types of economic growth, moreover, can be counterproductive, both for the world at large—as when it damages important world resources such as tropical forests or the atmosphere —and for the country in question—as when it consumes the natural resource base that is needed for economic growth.

These changes are important to the United States both because the United States inevitably will be affected by them, and because the United States is in a stronger position than any other nation in the world to promote international remedies. But the United States' ability to deal with these global changes in the conventional manner appears to be waning, in part because of demographic factors.

CHAPTER 9

The United States' International Standing

THE MOST important demographic reality affecting the United States' standing in the world is not a trend or future projection but an established fact: Americans represent only 4.6 percent of world population. Under moderate projections, the U.S. population will continue to grow for the next 40 years. But because the rest of the world will grow at a more rapid rate, the United States' share of world population will probably drop to about 3.9 percent by 2010.[1]

How will these and other demographic factors affect the United States' standing in the world, and how, in particular, do they contribute to the debate over whether America is in a state of decline or renewal?

The United States' relatively small share of world population has not been a determining factor in U.S. world influence in the past. At the peak of its economic and military power following the Second World War, the United States had only about 6 percent of world population, not much more than it has today or will have in the future. But in the past, the United States enjoyed relative geographic and economic isolation, and extraordinary economic, technological, and military predominance. In the future, by contrast, the United States will be inescapably part of an increasingly interdependent world, and other nations could well attain, if not surpass, its level of productivity. Some may already have done so. In these circumstances, the United States' relative economic strength with respect to some nations could continue to decline. But the extent to which that will occur, and with what consequences, depends on numerous other factors.

America's Relative Economic Strength

The United States' relative share of world Gross National Product (GNP) has declined from its extraordinary predominance following the Second World War largely because other countries have been

158

catching up to American standards of productivity. As figure 15 shows, even though U.S. productivity growth in manufacturing grew at a healthy 3.4 percent annually between 1979 and 1989, that performance still lagged behind those of Japan, Britain, and Italy. The Manufacturing and Allied Products Institute estimates that complete productivity convergence has now occurred at the aggregate manufacturing level between the United States and Japan.[2] And, as figure 16 shows, the trends suggest that Japan could be taking the lead.

The United States has not lost absolute economic strength; to the contrary, between 1950 and 1985 its real GNP roughly tripled. But whereas immediately following the Second World War the United States accounted for about 40 percent of total world GNP, by 1970 that share had dropped to about 24 percent and has vacillated in the

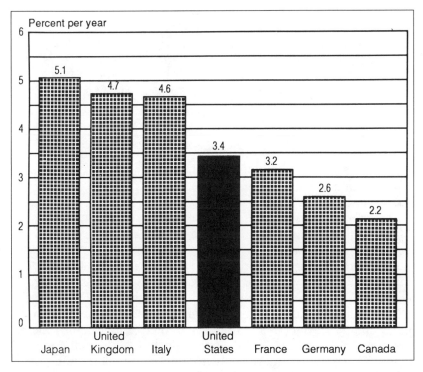

FIGURE 15.   Growth in Manufacturing Productivity in Leading Industrialized Countries, 1979–1987

Source: U.S. Bureau of Labor Statistics.

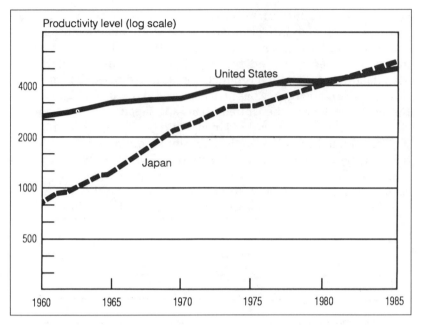

FIGURE 16.   Productivity in Manufacturing: United States and Japan, 1960–1985

Source: Manufacturing and Allied Products Institute.

vicinity of 20–23 percent throughout the 1970s and 1980s.[3] By contrast, over the same period, Japan's share of world GNP soared more than fourfold from 2 to 9 percent.[4]

Does this matter?

In economic terms, there is no ostensible reason why the United States should be concerned about the fact that other countries are becoming as productive as we are. In fact, it has been American policy since the Second World War to encourage this to happen. The Marshall Plan was consciously designed to assist allies and former enemies alike to rebuild their wartorn economies. The United States has contributed billions of dollars and its technical expertise toward the economic development of the rest of the world. Not only recipient countries, but the United States and the world economy as a whole have benefited enormously from the general economic growth enjoyed by much of the world in the four decades since the Second World War.

Even if other countries surpass the United States in per capita

GNP or economic leadership in specific industries, this development would not necessarily be a disadvantage for Americans. Just as other countries have benefited from U.S. economic growth and adopted its technological innovations, so the United States theoretically could benefit from the economic and technological advances of other countries in the future.

But as a practical matter, the relative decline in economic strength does mean that the United States is not likely to retain the economic edge that it has had over the past half century, nor will it have the same power to pursue its international interests and to influence world affairs.

The United States today is a far wealthier and more powerful country than it was nearly a half century ago. Its annual defense spending has roughly tripled in real terms (even though the defense budget consumes less than 6 percent of U.S. GNP today, compared with levels of 10 and 11 percent in the 1950s and 1960s). The United States also remains the largest economy and the most powerful military nation in the world, and is likely to continue to be so into the foreseeable future. But the relative size and direction of national economic strength is also important in determining world influence.

Paul Kennedy, whose book *The Rise and Fall of Great Powers* has received great visibility as a warning of American decline, argues that throughout history shifts in relative economic strength have been the principal determinants of international power.[5]

> The Netherlands in the mid-eighteenth century was richer in absolute terms than it had been a hundred years earlier, but by that stage it was much less of a Great Power, because neighbors like France and Britain had more power and riches. The France of 1914 was, absolutely, more powerful than the one of 1850—but that was little consolation when France was being eclipsed by a much stronger Germany. Britain has far greater wealth today than it had in its mid-Victorian prime, and its armed forces possesses far more powerful weapons, but its share of world product has shrunk from about 25 percent to about three percent. If a nation has "more of it" than its contemporaries, things are fine; if not there are problems.[6]

Samuel Huntington, arguing that, contrary to the positions of the "declinists," the United States is really in a state of renewal, responds that Kennedy overstates the extent to which the United States fits this historical pattern. He notes that far from losing its share of world gross product, the United States—with the exception of its drop from the abnormally high share of world GNP it enjoyed just after the Second World War—has held its own. Moreover, he notes that while the average annual growth rate of Gross Domestic Product in Japan between 1980 and 1986 was only 58.7 percent of what it had been between 1965 and 1980, the U.S. average annual growth rate for 1980–86 was 110.7 percent of what it had been from 1965 to 1980.[7]

Kennedy argues that historically great powers have undermined their economies by spending too much on military forces required to maintain their empires, a form of "imperial overreach." Huntington responds that the United States spends relatively little on defense, less than 7 percent of GNP, and that a greater danger for the United States is that its productive investment will be sacrificed to consumption. Still others argue that the key point is that the United States is underinvesting, and that the United States has sacrificed long-term economic strength for short-term economic growth.

Whether the United States will be able to sustain its relative share of world gross product at 20 percent or more, even though it has less than 5 percent and a declining share of world population, remains to be seen. The growing interdependence of the world economy and the tendency toward productivity convergence among nations would seem to militate against it. For the United States to maintain its recent position will require an extraordinary economic performance.

Even if it were to sustain its current share of world gross product, the United States still would have to contend with the mismatch between the security decisions it made years ago when it enjoyed substantially greater relative economic strength, and the capacity it has today. Following the Second World War, the United States undertook a broad array of security obligations, including formal treaties and the staking out of de facto strategic positions. During that period, the United States produced more than half the output of the industrial world, and its military strength was unequaled. U.S. productivity was increasing at a rate of about 3 percent per year, and its trade, fiscal, and financial positions were all strong. Four decades later, the United States retains most of those international commitments, and continues to maintain over a half million military personnel abroad to support its foreign strategic interests. But its economic and financial position has changed substantially. The fact that its share of world GNP has fallen by nearly half, and its industry is subject to intense competition from other countries, is probably partly caused by the fact that the United States has only a moderate share of the skilled proportion of world population in an increasingly interdependent world economy. However, the added economic and financial vulnerability brought on by running large budget and trade deficits, and by failing to compete in specific industries, is principally the consequence of actions over which Americans do have control.

Another, potentially more important challenge will be to maintain a stable international economic system.

World Economic Leadership

The Bretton Woods system for stabilizing exchange rates and liberalizing trade, established and maintained through U.S. leadership, provided the foundation for post–Second World War global economic growth. Since the mid-1970s, however, that system has faltered. Protectionism has spread, monetary and financial markets have been unstable, and national economic policies have taken divergent courses. Numerous factors have contributed to this situation, including the restructuring and globalization of the economy. But one factor that seems especially important is the inability, or unwillingness, of the United States or any other single power to play the leadership role that has been the cornerstone of the international economic system.

Some theorists believe that for the past several centuries the international economic system has depended on the leadership, or hegemony, of a single dominant economic and military nation. Great Britain played that role throughout the nineteenth century and beyond the First World War into the 1920s. The United States assumed the leadership role from the British, but only after a lapse during the 1930s when there was no clear international leadership. The choppiness of this transition may have taken its toll. Charles P. Kindleberger, in his classic study of the Great Depression, concludes that "the 1929 depression was so wide, so deep, and so long because the international economic system was rendered unstable by British inability and U.S. unwillingness to assume responsibility for stabilizing it."[8] Political economist Robert Gilpin attributes the current instability in the international economic system to the failure of the United States to continue to play the role of hegemon, and the failure of any other nation to assume that role.[9]

What proportion of world economic strength must a nation claim in order to exercise effective leadership? Great Britain at its peak never accounted for more than 25 percent of world gross product, about the same magnitude of the United States' share today. Certainly the U.S. share is not likely to fall to anywhere near 3 percent as did Great Britain's, if for no other reason than the U.S. population is more than four times that of Great Britain.

If the United States is unable or unwilling to exercise world economic leadership, which other country might do so? Japan is the most likely candidate, given its ascendant economic and financial strength. But Japan appears to be unwilling, and may well be unequipped, to do so for several reasons. Prominent among these is that for all its economic vigor, Japan has a smaller economy than the United States. Even if overall Japanese productivity were to rise substantially above that of the United States, the Japanese economy would still be smaller than the American economy, if only because its population is about one-half the U.S. population. Despite its powerful financial position, and the United States' currently weak financial position, Japan's overall economic weight is not likely to approach that of the United States. The demographic reality that dampens Japan's potential for world leadership is even more telling for West Germany, whose population of nearly 60 million is about half that of Japan's, and even with East Germany's 17 million people would still leave its population less than one-third that of the United States.

The fact that both the Japanese and West German populations are aging far more rapidly than the U.S. population would also seem to put a damper on the potential of either country for world leadership. Both are increasingly concerned with the need to provide for their rapidly growing elderly populations.

Nor is either Japan or West Germany likely to be in a position to develop the military posture that has historically gone hand in hand with world economic leadership. Japan may begin to increase its military budget above the 1 percent of GNP limitation that it set in 1976. In fact, with formal military expenditures of over $40 billion plus associated military infrastructure, the Japanese may now have the third highest defense budget in the world behind the United States and the Soviet Union. But even if the Japanese should decide to accelerate this military buildup, they are not likely to reach a level of strength anywhere near that of the United States.

West Germany is even less likely to do so, given its far smaller and declining population, and numerous other more influential factors that limit its military potential. The decline in the number of young Germans will require a higher proportion of them to spend longer tours in the military if personnel levels are to be maintained, a situation that has already caused mild political stress in Germany.

In sum, however economically vigorous and financially strong Japan or Germany currently may be compared with the United States, it seems implausible that a smaller country with a smaller economy, a more rapidly aging population, and a substantially weaker military capacity would take over a leadership role that seems to be too big for the United States.

Of the other candidates with the population weight to provide economic leadership, the European Community currently lacks the political cohesion, the Soviet Union currently lacks the economic and financial potency, not to mention the political cohesion, and such populous countries as China, India, Brazil, and other Third World countries are still far from commanding the resources necessary for world leadership.

The Presidential Commission on Integrated Long-term Strategy in its 1988 report, *Discriminate Deterrence*, projected that by the year 2010 the United States would have a GNP of nearly $8 trillion, the Chinese and Japanese each would have GNPs somewhat short of $4 trillion, and the Soviet Union would lag behind with a GNP of slightly under $3 trillion.[10] Such projections are, of course, speculative, but they provide a plausible basis for long-range thinking. The population dimension of these estimates is instructive: all the leading countries have large populations; China's unusually huge population puts it in contention with the two most advanced economies, the United States and Japan, even though its productivity will continue to lag far behind both; and the Soviet Union, with the second largest population among the four, nonetheless loses ground and will eventually fall to the rear because of its deficient economic system. In short, population matters, but only up to a point.

If historical patterns are applicable (and they may not be, given the dramatic changes in the world economy), it would appear that a U.S. share of around 20 percent of world gross product may be sufficient for the task of exercising international economic leadership. Nor is it inconceivable that the United States could maintain that proportion, even though it is nearly five times its share of world population. It has done so over the past two decades, even if the economic and financial foundations of U.S. growth in productivity over that period have been tenuous. However, low savings, the dependence on foreigners for investment and short-term financing of domestic and foreign debt, and the erosion of technological and economic leadership in key industries all raise questions as to whether the United States can sustain its relative economic position in the world.

One is left with the conclusion, therefore, that unless the United States makes a concerted effort to rebuild its economic and financial capacity and reassert its leadership, no single country may have the combined demographic, economic, and military weight necessary to exercise the kind of leadership upon which the world economic system has been based.

If this should prove to be the case, a major adjustment may be in store for the international economic order. It could take numerous forms: pluralistic leadership among two or more nations; more effective international cooperation; stronger international institutions; more flexible and skillful unilateral adjustment of individual national policies; the division of the world economy into regional economic and trading blocs; or adjustment to a higher degree of economic turbulence.

East-West Relations

The dramatic economic and political developments in the Soviet Union and Eastern Europe suggest the potential for major shifts in economic and strategic relationships both within and among the Western and Soviet alliances that have defined international affairs for the past half century. These developments have called into question the contemporary validity of the premises upon which the North Atlantic Treaty Organization (NATO) and the Warsaw Pact were established. Still, it is useful to view those alliances from a demographic perspective, both because they define the historic relationship between East and West and because they will continue to form the base for future changes in relationships within and among more traditional alliances.

At the core of America's political, military, and cultural alliances in the world are the Western industrial democracies. Together with the United States, they make up about 15 percent (or 742 million people in 1985, including Japan) of the total world population.[11] That proportion is down from 22 percent in 1950, and at current fertility rates is projected to fall to 13 percent by 2010, and to 8 percent by 2035.[12]

Fertility rates in all the Western democracies are currently below the replacement level. According to one projection, if they were to maintain their current fertility rates and current rate of net immigration, the Western democracies would increase their collective population from 742 million in 1985 to a peak of 795 million in 2020 before beginning to decline. Two countries, Germany and Denmark, have been declining in population for several years, and several others may soon have declining populations.[13]

Nonetheless, the Western democracies collectively have a substantially larger population than the socialist industrial countries. In 1985, the Soviet Union and Eastern Europe had a combined population of 393 million people, including 277 million Soviet citizens. That is 8 percent of world population, or only a little more than half the population of the Western democracies.[14]

The socialist countries are also experiencing fertility rates below replacement level, although their rates are not as low as those in the West. Their slightly higher fertility may be due in part to the strong pronatalist policies pursued by some of the socialist nations. It is also the result of substantially higher fertility rates in some of the non-Russian areas of the Soviet Union. This compensates for the lower fertility of the Russian population, but is also cause for concern among Soviet leaders who fear the potential for further political unrest among the Soviet Union's numerous ethnic minorities and regions, especially among the Muslim population, where growth is highest.

In 1979, the Russian population represented 52.4 percent of the total Soviet population, but Russian fertility was only 1.9, below the replacement level and almost identical with American fertility. Meanwhile, in the Central Asian republics, fertility in 1979 ranged from an extraordinarily high 4.1 in Kirgiz to an even higher 5.8 in Tadzhikistan. At these rates, the Russian population will decline to 46.7 percent of the total USSR population by the year 2000, while the population of Muslims (who are concentrated in the Central Asian republics), will increase to 21.3 percent.[15] Political dissent and public demonstrations in these regions in 1988 and 1989 suggested why their high population growth may be a mixed blessing for overall political cohesion and military Soviet strength. The diverse demographic mix of the Soviet Union and the consequent political problems it poses under conditions of economic stress present a formidable challenge to Mikhail Gorbachev's policies of *perestroika* and *glasnost'*.

Even if the socialist countries grew to 467 million by 2020, as they would according to one medium projection, they would still have less than 60 percent of the population of the Western allies in that year.[16] The Western democracies, in sum, have a commanding lead in population over the socialist countries that is not likely to diminish significantly for the next half century.

Of course, there is no guarantee that the current national alliances in either the West or the East will be sustained. While the Western democracies have certain common political institutions and traditions, each is a sovereign nation-state with substantial differences in cultural and social character. Recall that they fought the bloodiest war in history among themselves only a generation ago. And certainly the turbulence in the Soviet Union and Eastern Europe raises questions about the strength and durability of the Warsaw Pact. Countries and regions in both camps appear to be seeking more independent political identification, stronger trading ties, and a relaxation of tensions with countries in the other camp. Meanwhile, as the Soviet Union struggles to modernize an archaic economy and make the political adjustments necessary to hold together a weak economy, it cannot help but notice that the far more populous "Third World" nations to its South are showing signs of remarkable economic vigor.

The Shrinking Industrial Minority

A more telling demographic factor in world strategic relationships than the minor shifts in population advantage among East and West is that the industrial countries together—including the Western democracies and the socialist countries—now account for less than one quarter of total world population. Three-quarters of the world's population is comprised of the 3.7 billion people who live in Africa, Latin America, and Asia (excluding Japan, which is counted here among the Western democracies). The populations of these regions are growing at a rate that adds the equivalent of the United States' population every four years. By one projection, they will reach a combined population of 4.95 billion by the year 2000, and 6.53 billion by the year 2020, at which point the West and the socialist countries together would constitute only 16.4 percent of the world's population.[17] (See figure 17.)

For half a millennium, the imperial countries of Europe were the world's preeminent military powers, and for much of the past century directly controlled the majority of the world's population through their colonial empires. Then, in the course of two decades, following the Second World War, they lost both their colonies and their position of world economic, political, and military leadership.

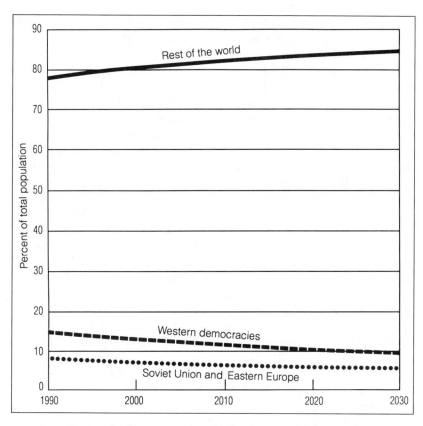

FIGURE 17.   Projected Composition of World Population, 1990–2030

Source: K. C. Zachariah and My T. Vu, *World Population Projections, 1987–1988 Edition* (Baltimore, Md.: Johns Hopkins University Press, 1988).

Dominance of world affairs passed from Western Europe to the United States and the Soviet Union. The colonies, for their part, gained independence and a growing measure of political influence that has prevented any superpower or a combination of superpowers from exercising the degree of control once held by the European imperial nations.

This shift in political and military power in its magnitude and swiftness is among the most dramatic in history.

In 1800, the per capita income of Europe was estimated to be about twice that of the rest of the world. After a century of unprecedented economic growth fueled by the industrial revolution, the per capita income of the industrial world had soared to approximately eight times that of the nonindustrial countries. Clearly, it was this magnitude of economic superiority, in combination with the technological sophistication and political organization with which it was associated, that enabled European civilization to establish political and military dominance over most of the world.

The United States benefited from the European industrial revolution, and by the early twentieth century had become its leader. Not only was the United States a member of the club of nations that had attained extraordinary economic superiority over the rest of the world, but also by the early twentieth century, the combination of its population size and productivity had placed it at the head of that exclusive club in raw economic power. The devastation of Europe during the Second World War left the United States in a class by itself—the sole survivor of the world's economic elite. But the historical circumstances of this unique position were ephemeral. Europe more than recovered its former economic strength in absolute terms. Japan, which to date has been the most successful of the major non-Western nations in applying European technology, recovered from the devastation of the Second World War and resumed the trajectory of its startling economic advance. The gap between the United States and the other industrial countries caused by the war was thus quickly narrowed after a postwar high.

Meanwhile, much of the rest of the world started down the road toward industrialization. Virtually all countries have strengthened their economies since the Second World War, but their performance has been highly uneven. Some, such as the newly industrial countries of Asia—South Korea, Taiwan, Hong Kong, and Singapore—have grown to the point that their per capita GNP is now about one-fourth that of the industrial world. They have thus reduced the West's former per capita economic advantage by one-half, and are continuing to narrow the gap rapidly.

At the other extreme, the economic advantage of the industrial world over the poorest countries is even greater today than it was nearly a century ago, and the gap may actually be widening. In 1980, the average per capita GNP of the industrialized countries was $10,660, while for the poorest nations, such as Zaire, it was as low as $250.[18] Thus, the richest nations in the 1980s had a shocking *fortyfold per capita advantage* over the poorest nations.

For the aggregate of the world's nonindustrial countries, however, the gap with the industrial leaders has been closing at a slow if not always steady rate. The less-developed countries' share of total world GNP increased from 11.1 percent in 1960 to 14.8 percent in 1980.[19] This does not include China, whose share of world GNP, by one estimate, grew from 3.1 to 4.5 percent over that 20-year period.[20]

The economic, technological, and military advantage enjoyed by the Western powers in the late nineteenth century thus appears to have been substantially reduced. Even relatively poor countries possess the material, organizational, and technical capacity that can make them a military match—at least on a defensive basis—for the military power that the industrial powers have been able or willing to commit against them. The shrinking military advantage of the industrial countries is reflected in the failure of the United States in Vietnam, the withdrawal of the Soviet Union from Afghanistan, and the embarrassingly close call that the once mighty British Empire had before retaking the Falkland Islands from Argentina.

The increasing economic and military potential in the Third World frequently combines with the demographic, political, and cultural diversity of those regions to generate turbulence. As former Secretary of State George P. Shultz once noted: "The spread of modern technical skills coincides with the modern resurgence of age old ethnic, religious, and communal conflict. Beyond the Iran-Iraq war we see fighting in Sri Lanka, ethnic conflict in Fiji, the devastation of Lebanon, Sino-Indian border tensions, the New Caledonia and Cyprus Disputes, the continuing Arab-Israeli conflict."[21]

The capacity for dealing with such a world cannot be gauged simply by numerical measures of economic and military strength. Numerous other factors affect a nation's military strength and overall power, including political will, geographic position, and character of leadership.

But sheer weight of population is also an element in this equation. China, for example, has one of the lower per capita GNPs in the world, but is a significant economic and military power by virtue of its massive and adaptive population. It has sufficient wealth and technological capacity that it is a nuclear power. And it need only achieve a level of productivity one-quarter that of the United States to become the largest economy in the world. Taiwan has nearly achieved that level of relative economic capacity. The economy of the People's Republic of China, meanwhile, has been growing at a rate of 8 percent per year.

By the year 2000, 70 percent of the population in the Third World will be concentrated in eight countries: China, India, Indonesia, Brazil, Pakistan, Bangladesh, Nigeria, and Mexico.[22] By 2025, the United States is projected to be surpassed as the fourth most populous country by Nigeria, and possibly by Indonesia as well. (See table 7.)

A large population by itself is no guarantee of significant international influence, as illustrated by Bangladesh. Furthermore, demographic diversity within countries can be a source of political tension and potentially of national weakness; this holds true no matter the economic wealth or military capacity of a country, as evidenced by periodic ethnic and regional rifts in nations as diverse as China, the Soviet Union, Nigeria, and the United States. However, several of the populous Third World countries are demonstrating the capability to combine human and technological resources in an increasingly productive fashion. Their size and growing economic and technological capacity cannot but help make them increasingly influential in world affairs.

American Population Dynamics and National Security

It should be underscored that the principal demographic factors influencing the United States' standing in the world are not trends so

TABLE 7
Population Projections for the Eleven Most Populated Countries, 1990, 2010, and 2025
(population in millions; percent of world total)

	1990		2010		2025	
	Population	*%*	*Population*	*%*	*Population*	*%*
China	1,117	21.2	1,386	19.7	1,537	18.8
India	843	16.0	1,130	16.1	1,312	16.0
USSR	289	5.5	324	4.6	344	4.2
United States	249	4.7	273	3.9	285	3.6
Indonesia	179	3.4	242	3.4	283	3.5
Brazil	150	2.8	203	2.9	236	2.9
Japan	124	2.4	131	1.9	130	1.6
Nigeria	118	2.2	217	3.1	298	3.6
Bangladesh	113	2.1	168	2.4	205	2.5
Pakistan	112	2.1	183	2.6	242	3.0
Mexico	89	1.7	128	1.8	154	1.9

Source: K. C. Zachariah and My T. Vu, *World Population Projections, 1987–1988 Edition* (Baltimore, Md.: Johns Hopkins University Press, 1988).

much as preexisting realities. In particular, the trend toward economic and technological convergence among important parts of the world's population increases the weight of population size as a determinant of relative economic, military, and political influence. But an additional question is whether population dynamics within the United States play a role in this equation.

In recent years, alarms have been raised by commentators such as Ben J. Wattenberg in his book *The Birth Dearth* that low American fertility could have negative consequences for the United States' strategic interests.[23] This concern seems to focus on two types of issues. One is that as the American population grows more slowly than its adversaries', or actually declines, the United States' military and economic advantage will gradually be eroded. The other is that the population dynamics of low fertility—slow growth, decline, and aging—will sap the economic and cultural vitality, the military capacity, and the political will of the United States.

History serves up numerous examples of nations concerned that their population was inadequate to support their strategic objectives. It was a concern of the Greeks and Romans; it has preoccupied the French since the Napoleonic era; Hitler and Mussolini promoted pronatalist policies; and the Eastern European countries have aggressively promoted childbearing in recent decades.

Concern about population decline—in contrast to lagging rates of population growth—is relatively new in historical perspective. It was first raised in the last century when it appeared that some European countries might soon stop growing. One of the few systematic studies of the subject, undertaken by Michael S. Teitelbaum and Jay M. Winter, concluded that "population decline—however defined—has evoked fear, confusion, and misunderstanding among a broad community of politicians, scientists, churchmen, and novelists in many different countries."[24] The study found that traditionally much of the fear has been based on misperceptions, misinterpretations, and ideological advocacy.

In the years prior to the Second World War, there was great alarm in France that slow birth rates posed a threat to French military strength and presaged the fading of the French nation. The *denatalité* debate in the 1930s prompted widespread philosophical considerations that sparked the existentialist movement and engaged Catholic and Socialist parties in competition for pronatalist policies. The Catholics advocated legislation against abortion and the Socialists proposed day care centers and youth programs. When, in 1940, France was unable to defend its Belgian frontier against German invasion, many attributed the military deficiency to low French fertility.[25]

Concern has been expressed in the past about declining birth rates in the United States, most notably before the baby boom surprised everyone with a sudden surge in population. The most recent alarms about an absolute or relative decline in American population are similar to many of the concerns that have been raised in this country and in Europe in the past. Fewer babies mean fewer soldiers, smaller-sized economies (which reduce military potential), and declining world influence of the national culture.[26] These concerns are not to be lightly dismissed, but, as argued earlier, they tend to obscure the far more important and immediate demographic reality that America's population is *already* a small share of the world total and would likely remain so even with a substantial upturn in birth rates.

The alarms also give the impression that because fertility in the United States is below the replacement rate of 2.1, the nation's population is likely to soon decline. The reality is that even if U.S. fertility stayed constant at its 1988 estimated rate of 1.8, the U.S. population would continue growing until the year 2030, when it would reach a peak of 290 million people. Moreover, that projection makes no allowance for increases due to immigration, or for an unforeseen upturn in fertility. Even if fertility were to *fall* to 1.630, the U.S. population would still continue to grow to 275 million by the year 2020.[27]

To be sure, a large population is an important component of national strength, military and otherwise. Even in an age of nuclear weapons, awesome conventional firepower, and sophisticated defense and weapons delivery systems, the number of personnel still counts in determining military effectiveness. Indeed, given that a stalemate in the production of nuclear weapons increases the importance of conventional forces, it is arguable that fielding large numbers of combat personnel is as important today as it was in the prenuclear period. The signing of the Intermediate Nuclear Force Treaty in 1988 made conventional force alignments an even more important strategic consideration in Europe.

Low American fertility, however, does not currently loom large as a factor in American military strength. It is true that the pool of 18- to 24-year-olds in the United States hit a peak of 30.4 million in 1980 and will continue to decline until 1995. Then, according to some projections, it is expected to rise slightly until about 2010, when it will begin a gradual but steady decline. However, practically no one expects it to dip as low as 16 million—the point it reached in 1950, when the United States was at the peak of its military influence in the world—until late in the next century.[28] A compensating factor for the declining pool of eligible male soldiers is the entry of women into an increasing number of military positions, including many that are close to combat duty.

Until the latter part of 1988, the armed services, with a few exceptions, claimed they were not experiencing problems in filling their ranks with qualified people. In fact, there was an apparent resurgence of interest in military service among younger people during the 1980s, after it had fallen in the aftermath of the Vietnam War. Enlistment in ROTC, for example, rebounded strongly following its decline in the 1970s. To maintain current levels of qualified personnel in the armed services in the face of mounting labor shortages could eventually require more aggressive recruitment, higher pay to attract and retain personnel, extension of tours of duty, use of women in combat positions, or even conscription.

Still, given its only slightly smaller population vis-à-vis the Soviet Union, the only thing that prevents the United States from fielding a strategically adequate level of military personnel is the political choice not to do so. That choice is based in part on a U.S. military strategy heavily dependent on nuclear weapons. This may or may not be a wise strategy. In fact, it may be based in part on a political disinclination to the draft. But such decisions are not constrained in any objective or strategic sense by the size of the 18- to 24-year-old cohort.

In the meantime, as we have seen, the Western democracies as a whole maintain a substantial population edge over the Soviet Union and Eastern Europe. The collective decision of the West regarding appropriate levels of conventional forces is a political and strategic choice that cannot be attributed to overall population ratios.

Population size is probably as important in determining the economic base required to support costly military systems as it is in supplying military personnel. In this respect, the West has an even more commanding lead. In 1986, the Western democracies together accounted for about 66 percent of world GNP compared to 19.2 percent for the Soviet Union and Eastern Europe, better than a three-to-one economic advantage.[29] Given the weakness of its economy, it is unlikely that without its large population base the Soviet Union could sustain the heavy economic burden of maintaining a military capability competitive with the United States. As it is, the Soviet

Union expends a much higher proportion of its GNP on the military than the United States (estimates generally vary between 15 and 20 percent). There can be little question that the high rate of military expenditure required from the Soviet perspective to compensate for an economy that lags far behind that of the Western capitalist system has taken its toll on the ability of the Soviet Union to meet fundamental consumer and other civilian demands. The economic and political restructuring underway in the USSR is certainly attributable at least in part to the inability of the centrally planned Soviet economy to support a military establishment competitive with those of the NATO countries. Meanwhile, the U.S. defense budget (plus minor additional expenditures for international affairs) stood at 6.6 percent of GNP in 1988, far lower than the 11.1 percent that the United States allocated to defense in 1958, and substantially below the Soviets' proportional allocation from a far weaker economy.

It bears repeating that a nation's population size and economic base are but two of many factors that determine its military capability. Technology, training, morale, political will, diplomatic skill, strategic mastery, and generalship, to name the more obvious factors, are all important. Critical in every case is matching resources to strategic objectives. North Vietnam achieved its military objectives against the United States, an opponent that was far superior in economic strength, population size, military technology, and the size of its military establishment. So has Israel defended itself against adversaries with an overwhelming population advantage, albeit at a high cost. Both of these small countries have been successful because they effectively mobilized and applied the resources they had (including the military equipment they were able to get from other countries) to meaningful strategic objectives that were capable of being achieved with those resources.

In sum, the alarm that the United States' low rate of population growth is eroding its military capability seems overwrought. The far more immediate and important demographic factor affecting the nation's overall world influence is that much of the rest of the world, with vastly greater population, has gained in per capita economic strength and military capability relative to the United States. Even an unprecedented surge in the U.S. birth rate would not alter the enduring reality of America's small share of world population. There are many practical ways the United States has compensated, and could continue to compensate, for that demographic reality, but attempting to change it by increasing the nation's absolute or relative population does not appear to be among the more productive or feasible choices.

But if a small and shrinking population share is an unalterable fact of life for the United States, the internal demographic dynamics associated with low fertility—in particular, the aging of the population—merit closer attention as a factor in determining the cost, the capacity, and the will to maintain America's international position.

CHAPTER 10

An Aging World Power

T HE AGING of the United States' population will be a major—and perhaps determining—factor in the United States' world standing and international leadership. It will affect both the capacity of the nation's economy and the political will to play a leading world role. Even if the United States cannot or chooses not to play a leading international role in the future, the aging of the population will nonetheless profoundly affect American politics and institutions.

The effect of aging on national politics and institutions involves a complex mix of numbers, perceptions, and attitudes. While the aging of the U.S. population is perceived as something new, it has been a prevailing trend for most of the country's history as life expectancy has increased and fertility rates have declined. Between 1900 and 1986, life expectancy at birth increased from 47.3 to 74.9 years, while fertility declined from 3.9 to 1.8 births per woman.

The sudden "discovery" of aging results in part from the fact that the long-term aging trend was obscured by the aberration of the baby boom. Between 1946 and 1964, the fertility rate grew to a peak of 3.8 and produced the baby boom population of 77 million people which has defined the demographic character and self-perception of the American population since the 1950s. So long as the baby boomers were *below* the average age of the population, they *retarded* the long-term aging trend. From 1960 to 1980, the average age of the American population rose from 29.5 to 30.0, or less than 2 percent. Now, as the baby boomers are growing older, exceeding the average age, they are *accelerating* the long-term aging trend. From 1980 through the year 2000, nearly the entire baby boom generation will pass the average age of the total population and sweep it upward from 30.0 to 37.3 years, an increase of 24 percent.

It's been like three kids on a seesaw. When two of them sit together at one end, they touch the ground and the third at the other end is perched high in the air. But when one of the two at the low end gets up and runs toward the high end, the moment he steps over the

178

fulcrum, the seesaw suddenly tips in the other direction, and he and his new partner plummet to the ground while his old partner is thrust into the air.

The sudden acceleration of the increase in the average age of the U.S. population would have been jarring if it had simply reflected a return to the historical trend. But its impact is further exaggerated in being superimposed on a pattern of increasing longevity and declining fertility. The consequence of this conjunction of forces is an increase in both the absolute number *and* the proportion of the elderly population.

As noted in earlier chapters, the size of the U.S. population 65 and over is projected to be 34.9 million in 2000. It will edge up to 39.2 million in 2010 when the first baby boomers reach age 65, and then soar to 64.6 million in 2030 when all the remaining baby boomers will have reached 65.

At the other end of the age spectrum, births are not keeping pace with the growth in the elderly population, even though birth rates have increased slightly as the baby boomers have moved into their childbearing years. The number of children age 5–17 is expected to increase to 48.5 million in 1995, an 8.5 increase over 1985. However, the number of 14- to 17-year-olds will actually decline slightly during that period.[1] The 18–24 age group, which reached an all-time high of 30.4 million in 1985, will decline to 14.6 million in 2001, before climbing again to 27.7 million in 2010.[2]

The consequence of the difference in growth rates for the elderly and for the young is that the age group of those 65 and older, which comprised 12.0 percent of the population in 1985 (contrasted with only 4.1 percent in 1900), is projected to rise to 13.9 percent in the year 2010—a relatively mild rise—and then surge to 17.3 percent in 2020 and on to 21.2 percent in 2030.[3]

Cost-Capacity Ratio

A rough estimate of how the changing age structure is likely to affect the cost-capacity equation is reflected in the dependency ratio that compares the predominantly dependent age groups (65 and over, and 18 and under) with the predominantly working-age groups. This ratio and its limitations have been discussed in earlier chapters, but it is worth highlighting the key points.

In 1950, the ratio stood at 64.4 people in the young and old groups for every 100 people in the working-age group. It rose to a peak of 83.1 in the 1960s, reflecting the sharp rise in the number of young dependents, and then declined to 62.9 by 1982. The ratio is projected to drop further to 58.1 in 2010. In other words, the total number of young and old people compared to those in their middle years actually has been declining and will continue to decline for the next two decades. It is then .projected to begin rising again, reaching 78.1 by 2080. But even at that point, the ratio will still be below the peak of 83.1 that was reached in 1965.[4]

There is a major change, however, in the proportion of children and elderly in that ratio. In 1950, 51.0 of the 64.4 dependents were children. By 1982, the children's share had fallen to 44.1, and by 2080 it is projected to fall to 36.2. Meanwhile, the elderly share rose from 13.3 in 1950 to 18.8 in 1982. It is projected to grow to 20.7 in 1990, and then will rise very slowly for the next two decades, only reaching 21.9 in 2010.[5]

These trends suggest a generally favorable ratio of dependents to workers for the foreseeable future, while signaling a decisive increase in the proportion of elderly to young in the dependent age groups. What these ratios do not reveal, however, is how many people will actually be dependent and at what cost, and how many people will actually be employed and at what level of productivity.

Cost Impact of the Changing Age Structure

Because they are central to the political question, let us summarize the costs associated with the changing age structure that are discussed more fully in chapter 5.

The cost of programs for the elderly has increased dramatically, in part because of the growing number of elderly people eligible for benefits, and in part because of rising benefit levels. The proportion of the federal budget devoted to those 65 and over increased from 2 percent in 1940 to 25 percent in 1982.[6] The federal government in 1982 paid 78 percent of all retirement and survivors' benefits and 54 percent of the medical costs for the elderly. By comparison, the private sector paid 15 and 37 percent, respectively.[7] In 1988 nearly 30 percent of the federal budget was allocated to programs for the elderly.

Major federal transfer payments to the elderly grew from $63 billion in 1965 to $260 billion in 1985 (in constant 1985 dollars), when they accounted for one-half of all outlays for federal domestic programs. On an elderly per capita basis, this was equivalent to $3,400 in 1965 and $9,000 in 1985. Most of these payments were exempt from federal income tax. About one-half of the elderly pay income tax, compared with 90 percent of adults under 65.[8]

While the growth in the number of elderly people in absolute terms and as a proportion of the population will be relatively slow until 2010, the number of the "old elderly"—85 and older—is growing rapidly, with major cost implications. While in 1965, life expectancy at birth leveled off at 75 years, the life expectancy for those 75 and over began to increase dramatically. In 1985, the 65–74 age group of 17.0 million was nearly eight times larger than in 1900, while the 75–84 age group numbering 8.8 million was 11 times larger, and the group of 2.7 million people 85 and older was 22 times larger.[9] The 85-and-over group is expected to nearly double to 4.9 million in 2000, and increase to 6.6 million in 2010.[10]

The cost of medial and long-term care for this group will be substantial. The proportion of elderly people living in institutions increases dramatically with age: it is currently 2 percent for those 65–74; 7 percent for those 75–84; and 23 percent for those 85 and older.[11] In 1986, $26 billion was spent on long-term care for the chronically ill among the elderly. This cost will rise as the nursing home population grows from 1.2 million in 1980, to a projected 2.2 million in 2000, and to 3 million in 2020.[12] Meanwhile, the number of elderly people receiving home health care is projected to increase from 4 million today to 6.8 million in 2020.[13]

The increase in costs to support the elderly may be offset to some extent by the absolute and relative declines in younger age groups. But this advantage could in turn be offset by two other factors.

First, the U.S. government typically has spent far more on the average elderly person than on the average child. According to one estimate, in 1984 the federal expenditure per child was about one-tenth the expenditure per older person.[14] This does not account for the largest proportion of government spending on children, which is spent by state and local governments for education. Still, a 1975 estimate of spending by all levels of government found total per capita expenditures for the elderly to exceed per capita spending for children 17 and under by at least three to one.[15]

Second, it may be necessary to increase substantially the amounts spent for educating and training the young. Recent studies have found U.S. high school students to be woefully ill-prepared for productive employment in a knowledge-based economy. Eighty percent of high school seniors have inadequate basic writing skills; 50 percent read below levels required for carrying out even moderately complex tasks; and U.S. students show mediocre mathematics skills compared to students in 19 other countries.[16] It will be essential to remedy these deficiencies in order to provide the productive capacity needed to carry the higher costs of the elderly.

The Workforce

On the capacity side, the demographic influences will be similarly mixed. The U.S. labor force in 1988 was about 123 million, up from 94 million in 1975. It is projected to reach 135 million by the year 2000.[17] The working-age population (age 16 to 64) increased 1 percent per year in the 1950s, but accelerated to a 1.8 percent per year increase in the 1960s and early 1970s as the baby boom population moved fully into their working years. The steady increase in the percentage of women entering the workforce accelerated labor force growth to 2.5 percent per year by the late 1970s and early 1980s. (Part of this growth was in part-time workers, who increased from 7 percent of the labor force in 1950 to 14 percent by the middle 1970s.) Meanwhile, now that the baby boom cohort has moved beyond the work-entry years, and the growth of women's participation has decelerated, labor force growth has fallen to 1.5 percent per year.

It is unclear how a maturing baby boom workforce will affect U.S. productivity. One school of thought holds that improved skills, experience, and maturity will increase their productivity as it always has for workers moving into their prime working years.[18] However, workers in the past have had relatively stable career patterns in relatively stable industries; workers could build considerable skill and knowledge of the industries, firms, vocations, and jobs in which they were rooted. It remains to be seen if the baby boomers will be willing to upgrade their skills in order to keep pace with a rapidly changing economy, to move to other localities in search of better jobs, or to change vocations altogether.

Meanwhile, the numbers of entry-level workers will be declining, even as the need for qualified labor is projected to grow. By one estimate, the private-sector demand for 152 million workers in 1990 will not be met by the projected workforce of some 129 million.[19] The consequent labor squeeze was already being felt in many regions by the late 1980s.

Moreover, a growing proportion of the shrinking pool of entry-level workers will come from minority groups that have traditionally experienced greater poverty and family dislocation and therefore have not received an education adequate to their employers' needs. The Bureau of Labor Statistics estimates that between 1987 and the year 2000, 57 percent of the net new entrants into the labor force will be from minority groups. As already noted, unless the investment is made to remedy the educational disadvantages of these workers, the labor force will be that much less productive.

In 1987, nearly 1 million students were estimated to have left the nation's schools without graduating, and without employable skills.[20] Another 700,000 remained in school to get their high school diplomas, but graduated with a deficiency in fundamental employable skills. At this rate, unless changes are made in the way we educate the disadvantaged, by the year 2000 the nation will have an additional 20 million people with little prospect for productive employment.[21]

The elderly themselves constitute a growing potential labor pool. The number of employed elderly people has increased, but only because their overall numbers have grown enough to offset a sharp decline in their rate of labor force participation. In 1900, two of every three elderly men worked, while today the ratio is one in six (or 16 percent). The labor force participation rate for elderly women increased slightly from one in twelve in 1900 to one in ten in 1950, but dropped to one in fourteen (or 7 percent) in 1985.[22] The average length of retirement increased from 7 percent of adult life expectancy in 1940 to 23 percent in 1982.[23]

The Political Impact of Aging

On balance, the forces associated with the aging trend appear likely to push up costs more than they will increase capacity. This cost-capacity gap will tend to widen gradually over the next two decades, and then expand rapidly early in the next century as the baby boom generation retires. To support the higher costs, action could be taken to restrain the cost increases, or to extend the government's revenue base, or to strengthen the economy. Alternatively, other government programs could be cut to make additional resources available for the elderly.

The political equation by which these choices will be made has three key variables. The first is the political strength of those who stand to benefit from sustaining or expanding programs for the elderly. The principal beneficiaries, of course, are the elderly themselves who receive Social Security, Medicare, and other benefits. Secondary beneficiaries include the children of the elderly who care about their parents and who would otherwise bear a greater burden for them in the absence of government assistance. Other indirect beneficiaries include citizens in general who want the elderly to be properly cared for.

The second variable is the political strength of those who have alternative claims on the resources required to support elderly programs. This includes taxpayers who pay the Social Security payroll tax as well as other taxes. It also includes those who benefit, or would benefit, from other government programs that seek higher budget shares. Such programs directly benefit specific constituencies, such as the poor, college students, contractors, and so forth. They may also benefit all citizens to some extent by promoting national economic health or strategic interests.

Most people, of course, fall into both categories, but the intensity of their interest varies. Thus the elderly are concerned about national defense and the education of the young, but they are likely to be more crucially interested in their own Social Security payments and medical insurance. Young workers, meanwhile, want to be sure the elderly are properly cared for, but they are likely to be more intensely interested in education for their children and in the size of their tax burden.

The third important variable is the political culture in which these varying interests are contested and resolved. There is a well-established national consensus in favor of supporting the elderly, and specifically Social Security and Medicare. It is based partly on custom, and partly on deeply embedded values that recognize the appropriateness of supporting elderly people who are retired, ill, infirm, or otherwise in need of assistance. But it is also based on perceptions and beliefs that are at odds with current facts and evolving reality. For example, while many people 65 and over conform to the traditional image of the elderly as frail and unable to support themselves, many others are affluent, healthy, and physically robust.

All three of these political variables are themselves affected by demographic forces.

The Elderly as a Political Constituency

The growing number and proportion of elderly people in itself would guarantee their increasing political influence. As shown in table 8, the elderly are a substantial and growing minority of the electorate; they currently account for 16.8 percent of the voting-age

TABLE 8
Population of Voting Age, 1960–1988
(in thousands)

	1988 (Nov. 1)[a]	1980 Census	1970 Census	1960 Census
Total population	182,628	162,791	133,568	115,121
18–24 years	26,556	30,022	23,697	15,604
25–44 years	79,377	62,717	47,995	46,899
46–64 years	46,098	44,503	41,810	36,057
65 and older	30,597	25,549	20,066	16,560
Percent of total				
18–24 years	14.5	18.4	17.7	13.6
25–44 years	43.5	38.5	35.9	40.7
46–64 years	25.2	27.3	31.3	31.3
65 and older	16.8	15.7	15.0	14.4

Source: U.S. Dept. of Commerce, Bureau of the Census, *Projections of the Population of Voting Age for States, Nov. 1988*, Current Population Reports, ser. P-25, no. 1019 (Washington, D.C.: GPO, January 1988).
  a. Projection.

population, a proportion that will steadily grow. But the strength of those numbers is enhanced by the fact that a higher proportion of older residents are citizens (and hence eligible to vote), are registered to vote, and actually do vote than is true of any other age group. The combined force of these factors was reflected in the March 8, 1988, "Super Tuesday" presidential primaries, when voters 60 and older accounted for 32 percent of total Democratic voters and 30 percent of total Republican voters.[24]

The political interests of the elderly as a group, moreover, are highly focused on a few major concerns. While the elderly themselves are a diverse group of people and reflect the varied interests of all voters across regions, racial and ethnic groups, and socioeconomic classes, they are also nearly all fundamentally concerned with the size and reliability of their pensions, the availability and cost of medical care, and the cost of living. These are the issues that most clearly distinguish voters in this age bracket in political opinion and voting behavior.

The elderly are also politically well organized. They are represented by the largest, most heavily funded, and one of the most effective political lobbies in Washington, the American Association of Retired Persons (AARP), which, in 1988, had an annual budget exceeding $100 million, and a membership of 27 million. Other groups, such as the National Council on Aging (NCOA), the National Council of Senior Citizens (NCSC), and the Gray Panthers add to the formidable strength of the senior lobby.

The political strength of the elderly is reflected in the solid support given by both parties to the Social Security system. In 1986, Social Security was the major source of income for 35 percent of older families and individuals, followed by asset income (26 percent), earnings (23 percent), public and private pensions (14 percent) and other government transfer programs (2 percent).[25] Ronald Reagan, the most conservative president since the advent of Social Security, was elected on a pledge to fully protect Social Security, confirming its acceptance as a basic responsibility of government. In fact, the evidence suggests that older voters who cast their votes for Reagan in the 1980 election did so out of conviction that he, an older American himself, would keep his promise not to tamper with Social Security, and that he, better than President Jimmy Carter, could reduce inflation and bring order to a turbulent economy. When, following the stock market crash of October 1987, President Reagan agreed to negotiate a budget deficit agreement with the Congress, he stipulated that "everything will be on the table, with the exception of Social Security." There is no indication that President Bush will be any less supportive.

Republican senators who lost their seats in the 1986 elections, which in turn resulted in the Republicans' loss of the majority in the Senate, were convinced they were defeated by elderly voters who perceived them as being unsatisfactorily supportive of Social Security.

To date, there has been only the slightest political support for reducing Social Security benefits. In the early 1980s, the question was whether the increase in nominal payments to beneficiaries could be held to something less than the full increase in the Consumer Price Index (CPI). When, in 1986, the CPI rose less than the 3 percent required by law to trigger any cost-of-living adjustment for Social Security benefits, Congress promptly amended the law to provide for an adjustment in benefit levels anyway.[26]

But despite their undeniable and growing political strength, the elderly nonetheless will remain a political minority. Political support for programs for the elderly ultimately will depend on the views and actions of the majority of voting adults under 65.

Support for Elderly Programs

In general, people under 65 are broadly supportive of programs that benefit the elderly. After all, many are their parents, grandparents, aunts, and uncles. Without government assistance, moreover, the burden for supporting their elderly relatives would fall more directly on them. And most people look ahead to the time when they themselves will be elderly and dependent on government assistance.

The growth of government support programs has not eliminated the sense of personal responsibility people feel for their elderly relatives. Many adult children support their parents and grandparents with both direct assistance and financial aid. In fact, given the extension of life and especially the growing number of frail elderly persons, the burden on adult children by some measures may be greater today than it has ever been, even with higher levels of financial assistance from the government. Thus, many adults view government support not as an alternative but as a complement to their own continuing support for their elderly parents, with the two—government and families—working in a partnership to provide the higher levels of support required for today's longer-lived elderly.

People under 65 are also potential future beneficiaries of programs for the elderly. They naturally become increasingly mindful of their own approaching retirement and dependence on government support as the years go by. Moreover, the longer they have supported the existing system of elderly programs, the greater the financial and moral stake they feel they have in it. What's more, many from the baby boom generation will have few (if any) children to depend upon for financial or other support as they grow old. As they age, they thus become increasingly aware that support for themselves in their old age will depend exclusively on their own assets and government assistance. Consequently, they are likely to show strong support for the national consensus on elderly programs, and even more so as they approach retirement. Their sense of "ownership" is especially strong toward Social Security, which is based on the notion that subscribers "invest" through the payroll tax in a personal account that will return their higher-valued shares to them at retirement. Of course, there is no such investment, except in the very broad sense that Social Security paryoll taxes help the United States government partially fund its obligations, but the perception of having made a personal investment is a powerful source of political support for the Social Security system.

Nonetheless, as the cost of programs for the elderly continues to grow and are perceived to be competing with such other programs as those for education, child care, and transporation, support among younger age groups could weaken.

People in their forties realize that they have already contributed heavily to Social Security and other elderly programs for about twenty years, and they are also only twenty years from retirement. Thus, their support is likely to be firm and to grow stronger as they move into their fifties and sixties. However, people in their twenties and thirties are still far enough removed from this critical age threshold that their personal support for the current system of support for the elderly is based more on cultural inheritance than a calculation of their own interest. As the younger members of the baby boom generation, and the baby bust generation behind them, become aware of the relatively high burden that they will bear to support the elderly, especially in comparison to the benefits they may look forward to in their own retirement years, the strength of their commitment could weaken.

As Jack Meyer and Rosemary Kern explain in chapter 5, the Social Security benefits that younger adults might receive when they retire could be far below what they might otherwise achieve by investing their contributions privately.[27] In fact, the terms of exchange could become so disadvantageous by the time they retire, given the extremely high proportion of retirees to workers projected for their retirement years, that Social Security benefits may have to be substantially reduced.

Current Social Security beneficiaries are receiving on the average far more in benefits than they contributed in their lifetime, and probably more than they could have expected to receive from a reasonable return if they had invested their contributions in bonds or equities. Most beneficiaries either do not understand this, or profess not to, fervently maintaining that they are entitled to their benefit checks because it is simply a return on the money that they invested over the years.

As payroll taxes have increased from their original 2 percent to 14.3 percent today to cover the rising benefit levels and the increasing number of beneficiaries, the terms of exchange in Social Security have turned less favorable. Most of today's contributors probably will receive benefits that will about equal their contributions, but that level of return will become progressively more uncertain for contributors in the future.

Most analysts agree that the Social Security amendments of 1983 shored up the system for the short term, and probably for the next twenty years. The Social Security Administration projects a $4.1 trillion "surplus" in the Old Age and Survivors Insurance (OASI) by 2010. Technically, the Social Security Trust Fund "lends" its "surplus" to the federal government. However, those "loaned" funds are not invested in any conventional sense, but are essentially accounting transfers of revenues from one federal government program used to cover the expenses of other government programs. The repayment of those "borrowed" funds in the future must come out of federal revenues, so whether or not any real Social Security surplus exists depends entirely on the political will of Congress to tax (or its ability to borrow) commensurately.

The extent to which the Social Security surpluses are "invested" depends on the wisdom of federal policy in funding programs that will promote the future vitality of the U.S. economy. The debate over whether the Social Security payroll tax should be left high enough to continue generating OASI surpluses, or whether the tax should be reduced to a level that would permit only actual liabilities to be covered—or whether it should be taken entirely out of the unified federal budget—is essentially an issue of accounting, public perception, and politics. Either way, future taxpayers will have to cover future Social Security benefits.

Even assuming that the projected surpluses in the trust fund are permitted to accumulate for the next 20 years, once the baby boomers begin to retire in large numbers, the fund will eventually be drawn down. Consequently, even under optimistic projections, the financial viability of Social Security under the current accounting system would once again be threatened.

Since the major burden of providing for the elderly for the next 20 years will be rising costs for medical and long-term living care, especially for those 75 and older and, most particularly, 85 and older, defining levels and modes of care for these age groups will be one of the most politically challenging issues of the next decade. Long-term care and catastrophic health coverage are certain to increase costs. New forms of medical treatment could also add to costs, as they have in the past, both by extending life (and hence dependency) and by establishing higher and more expensive standards of health care. The political implications here include not only determining who is to pay the cost, but who is to receive treatment. The moral issue of how long and at what cost to prolong the life of the very old and the very sick can be expected to emerge from the shadows of philosophical debate and muted decisions among doctors and families to become a major political issue confronting the relative importance of prolonging life and other public values. This is already occurring at the state level, as officials wrestle with the rising cost of health care.

No one knows for sure how young adults will react to the growing public awareness of these circumstances. There are far too many variables to enable anyone to predict with any accuracy the financial status of Social Security and other programs for the elderly in the distant future. A great deal depends on the strength of the economy and the distribution of income. Younger adults are likely to be more willing to accept a higher burden of support for the elderly if their incomes are also higher. For those in the baby bust generation, the fact that their relatively small numbers are likely to put them in a seller's labor market and thus improve their incomes increases the prospect that they will be more willing cost-bearers for elderly programs. On the other hand, compensation levels could be held back by world competition, immigration that expands the workforce and holds down wages, or sluggish-to-negative economic performance. As will be noted in the next chapter, in recent years the average real income of younger adults has not been increasing as rapidly as it did for their parents, and by some measures is actually falling. Moreover, a growing awareness of the mounting evidence that the elderly are increasingly better off financially compared to younger age groups could contribute to an erosion of political support for programs for the elderly among younger voters.

Still one other demographic factor could affect this political equation: the changing racial and ethnic mix of different age groups. The elderly are still by far predominantly white, while the younger age groups are increasingly black, Hispanic, and Asian. Thus, there exists the possibility that the economic and financial factors likely to diminish the younger age groups' support could be reinforced by racial and ethnic factors.

How are these various political forces likely to play themselves out?

Senator David Durenberger (R-Minn.) sees "the potential for real generational warfare in the next century."[28] He is one of the cofounders of Americans for Generational Equity (AGE), a nonprofit research group whose avowed purpose is to "preserve more economic and physical resources for future generations rather than spending them now."[29] In addition to reforming Social Security, AGE advocates

reducing the federal budget deficit, promoting savings and investment, and other measures to build economic strength as critical to the
country's ability to support elderly programs in the long run.

Groups such as the Gerontological Society of America have attempted to quell the talk of generational warfare with studies such as
Ties That Bind that demonstrate generational interdependence.[30] A
coalition to promote the common interests of children, youth, families, and the elderly has been established by the National Council for
the Aging and the Child Welfare League of America.[31]

Gerontologist Bernice Neugarten and public policy analyst Dail
Neugarten observe, "The few studies presently available indicate
that during the life-times of parental generations, a larger amount of
financial assistance flows down the family ladder than flows up that
ladder. . . . How many parents or grandparents are providing the
down payments on homes for young adult children? How many are
providing funds to help divorced daughters who have young children to support?"[32]

In the end, support for elderly programs will not be determined
by a simple political calculus of the different generations' assessing
how much they are likely to pay and receive in public assistance. It
will involve a far more complex set of considerations regarding the
responsibilities and capacities of different age groups and of members of society working collectively to meet common objectives.

New Perspectives on Aging

The extension of life expectancy and improvements in health increasingly will compel a rethinking of what it means to be "elderly." The
time-honored definition of "anyone 65 and over" is clearly obsolete,
since many people in their sixties, seventies, and even eighties are as
healthy and vigorous as people far younger. Many people 65 and
over are affluent, while increasing numbers of younger people and
children—and many other elderly people—live in poverty. These
new realities will enhance the reasonableness and the political appeal of using more objective criteria of income and health, rather
than simply age, in determining eligibility and benefit levels for
government programs. But it is also to be expected that a new ethic
will evolve that conforms to the changing reality of so large and
culturally powerful an elderly population. It will be an ethic that,
among other things, is likely to define new responsibilities for the
elderly that are more in keeping with their social, economic, and

political strength and potential. There is little precedent for such an "ethic of the elderly," and so its evolution is likely to be bumpy.

Aging has always been viewed as a mixed blessing. We strive for longevity, view it as a personal triumph when an individual achieves a great age, and count it as a social triumph when average life spans increase. And yet at the same time we regret the passing of youth, lament the physical deterioration attendant upon old age, and fear the approach of death. Traditionally, old age has been viewed as a resting place, a time of retirement, reflection, and withdrawal. To be sure, there have been exceptional examples of very old people who have remained fully productive and engaged in life into their nineties and even beyond. Indeed, it is probably no coincidence that most centenarians seem to be precisely those people who exude a continual delight with life. But these are the exceptions. While increasing numbers of people above 60 are challenging the conventional perception through their behavior, many continue to expect little of themselves, and little is expected of them.

If we persist in endorsing the conventional images and expectations of old age, the rapid and sustained aging of the population could become a heavy psychological and spiritual—as well as economic—burden that could weigh down and ultimately come to define the entirety of American society. And this could happen with unexpected force as the baby boom generation moves into the traditional retirement years, not just because that generation is so large in numbers, but also because it has been and will continue to be a powerful cultural force in defining the norms and moods of U.S. society.

The world of the twenty-first century will be a far more complex place, global technological and economic interdependence will be greater, and the United States' comparative strength among nations is likely to be diminished. And yet at precisely the time when the international challenge is getting tougher, the spirit of America may be increasingly defined by a generation of old folks, satisfied that they have made their life's contribution and contentedly retired from the world. Indeed, this tendency may be reinforced by the baby boom generation's current penchant for self-involvement, and the strong strain of isolationism always present in the American psyche. At the very moment the United States should be fully engaging the world in all its new complexity, it could instead turn inward and away from the world and leave its fate—and with it the fate of the U.S. experiment—in the hands of other nations that are more youthful, more energetic, and potentially more mischievous.

It need not happen that way. In fact, there are clear signs that the conventional habits of mind about old age are changing in quite practical ways. Many elderly people get bored with "retirement" and panicky at the prospect of 40 years of dependence and indolence, and so seek active lives in paid or unpaid activities. Labor-starved businesses are seeking to attract productive elderly persons into the workforce, or to keep them from leaving it in the first place. Small changes are being made in pension and health programs to define beneficiaries on the basis of need, rather than age. And thoughtful, caring, and eminently practical people over 60 are beginning to seriously redefine their own personal roles and responsibilities, to themselves, their families, and to society more generally.

But a more rapid evolution is required if these changes are to come about in time to counter the powerful demographic drift toward social old age in the conventional mold. Without denying the practical limitations on even the healthy elderly, and the special needs of those who are indeed frail and infirm, social thinking and public policy need to approach those in the upper years more as a resource than a burden. They are a resource of people with experience, capacity, energy, and creativity. They are above all a resource of wisdom. And there could be no more precious and needed commodity for the world of the twenty-first century than that.

The Formative Role of the Baby Boom Generation

The new politics of aging will be defined by the behavior and thinking of people from all age groups. But, as we have said, a pivotal role is likely to be played by the baby boom generation, because of its size, its position of emerging leadership, and—before long—its entry in massive numbers into the ranks of the elderly. How they choose to use that power remains to be seen.

The size of the baby boom generation alone has had and will continue to have a profound effect on American life. As they grew up, the boomers generated demand for pediatric services, baby food, toys, primary schools, secondary schools, colleges, consumer goods, automobiles, and houses. They caused crime rates, the labor force, and unemployment rates to rise. For the next 20–30 years they will probably supply the bulk of the nation's labor force. Beginning as early as the year 2000, when the first baby boomers reach the age of 55, they will begin to swell the ranks of America's retired, a trend that will accelerate for the ensuing 30 years, until most of them are retired by the year 2030.

The potential political strength of the baby boomers is reflected in their share of the electorate: people between the ages of 25 and 44 represent 43.5 percent of the voting-age population, compared with the 25.2 percent in the 45–64 age group. For the past 20 years, political analysts have predicted that the baby boom generation would be the decisive factor in each coming election. It never happened, or if it did, it certainly did not produce the expected result. Few would have predicted that a generation popularly characterized as the flower children, antiwar demonstrators, and civil rights activists of the 1960s would cast the majority of their votes for Ronald Reagan.

Today, the baby boom generation is contradictorily characterized as both anti-institutional and dedicated to corporate careers; both cynical and idealistic; both having a short attention span and being performance-oriented; both favoring change and consumed with the need for personal security; both naive and media-savvy; both highly individualistic and seeking a stronger sense of community. The defining characteristic of this generation, in short, seems to be its very diversity.

What happened to the predicted political character and clout of this group?

In the first place, the baby boom generation was always far more diverse than the media-nurtured popular image held it to be. It should be no surprise that the children of a heterogeneous U.S. population reflect the diversity of their parents. They are the same composite of ethnic, racial, religious, income, and regional groups, and bear the particular cultural and political perspectives of that diverse heritage.

Another reason for their lack of political cohesion is that the demographic definition of the baby boom generation conflicts in important respects with its characterization as a political generation. A more apt delineation would probably distinguish between those whose formative political years were the 1960s—people today in their mid-thirties to late forties and even early fifties—and those whose formative political years were the 1970s—people today in their early twenties to mid-thirties.

But even the sixties generation is far more diverse than popularly characterized. The flower children and hippies of the sixties were a colorful but minuscule minority whose survivors today are barely identifiable. Most baby boomers never participated in the civil rights marches and antiwar protests of the 1960s. Some were too young, others were opposed to the demonstrations, many were indifferent, and most did not act on their views one way or the other.

But for all their diversity, baby boomers as a generation have had certain common experiences. They have always been the center of attention. They were the consuming daily preoccupation of their mothers, women who had assumed responsibility for holding down the home front during the Second World War, including taking traditionally male jobs, and then were suddenly returned to the home when the war was over. (Contrast this with the incidence of working mothers, day care preschoolers, and latchkey children today.) Children were the predominating influence in their neighborhoods, and the beneficiaries of massive new school programs, including an outpouring of resources for public instruction following the Russian Sputnik in 1957. The boomers were the first generation of Americans (or human beings) to establish the television habit from childhood. At the same time every day, in cities, suburbs, towns, and farms across the country, they would gather to watch the same children's television programs.

Since the turbulent years of the sixties, the baby boomers as a generation have concerned themselves with the private interests of career, marriage, home buying, children, and personal affairs. For women, the massive entry into the labor force and into careers other than teaching and nursing has offered an experience totally different from that of their mothers. Men, largely as a consequence of changing women's roles, have also found that their roles are significantly different from those of their fathers, especially insofar as they are less likely to have children at home or be the exclusive breadwinners for those children. Gender may be a more significant factor in voting behavior among the baby boom population than among other age groups. In the 1984 presidential election, for example, an ABC exit poll found 12 percent more male baby boomers voting for President Reagan than females in their age group.

Compared with previous generations, baby boomers are more likely to be single, divorced, or part of a two-wage-earner household. They are more likely to have fewer children, or none, and to become first-time parents at a later age. And, as will be discussed in the next chapter, they are less likely to experience a sizable increase in real income, as their parents did. Contrary to the media-nurtured image of the "yuppie"—young, upwardly mobile professional—the baby boom generation as a whole may be the first downwardly mobile generation since the Civil War.

Perhaps some guides to the future of this generation can be gleaned from Sweden, whose own baby boom began in the late 1930s—about six or seven years before the United States—and had ended by the late 1940s—about fifteen years before the United States. The leading edge of the Swedish baby boomers are now moving into their fifties. They rose quickly in their careers and achieved financial success and responsibility at an early age. Today, many are said to be feeling some sense of burnout, boredom, or restlessness for lack of new goals to aspire to. Meanwhile, the large cohort of people in their forties immediately behind the leaders is said to be feeling intense frustration at having few openings in the top leadership positions, which are filled by their slightly older brothers and sisters. Nor do they have any realistic prospect that those positions will be open until late in their careers, if at all.[33] It remains to be seen whether similar patterns will develop in the United States.

During the next 20 years, the baby boom generation will dominate the workforce, consumption patterns, and increasingly, positions of economic, political, and intellectual leadership in the United States. They are thus likely to shape U.S. culture and institutions in the next two decades even more strikingly than they already have in their childhood and youth.

By the time they are elderly themselves, the voting strength of the baby boom generation will be roughly 50 percent greater in proportional terms than today's already politically powerful 65-and-older age group. If the tendency for elderly voters to vote in high numbers and to concentrate on a few major issues of importance to them as a generation hold true, the baby boomers could exercise unprecedented political influence, acting with a cohesion that they never achieved in their earlier years. They will thus be in a position in their later years to consolidate the changes in national policy and character that they will shape over the next two decades. And they, along with the rest of the country, will live with the consequences of those changes for the duration of the twenty-first century. Perhaps their most significant influence will lie in defining the United States' role in a rapidly changing world.

Generational Perspectives on the U.S. World Role

How Americans will resolve the growing mismatch between costs and capacities associated with structural aging is intimately tied to the United States' role in the world. The net effect of demographic forces both nationally and worldwide is to squeeze U.S. resources for both domestic and international purposes. Effective action in international affairs will be critical to American security and economic well-being. But the costs associated with aging—as the federal budget context is currently structured—could gradually crowd out resources allocated to international affairs or to the investment needed to keep the United States competitive in global markets. How the United States deals with these pressures will depend in part on the reconciliation of differing generational perspectives on the nation's world role.

The generation that grew to adulthood between the First and Second World Wars developed its view of the world during a period of dramatic U.S. ascendency in a turbulent and violent world. They endured the Great Depression, watched as the appeasement of Munich was followed by Nazi aggression, and fought the Second World War to a successful conclusion, ushering in the atomic age in the process. Thereafter, they confronted the Soviet Union and Communist pressure throughout the world, while building the most highly productive and bountiful economy in history. They were, in short, a generation that confronted and met challenges of heroic proportions.

The experience of their children, the baby boomers, has been quite different. Born at the peak of American world power and economic abundance, the baby boomers were taught implicitly (if not explicitly) that the United States had a right to be number one in the world because of its national virtue. This lesson was mixed with fear of the Soviet Union and Communism, a fear that was reinforced by an acute awareness of the potential for instant annihilation by Soviet atomic weapons. The threat was brought home through the power of television, which instructed children in the 1950s to take cover at the first sign of the white flash of an atomic explosion, and by air raid drills that were regularly held in elementary schools.

The 1960s proved to be a turning point both for American power in the world, and for generational perspectives on the United States' role in it. John F. Kennedy assumed the presidency in 1961 promising that American power would be used anywhere in the world at any cost to defend the interests of the United States and its allies. The validity of that bold claim was called immediately into question when the United States failed to support the Bay of Pigs invasion that was intended to drive Communism out of Cuba. Kennedy appeared to restore America's prestige during the Cuban missile crisis of 1962. The foreign policy significance of that event is much in dispute. But the event itself had a powerful effect on the political and world views of the sixties generation. It was perceived as a moment of supreme American vulnerability, and transformed President Kennedy into a hero for millions of young Americans who believed he single-handedly stared down the Russians and saved the United States from nuclear attack.

Kennedy's assassination was in many respects as emotional an event to young Americans of that era as the Japanese attack on Pearl Harbor had been to their parents. In the minds of an entire generation, the symbolic embodiment of American vitality, strength, and idealism was destroyed. The frailty of that symbol hinted at the vulnerability of the broader national strength and purpose that Kennedy personified for an impressionable young generation.

The Kennedy legend and political style thereafter became a benchmark that is almost embarrassingly mimicked today, a quarter century later, by politicians appealing for the votes of baby boomers. The significance of that legacy tends to be obscured in the cross fire of bloated myth and lingering political hostility toward the Kennedys. The enduring reality is that President Kennedy had become a momentary political and cultural bridge between two generations, one defined by the Depression and the Second World War, the other defined by the cold war and the social revolution of the sixties. And when he was assassinated, that bridge collapsed.

The Vietnam War then drove a wedge between the two generations that in some respects has yet to be dislodged. Vietnam defined and tested American strength and purpose. The cost in lives and national prestige, and the inability of the United States to impose its will on a far smaller country, left a strong image in the minds of young Americans. Just as the experience of Munich cautioned their parents' generation against the appeasement of aggression, so the experience of Vietnam cautioned the baby boom generation against the overcommitment of U.S. power in the world.

Now another generation of Americans is coming to adulthood with a far more mixed picture of their country's international role. Their adolescent experiences have included an awareness of growing foreign economic competition, repeated attacks on the prestige of the United States abroad in the form of terrorism and the taking of hostages, and the image of Ronald Reagan seeming to stand tall in the world. But it is not apparent that any single event or intense experience has molded their world view.

In sum, the varying generational perspectives have yet to be blended into a common vision of America's role in the world that commands a consensus among all age groups.[34] The election of George Bush as president in 1988 continues the national leadership of a generation whose world view was molded by the threat to democracy of extreme ideologies and the rise of the United States to world leadership in the Second World War. But the bulk of American electoral strength is progessively shifting toward two younger generations that have quite different global perspectives.

Choices

Until the late 1980s, the United States was able to substantially increase funding to support its growing elderly population, while also building up its defense capability. But the sustained increase in budget appropriations for defense and entitlement programs began to encounter political resistance in the mid-eighties, prompted by rising concern over the nation's chronic budget and trade deficits. Programs for the elderly continued to expand in real terms and as a proportion of federal spending, but defense expenditures leveled off and began to decline as a proportion of the federal budget and of GNP. Meanwhile, neither the federal government nor the private sector has invested at levels required to build an economy capable of supporting both the rising costs of caring for the elderly and sustained levels of national defense.

The budget tradeoff is not simply between programs for the elderly and defense. Nor is it necessarily the case that increased defense spending buys additional national security or international influence; equally important is the strategic and tactical effectiveness of our military forces and the strength of the economy. Yet there is no escaping the fact that a growing elderly population will continue to place ever higher demands on national spending and is likely to consume a growing proportion of national resources, whether funded in the federal budget or in other ways. To be sure, the more productive the economy, the less stressful those demands will be. And it is easily within our capabilities to achieve the proper mix of consumption and investment and other policies that will foster a productive economy.

But even with a reasonably growing economy, the rising cost of elderly programs almost certainly will force a political choice as to how much of that cost should be accepted, and which other sectors of the U.S. economy and society should have their share of resources reduced commensurately. The outcome of that choice will be affected not only by the political dynamics and generational perspective of an aging society, but also by other demographic forces that are changing the composition and political character of the population.

CHAPTER 11

Assertive Diversity

D IVERSITY HAS always been a celebrated feature of U.S. society. It is rooted in the cult of individualism and has been nourished over the years with repeated waves of immigrants from diverse cultures. The central problem of American politics from the beginning has been how to marry the energies and appetites of assertive individuals and factions to the broader needs of the community as a whole.

Demographic trends continue to increase the diversity of the U.S. population, as they have throughout the nation's history. Some of these, such as the dramatic increase in the ratio of older women to older men, have little to do with social choices. But others, such as the increased divorce rate, reflect significant changes in social behavior.

As has always been the case, the unleashing of energy and pursuit of personal and group interests has both expanded capacities and generated costs. For example, the rapid growth in government benefit programs has expanded the capacity of students, the elderly, businesses, the poor, and the disadvantaged. But it has also increased the cost of government. The loosening of traditional family obligations has permitted individuals to escape from confining situations, but one consequence has been a shift of family responsibilities to schools and other social institutions.

The demographics of diversity are also affecting the character of political institutions. While the United States has never been the thoroughgoing melting pot of legend, its prevailing civic culture has traditionally encouraged the assimilation of diverse economic, ethnic, and political interests. In recent years, however, the assertiveness of individual and group interests seems to have been overpowering the common goals and interests that define the community of which they are a part.

The balance between assertiveness and assimilation has always been a tenuous one in American society. As individuals and groups have sought to become part of the national mainstream, they have both drawn upon the characteristics that defined their uniqueness and adapted themselves to the prevailing civic culture. In the process, they have contributed to and helped to redefine the prevailing culture.

In recent years, there appears to have been a tilt in the balance, from assimilation toward assertiveness, caused by changes on both sides of the equation. On the one side, the defining character and assimilative pull of the prevailing civic culture has weakened. And on the other, the strength of individual and group definition and the legitimacy of assertiveness has been in the ascendant.

This shift may have been accelerated by the economic strength of the United States in the years following the Second World War. Groups and individuals could pursue their own interests with intensity, secure in the belief that the economic wealth and political cohesion of U.S. society could accommodate them. National energies were no longer consumed in coping with economic depression or fighting a war, and so the opportunity was ripe to pursue the unfinished agenda of the American Dream: economic gain, the loosening of confining social conventions, the promise of civil rights for all, and the pursuit of personal goals and ideals.

These changes have produced abundant benefits for millions of individuals. They have also created stress. In the future, demographic forces can be expected to reinforce the diversity of American society, test the resilience of institutions they affect, and reshape the political culture from which they are derived.

Income and Wealth

A basic expression of individual diversity in the American culture is the freedom to pursue economic gain. And, inevitably, such freedom creates concentrations of income and wealth among some groups more than others.

In his assessment of income distribution in the United States, Frank Levy concluded, "Family income inequality is very large." He also found that the degree of inequality had remained relatively constant since World War II, although "there was a trend toward equality in the sixties, away from equality in the seventies, and a somewhat sharper trend away from equality in the eighties."[1]

As shown in table 9, the share of household income (before accounting for taxes and government benefits) received by the upper one-fifth of U.S. households increased from 43.3 percent in 1970 to 45.7 percent in 1985. During the same period, the shares of the mid-

TABLE 9
Proportion of U.S. Income Received by Households Before Taxes and Transfers
(in percent)

	1970	*1975*	*1980*	*1985*
Upper 20 percent	43.3	43.7	44.2	45.7
Middle 60 percent	52.7	52.1	51.8	50.4
Lower 20 percent	4.1	4.2	4.1	3.9

Source: U.S. Dept. of Commerce, Bureau of the Census (Washington, D.C.: GPO, 1988).

dle three-fifths of households declined from 52.7 to 50.4 percent, and those of the lower one-fifth declined from 4.1 to 3.9 percent. These changes are relatively small, and they do not account for the government benefits that keep many households above the poverty line.

Overall, the shifts in income distribution since the Second World War have been modest compared with the relative constancy in the inequality of income: the top fifth of families received 43 percent of total family income in 1947, 41 percent in 1969, and about 46 percent in 1987. Meanwhile, the lowest fifth continued to receive a very small share, around 4 percent of the total. In Mexico, as noted earlier, the lowest one-fifth of households receives about the same share, 3 percent of national income.

The aggregate distribution figures alone do not tell the whole story. Equally important is the direction and magnitude of overall income and the changing distribution *within* the various quintiles.

From the end of the Second World War through 1973, inflation-adjusted wages grew by 2.5 to 3.0 percent per year. Real income for the average family increased 30 percent during the Eisenhower years (1952–60) and 30 percent again during the Kennedy-Johnson years (1960–68). From 1973 through 1980, however, the average family real income actually declined by 7 percent, and it declined by another 5 percent through 1984. The movement of the baby boom population into the workforce may have contributed to this poor performance, since the increased supply of labor could be expected through normal demand/supply dynamics to have had a dampening effect on average wages, no matter how robust or anemic overall economic growth may have been.

A Census Bureau study that attempted to measure the effect of benefits and taxes as well as income indicated that the disparities in broader measures of compensation may not be as great as the above figures suggest. By accounting for income and payroll taxes and estimating the value of such benefits as Social Security, Medicare, Medicaid, food stamps, and housing assistance, the study concluded that the top quintile's share of total income would decline by about 1 percentage point to 45 percent, and the bottom quintile's share would increase by about 1 percentage point to 4.7 percent. The report concluded that the official poverty rate would drop from 13.6 to 11.6 percent under this method of calculation. Government programs, it found, reduced poverty among those over age 65 from 47.5 to 9 percent and among children under 18 from 24 to 17.1 percent.[2]

In an apparent reversal of the traditional American notion that each new generation will do better than the last, younger families have been moving down the income scale, while the elderly have been moving up.[3] A study by the Congressional Budget Office found that median adjusted family income (accounting for differences in family size and inflation) rose by 20 percent between 1970 and 1986. However, the gains varied significantly by family type. Elderly family income rose by half to over three times the poverty threshold, while the income of single women with children saw only slight growth and remained just above the poverty threshold.[4]

In 1950, fully employed men in their early twenties had median incomes equivalent to 93 percent of fully employed men age 45–54, in part because the younger generation was increasingly better educated. By 1984 that ratio had plummeted to 47 percent. Members of the baby boom generation have continued to improve their education compared to the older workers ahead of them, but this has not prevented each successive cohort from falling further behind in its share of family income.[5]

Still, in terms of absolute real income, the family of today's average 30- to 40-year-old is about 50 percent better off than a comparable family 30 years ago.[6] Because of the overall size of the baby boom generation, moreover, the total personal income of the 35- to 50-year age group is projected by the Conference Board to climb by 90 percent in real terms by the turn of the century. By contrast, the total personal income of households headed by people under 35 is projected to increase hardly at all during that period, while households headed by people over 50 are expected to experience average growth.

Younger families also appear to be losing ground in the wealth distribution. The average real net wealth of U.S. households increased from $41,000 to $47,000 between 1977 and 1983. But net wealth declined from $18,804 to $16,651 for households headed by a person age 25–34, and from $44,359 to $40,710 for those headed by someone age 35–44.[7] Meanwhile, people 65 and over owned 40 percent of the nation's personal financial assets, about $1 trillion in 1987, while they represented only 20 percent of all households.[8] It is to be expected, of course, that older people will have accumulated relatively greater wealth than younger people. Many among the younger generation, moreover, stand eventually to inherit much of their parents' wealth. And yet the stark fact remains that 20 percent of children in the United States today live in poverty,[9] and children are seven times as likely to be poor as elderly persons 65 and over.[10]

Historians Will and Ariel Durant, in summing up the lessons they learned from a lifetime of historical study, observed that fluctuations in the distribution of income and wealth have been one of the constants of history. During periods of economic liberty, the clever, capable, energetic, and powerful acquire a relative material advantage, and hence income and wealth become more concentrated. At some point, however, extreme concentrations of wealth create resentment and instability.[11] Eventually there is an adjustment that redistributes wealth. The only question is whether those with the advantage in income and wealth make the adjustment voluntarily and in a measured fashion, or whether the adjustment occurs as a consequence of economic, social, or political turmoil.

While the aggregate distribution patterns have not changed greatly in the United States, extremes at both ends of the income spectrum have been highly publicized. The number of homeless people on the streets appears to be increasing and the wealth amassed by some on Wall Street has been much noted. The lesson taught to the young when they see widespread apparent indifference to the inequality revealed by these publicized extremes is that wealth is not only highly valued in society, but that the best and quickest ways to get it appear to have little to do with creating wealth for society as a whole or with service to others.

The immediate political issue is whether adjustments can be made to improve the situation of those who are in serious need, to eliminate the sources of the greatest social tensions, and to alter behavior—such as excessive consumption and underinvestment in human resources—that may undermine the long-term performance of the U.S. economy.

Family Structure

The distribution of wealth and income has been affected in part by changes in family structure. For example, the increasing number of children who live in poverty is associated with the rapidly increasing number of single-parent families headed by females.[12] And the increase in single-parent families is associated with the changing role of marriage.

The annual number of divorces per 1,000 married women doubled from 10 in 1965 to 20 in 1975. Since 1975, the divorce rate has increased more slowly and, in 1986 and 1987, declined slightly. The reasons for the recent decline from historic peaks are not altogether clear. It may have to do with the passing of the baby boom population beyond the years in which the incidence of divorce is highest. Some suggest it may be related to the AIDS epidemic, which could be diminishing nonmonogamous sexual relations and may encourage earlier and more enduring marriage. Or it may simply reflect a greater desire among more people for the benefits of marriage. Still, at the current rate, one of every two marriages now being contracted will likely end in divorce.[13]

Because people continue to remarry, the number of married-couple households has increased from 44.7 million in 1970 to 49.6 million in 1982. However, during the same period, the number of unmarried-couple households more than tripled from 523,000 in 1970 to 1,863,000 in 1982.[14]

In general, according to Thomas J. Espenshade, the tendency to postpone marriage or avoid it altogether, the increasing probability that marriage will end in divorce, and the leveling off or declining rates of remarriage all "are consistent with the view that marriage is weakening as a social institution."[15]

Coincident with the decline of marriage is the rising proportion of children born out of wedlock. One consequence of these two trends is that the proportion of children living with only one parent increased from 9 percent of all children in 1960 to 24 percent (or 14.8 million children) in 1986. For that year, 18 percent of white children were living with one parent, compared to 30 percent of Hispanic children and 53 percent of black children.[16] Eighty-nine percent of children in one-parent homes lived with their mothers.

The basic family unit has undergone such profound change that the concept of a "household" of unrelated individuals has become a more descriptive category of the basic living unit than a "family" of related individuals. One-person households now account for nearly 25 percent of all households, compared with 10 percent in 1950. Only half of today's households consist of married couples, compared with three-quarters in 1950. And average household size has plummeted from 3.7 people in 1960 to 2.7 today. In 1986, an estimated 2.2 million unmarried couples lived together, up from 1.9 million the previous year. This reflects a renewed growth in the number of unmarried couples after a leveling off in 1984–85, following a sharp increase in the 1960s and 1970s. At the same time, more young people are now living longer with their parents.[17]

To the extent that the family does not perform its traditional functions—bearing and raising children, organizing economic activity, ordering property, centering religious and social activities, and providing protection, companionship, and emotional warmth—the responsibility or consequences are shifted to other institutions. Schools in particular have been expected to perform many of the functions once performed by the family and to remedy the problems caused by family inadequacies. But without the support of strong family relationships to encourage and assist in learning and to reinforce students' aspirations, the schools are hampered in their ability to perform their principal function of education. The school dropout rate for children living in single-parent households, just as one example, is twice that for children with two parents at home.[18]

The family is a political institution in its own right, establishing relationships of authority, rights, and responsibilities among its members. But it is also a training ground that teaches people how to behave in social and political relationships, and a paradigm for the structure of other political institutions. In particular, people tend to view government and civic relationships in terms of their experience with family relationships. That paradigm once provided the vast majority of Americans with a common reference point: the traditional family with a mother and father and children. Today, however, there is a wide variety of family and household structures: different types of people living together, often temporarily, and with a wide range of relationships. Not only do these various structures suggest new patterns of social and political behavior, but also the fact that there is such a wide variety of new structures means that no single pattern is as likely to provide a common point of reference in defining social and political relationships.

This consequence of changing family patterns may be more far-reaching than all of the others. Not only are children being raised with a far different definition of social relationships learned in the family that will be translated into their habits and expectations for other social and political institutions, but also more people are likely to have far more diverse points of reference for such relationships than ever before.

Gender

Changes in family structure are closely associated with the changing role of women. Since the 1950s, women increasingly have turned to work outside the home and have become participating, and frequently principal, household wage earners. The Bureau of Labor Statistics predicts that 47 percent of the workforce will be female by the year 2000, compared with 42 percent in 1980 and 29 percent in 1950. In the year 2000, 60 percent of women are projected to be working, compared with 51.5 percent in 1980 and 37.7 percent in 1960.

The number of working mothers in 1985 was 18.6 million, nearly triple the number in 1960.[19] Between 1970 and 1982, the number of female-headed households doubled from 2.9 to 5.9 million, increasing their share of all households from 4.7 to 7.0 percent.[20]

In 1980, there were 15.5 million women 65 and over, compared to 10.4 million men, a ratio of 148 women for every 100 men in that age group. For the population 85 and older, the female-to-male ratio is 237.[21] The striking imbalance between the numbers of men and women is a relatively recent development in the United States. Prior to the 1930s, the sex ratios were about even because of the higher number of male immigrants and the higher mortality of women in the child-bearing years.[22]

Since 1970, life expectancy for both men and women has increased, but it has increased even more rapidly for women.[23] Revised Social Security estimates project that male life expectancy at birth will increase to 72.9 years in 2000 and rise to 76.7 by 2080. Comparable figures for females are 80.5 in 2000, rising to 85.2 by 2080.[24] Thus, the proportion of women in the older age groups is, if anything, likely to increase.

As a consequence, elderly women are more likely than men to be unmarried and to live alone. In 1985, 77 percent of elderly men were married, compared with 40 percent of elderly women. Half of all women (51 percent) were widows, and there were over five times as many widows (8.0 million) as widowers (1.5 million).[25] The remarriage rate for older widowers, moreover, is almost seven times that of elderly widows.[26] Slightly fewer than one-third of all elderly people lived alone in 1985, but this included 41 percent of the women and only 15 percent of the men.[27]

Today's older widows are women who are not likely to have had incomes of their own, and are more likely than older men or couples to be in poverty. Michael Hurd concludes that poverty among widows will only be reduced if Social Security benefits are substantially increased or, before becoming a widow, a woman and her husband reached the age of 65 with greater wealth.[28] Broad characterizations of "the elderly" tend to obscure such important distinctions; while the elderly as a class are financially well off compared to other age groups, many groups, such as older widows, are not.

The increasing "feminization of the elderly" could tend to fuse two powerful social and political movements: women and the elderly. Feminist leader Betty Friedan, author of *The Feminine Mystique*, has turned her attention to the issue of aging and says she has discovered many similarities between their problems and the concerns of the women's movement.[29]

Such a fusion, and its demographic underpinnings, reflects the growing political strength of women. Women have entered elective office in large numbers. In 1987, there were over 17,000 women in local elected positions, 42 in statewide elective offices including three governors, 1,101 in the state legislatures, and 26 congresswomen, including two United States senators.[30]

Ethnic and Racial Groups

The growth in racial and ethnic groups is testing the concept of "minority" in a country where there may eventually be no clearly identified "majority." (See figure 18.) In 1984, blacks and Hispanics accounted for 19.2 percent of the U.S. population. (See figure 19.) In 2020, blacks and Hispanics are projected to account for about 35 percent of the total U.S. population of 265 million. Some time in the next century, if current fertility patterns hold, the non-Hispanic white "majority" in the United States will become a minority. This has already occurred in numerous local jurisdictions throughout the country. It is projected to occur by the year 2000 in greater Los Angeles, and in California and Texas by 2010.

The black population was estimated to be 28.6 million, or 12.1 percent of the total U.S. population, in 1984. It is projected to increase to 33.6 million by 1995,[31] and to 44 million in 2020.[32] The

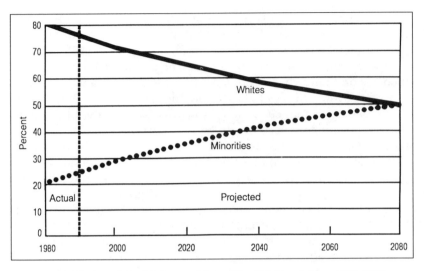

FIGURE 18.   Ethnic and Racial Composition of the U.S. Population, 1990–2080

Source: Michael S. Teitelbaum and Jay M. Winter, *The Fear of Population Decline* (New York: Academic Press, 1985).

black population as a whole is growing at nearly twice the rate of non-Hispanic whites, but there are important differences in the age configurations. The number of blacks in the 18- to 24-year-old age group is projected to decline by nearly 400,000 from 1984 to 1990, a rate reduction not quite as large as the overall population decline for that age group as a whole. This should ease the problem of finding employment for the chronically unemployed among the young black adult population. On the other hand, the number of 25- to 44-year-old blacks of the baby boom generation will increase even more rapidly than that age group as a whole, potentially exacerbating problems of discrimination in finding jobs and housing. Meanwhile, there is a sharp disparity in the proportions of the black elderly and of children compared to the entire population. By 1995, blacks are likely to account for only 8.3 of America's population 65 and over, but 17 percent of Americans under five years old.[33]

The elimination of barriers to voter registration for blacks and the emphasis by black leaders on registration and getting voters to the polls have had substantial success. This growing political strength is reflected in the increasing number of black elected officials, up to 5,606 in 1984, a figure that included 247 black mayors.[34] By 1987,

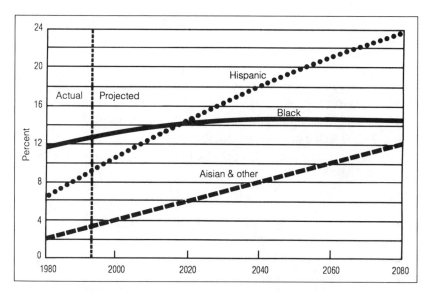

FIGURE 19. Minorities in the United States, 1980–2080

Source: Michael S. Teitelbaum and Jay M. Winter, *The Fear of Population Decline* (New York: Academic Press, 1985).

nearly 7,000 elected officials and 303 mayors were black.[35] And in 1989, Douglas Wilder of Virginia became the nation's first black elected governor.

The number of Hispanics was estimated to be 18.7 million in 1987, or 7.8 percent of the U.S. population.[36] While some 12 million fewer than blacks, the Hispanic population is growing at nearly twice the rate—or nearly four times as fast as the non-Hispanic white population—and is projected to reach 47 million in 2020, surpassing the size of the black population. While blacks and non-Hispanic whites 18–24 years old are declining, the number of Hispanics in that age group will continue to increase. The growing political influence of Hispanics is reflected in the 3,128 Hispanics in elected office in 1984.[37]

Fertility and age structure fluctuate widely among different ethnic groups. The fertility rate for non-Hispanic whites is 1.7; for blacks, 2.4; and for Mexican-Americans, 2.9. The Asian-American fertility rate of 1.3 is even lower than for whites. According to the 1980 census, the average white person was 31 years old; the average black, 25; and the average Hispanic, 22.

The growth in the number and proportion of racial and ethnic groups raises several issues of political importance aside from the shifting balance of voting strength.

The number of disadvantaged children is likely to grow because minority children on average start out with some distinct social disadvantages:

- Thirty-six percent of the children born in the United States in 1984 belonged to minority groups.

- By the year 2000, 38 percent of children under 18 will be from minority groups.[38]

- Forty-six percent of black and 38 percent of Hispanic children live in poverty.[39]

- Black children are five times more likely than white children to live in poverty.[40]

- Sixty percent of black children live in homes headed by a single parent, compared with 20 percent of white children.[41]

- In 1986, 75 percent of all black babies were born to single mothers, half of whom were teenagers.[42]

Now that the majority of net new entrants into America's labor force will be coming from minority groups, more than ever before the future of the American economy and society will depend on the status and education of its minority children.

The growing size and influence of racial and ethnic groups also raises the possibility of increasing racial or ethnic tensions in the United States. The evidence here is mixed. Such highly publicized incidents in New York as the attack by white teenagers upon blacks in the Howard Beach section of Brooklyn, the shooting of black teenagers in a New York subway by Bernhard Goetz, and the beating and rape of a female investment banker by a gang of black and Hispanic youths in Central Park may reflect a rise in racial tensions. The National Council of Churches released a report in 1988 claiming that racial and other forms of "hate violence" had reached "epidemic proportions."[43] The passage of Proposition 63 in California in 1986 declaring English to be the official language of the state, and similar measures in other jurisdictions, reflects the growing level of concern of non-Hispanic citizens over the growth in the influence of the Spanish-speaking population. Tension is also apparent among minority groups, as reflected in the clash between blacks and Cubans in Miami in early 1989, and the stress between Haitian and native American blacks in southeast Florida.

Racial and ethnic tensions could also be heightened by the widening differences in the age structure between different groups. The younger working-age population will become increasingly black, Hispanic, and Asian. Thus, any resentment associated with the growing burden imposed on the younger generation in bearing the cost of programs for the elderly could be exacerbated by ethnic tensions, with an increasingly minority workforce supporting a predominantly white retired population. In fact, the proportion of whites 65 and over is all the greater, since life expectancy for whites is longer than for blacks. For example, black males born in 1982 had a life expectancy of 64.9 years, six years less than the 71-year life expectancy of white males born in that same year. Not only will there be more young blacks supporting more white retirees, but also those blacks can expect to live a shorter life and receive a smaller return on their Social Security contribution than whites of the same age.

By many measures, U.S. blacks as a group have made enormous strides in recent years. The median number of school years completed by blacks increased from nine in 1968 to twelve in 1985. The proportion of blacks age 25 and over who finished high school doubled from 30 percent to 60 percent over the past 20 years. Black families with two wage earners had about 85 percent of the income of similar white families, up from 73 percent in 1968.

But while those blacks who are working are doing strikingly better, an increasing proportion are not working at all. Only 56 percent of black men were employed in 1987, down from 70 percent in 1968.

In fact, there seems to be a widening gap between prosperous, well-educated blacks and those who are poor and have little education. In some respects, the economic differences *among* blacks are more significant than the differences between blacks and other racial or ethnic groups. This is a positive development to the extent that it reflects black gains and diminishes the importance of race as a defining social and political characteristic. But it is disturbing in its implication that part of the reason for the disparity is that some blacks are even worse off than they used to be. Meanwhile, the widening economic and social division among blacks poses a serious challenge to the black political agenda. Karl Zinsmeister has observed that "current public policies on issues of race—affirmative action and quotas, electoral activism, and minority set-asides—provide aid almost exclusively to middle and upper class blacks."[44]

Diversity among Hispanics in the United States is reflected in their different countries of origin (in millions of people)—Mexico,

11.8; Puerto Rico, 2.3; Cuba, 1.0; Central and South America, 2.1; and other, 1.6.[45] National origin and the wide differences in education and income among Hispanics are frequently more defining factors than the shared culture and language that characterizes Hispanics as an ethnic group. These differences are reflected in the widely diverse and often openly adversarial political agendas of various Hispanic groups.

Perhaps no racial or ethnic group is as culturally diverse as Asian-Americans, whose numerous countries of origin have strikingly different religions, languages, and national cultures. In 1980, there were about 3.7 million Asian-Americans in the United States. While this is less than 2 percent of the U.S. population, Asians currently represent 44 percent of annual U.S. immigration, which continues to diversify the American population.[46]

Immigration

Immigration into the United States proceeded without restraint from the arrival of the first European colonists through the early twentieth century. It reached a peak of 880,000 immigrants per year in the 1910s (with peak legal entries of 1.2 million in 1907 and 1914) prompting the "national origin quotas" legislation of 1921 and 1924, which deliberately restricted immigrants from southern and eastern Europe.[47] The Depression of the 1930s and the Second World War further discouraged immigration, which averaged less than 50,000 per year from 1930 to 1945. The Immigration and Refugee Act of 1952 (the McCarran-Walter Act) codified previous national origins quotas, while its "Texas Proviso" facilitated the illegal immigration of Mexican farm workers as "temporary workers."[48]

In 1965, amendments to the Immigration and Nationality Act abolished the national quota system and replaced it with a new emphasis on family ties as a criterion for immigration. This favored Latin Americans and Asians, whose relatives had been among the most recent immigrants. The liberalization of American immigration laws occurred almost simultaneously with the precipitous drop in American fertility that followed the baby boom years. As a consequence, immigration in the 1970s and 1980s has accounted for as much as 30 percent of U.S. population increase, the highest proportion since the peak immigration years of the 1910s, when it reached 60 percent. The current level of legal immigration today—about 500,000–600,000 people per year—constitutes a far smaller increment of total population, less than 1 percent, compared with 10 percent in the 1910s. However, the rate of illegal immigration today is high. While the annual number of illegal immigrants is uncertain, estimates of the number of illegal aliens now living in the United States range from 2 to 8 million.[49]

The Immigration Reform and Control Act adopted in 1986 was intended to address the problem of illegal immigration by applying employer sanctions and requiring tighter identification to discourage the employment of illegal aliens. It also provides for the legalization of large numbers of aliens already in the United States. The law was opposed by employers who depend on illegal immigrants and by some Hispanic groups, but was passed by Congress on the strength of general public support for curbing illegal immigration.

The United States is more consciously and proudly a nation of immigrants than any other country in the world. The 570,009 new legal immigrants that entered the country in 1985 were greater in number than all of the immigrants accepted in that year by the rest of the world combined.[50] Yet each new group has faced hostility and discrimination from those who preceded them. In time, new groups are assimilated into the American mainstream and prejudices fade, or are rediverted toward the newest immigrants.

As people move up the socioeconomic ladder, they tend to become more tolerant of new immigrants, in part, no doubt, because their jobs and social status are not as directly threatened by them.[51] The Scots, Germans, Irish, Jews, East Europeans, and Italians all were subjected to discrimination, overcame barriers to upward mobility, and became part of the mainstream. Today, Hispanics and Asians are confronting similar patterns, and are responding much as past immigrants did.

Immigration continues to provide the United States with a rich infusion of human capital. Today's immigrants from Africa, Asia, and India, in fact, include a higher proportion of high school graduates than is found in the U.S. adult population.[52] Mexican immigrants have had substantially less education, but are a source of energetic labor and entrepreneurship. As Joel Kotkin and Yoriko Kishimoto have shown in *The Third Century*, immigrants continue to bring fresh energy and initiative to the American economy, and offer the United States a unique source of knowledge and skill with which to compete in the world marketplace.[53]

A study by the Rand Corporation concluded that many of the public concerns regarding Mexican immigration in California have been exaggerated. It found that Mexican immigrants provide economic benefits to the state and contribute more in public resources than they consume in public services (although immigrant youth produce a net deficit in educational expenditures). The study also concluded that contrary to the belief that Mexican immigrants were developing an isolated and exclusive Spanish-language enclave, they "are following the classic American pattern for integrating into U.S. society, with education playing a critical role in this process."[54]

However, the study also found that Mexican immigration raised some long-term issues, including the possibility that "continued rapid immigration from Mexico and projected shifts in the industrial and occupational structure of California could disrupt the traditional mobility process of immigrants." Education, it concluded, will be critical to occupational and social mobility.[55] The study also found that while Mexican immigrants tend to learn English once they become assimilated into the American mainstream, much as immigrants have always done, they are also likely to retain and use their Spanish language within the local Hispanic community.

The Multicultural Mosaic

The increasing racial and ethnic diversity of the U.S. population poses both challenges and benefits. Arnold R. Weber, president of Northwestern University, has summed it up thus: "How do you manage a truly multi-racial society? How [are we] to permit the richness and diversity associated with ethnic cultures while at the same time trying to understand those elements that hold us all together as a people?"[56]

This challenge is reflected in the delicate issue of demographic labeling. What are we to call ourselves and each other?

The U.S. Bureau of the Census currently uses the designations of *white, black, Hispanic,* and *Asian* to define the major racial and cultural groups in the United States. As William Alonso notes, those designations are simply social conventions. They derive from common usage, and have varied over the years. Today, there are Hispanics who would prefer to be called *Latino,* blacks who would prefer to be called *African-American,* Asians who would prefer to be designated more precisely by their national origin (such as Japanese or Chinese), and many Americans across racial and ethnic groups would prefer to have no label at all to define what kind of American they are.

That is not to say that the matter of demographic designations is trivial. It has important legal implications, since many laws and their administrative vehicles for implementation—such as affirmative action and minority set-aside programs in government procurement—make specific reference to race, cultural background, and national origin. It is a matter of practical political consequence, as reflected in the 1989 Chicago Democratic primary for mayor, where an estimated 93 percent of blacks voted for the incumbent black acting mayor, Eugene Sawyer, and 82 percent of the whites for the white challenger and eventual winner, Richard Daly. And it is socially important in determining how people think of themselves and are perceived by and interact with others. Even more important are the underlying perceptions, feelings, and social relationships reflected in these designations.

Perhaps a more telling trend in demographic labeling lies not in the designation of minority groups, but in the new labels that are being used to describe the white majority, including, for example, *Anglo* and *European-American*. This is significant in part because the newer designations constitute a cultural rather than racial characterization. But even more significant is the implication that *white* is no longer automatically assumed to be equated with the majority of the population. The two points are closely related.

The racial designation of *white* is of limited use in distinguishing between Hispanic and non-Hispanic whites, since most Hispanics are also white. So it would be demographically more precise to find a nonracial term to define non-Hispanic whites. Moreover, the shift from *black* to *African-American* would also be a shift from a racial to a cultural label, and indeed many blacks prefer it precisely for that reason. If blacks prefer a cultural to a racial label, and other minorities are already designated in terms of their cultural or national background and prefer to be so designated, then a nonracial label for whites would also seem to be appropriate as a way of both moving away from the racial labels and bringing all the designations into some conformity of type.

But more to the point is the fact that the use of *Anglo* in lieu of *white* has occurred in areas that have large Hispanic populations, especially Texas and southern California. In several communities in those areas, the Hispanic population is either a majority or a very large minority of the population. In such circumstances it becomes less precise and more objectionable to use the term *white* to define only one part of the population but not another large segment that is also white. Hence the term *Anglo* has come into use as a counterpart to *Hispanic* because of a change in the size and preferences of the Hispanic population. Similarly, many blacks, now preferring the cultural label of *African-American*, believe that whites should also be designated by a cultural label; one occasionally hears blacks referring to whites as *European-Americans*, for example. Here as well, the change in designation of whites derives not from a desire for change on the part of whites themselves, but rather from the changes and preferences taking place among blacks.

The key point is that whereas in the past minorities tended to be defined by the majority, the more recent tendency has been for the majority to be defined by the minorities. The reasons are both demographic—the majority is no longer so large a majority and in fact in many areas has become itself a minority—and the result of preference—minorities are more inclined to define themselves and to insist on a more satisfactory and less apparently discriminatory system of designations all around.

Do these trends reflect a maturing of U.S. society regarding questions of race and culture, or a deepening of diverse racial and cultural identities? How will the white majority react as its majority status is eroded? Will it begin to think of itself as a minority group, and organize in the manner of other minority groups? And when there is no clearly recognized racial or cultural majority, will there be a tendency for the various minorities to identify even more strongly with their group, or will minority affiliations begin to lose their appeal, and the day of the "hyphenated American"—once deplored by President Theodore Roosevelt—pass?

As is true of other demographic forces, the answers to these questions lie not in a preordained destiny, but in how people choose to shape those forces to their own desires. The challenge will be to adapt the American civic culture in a way that accommodates the new diversity while holding fast to a core of common values that defines the highest character of the evolving U.S. experiment. A large part of that effort will take place in the practical world of politics.

Political Affiliation

The national political parties in the United States historically have been among the most broadly based, heterogeneous, and nonideological parties in the world. Both the Republican and Democratic parties traditionally have been loose coalitions of political groups whose constituencies overlapped with one another. The basic strength of both parties traditionally lay in a diffuse system of largely autonomous state and local political organizations. In recent decades, however, there has been more of a tendency to build on nationally affiliated constituencies.

For most of the post–World War II era through 1980, the Democrats held about a 20-percentage-point plurality over the Republicans in party identification. That margin fell as low as 15 percent during the Eisenhower administration and rose as high as 27 percent after Lyndon Johnson defeated Barry Goldwater in 1964. Both of these turned out to be temporary swings from a fairly stable 20-point Democratic advantage in voter identification, until recently.

Party affiliation is usually a reliable indicator of how people tend to vote for local, state, and national candidates. The important exception has been that, despite their disadvantage in voter identification, the Republicans have won every presidential election since 1952 except for the elections of 1960, 1964, and 1976. For most of these years, however, the Democrats controlled the House and Senate, as well as a substantial majority of governorships and state legislatures.

Ronald Reagan's election in 1980 occurred while the Democrats still enjoyed a 17-point preference. When President Reagan was reelected in 1984, the Democratic advantage in voter identification had fallen to 10 percentage points. Since then it has fluctuated and been variously reported by different polls, some finding it increasing and others finding the advantage virtually disappearing. It is still too early to tell whether this is a temporary swing associated with the party and popularity of the incumbent president, as appeared to be the case in the Eisenhower and Johnson administrations, and hence may fade if President Bush's popularity falls. However, there are indications that deeper changes in party affiliation, and perhaps in political structure, have indeed occurred in the United States.

The sharp reduction in the Democratic plurality is principally due to a drop in Democratic voter identification from 47 percent in 1952 to 37 percent in 1984. This did not reflect a net shift to the Republican party, but a net reduction in the percentage of voters who identified with either major party. During the same period, Republican voter identification also fell, but by only one point, from 28 percent to 27 percent. Between 1980 and 1984, the Democrats suffered a decline from 40 to 37 percentage points, while the Republicans were gaining 3 percentage points.[57]

REGION

Virtually all of the Democratic-decline can be accounted for by the loss of the party's historical regional advantage in the South. Whereas in the 1950s, 71 percent of all southern whites identified themselves as Democrats and only 22 percent as Republicans, by 1984, 46 percent called themselves Democrats and 42 percent Republicans.

While the Democratic loss in the South has been dramatic, Democrats nonetheless have retained the allegiance of a majority of southern whites. The unusually high Democratic affiliation in the South was probably something of an historical anachronism dating back to the Civil War. It endured in large measure due to a combination of Democratic affiliation in local politics and national political strength perpetuated by the southern states through the skillful use of the old seniority system in Congress. The strong advocacy of the civil rights movement by the Democratic party in the 1960s strained party ties with traditional southern whites, many of whom were already uneasy with the increasingly liberal tendency of the Democrats.

What has occurred in essence, however, is that the South has been loosening itself from a century-old tradition of overwhelmingly Democratic political affiliation and realigning itself more in keeping with the national political profile. Republican affiliation among southern whites today is also correlated with socioeconomic status, as it is nationally.[58] Southern whites in the lower socioeconomic levels have continued to identify in greater numbers with the Democrats than with the Republicans, whereas a majority of those in the middle and upper groups showed a preference for the Republicans.

There are indications, however, that the continued conversion of southern white Democrats to the Republican party could tilt the advantage further to the Republicans. Young whites reaching voting age have been choosing the Republican party in even higher proportions than their elders, at the same time that their age peers in other regions of the country have been more inclined to eschew both parties. Migrants to the South (largely from the North) also have added to the Republican numbers, although not in the same proportion as converting and newly mobilized southern whites.

Still, a strong base among whites and an 80-percent margin among blacks continue to give the Democrats a majority of voters in most southern states. It was this coalition, not a return by southern whites to their historical Democratic voting habits, that accounted for the loss of several southern Republican Senate seats in the 1986 elections, losses that were critical in giving the Democrats control of the Senate. Democratic strength in the South could increase as a consequence of two other demographic factors: the proportionately large numbers of young blacks (compared to young whites) that will soon be reaching voting age, and net in-migration of blacks into the southern states after many decades of out-migration.

RACIAL AND ETHNIC IDENTIFICATION

With the loss of a southern advantage, the Democrats' national plurality in 1984 was based almost entirely on a strong affiliation of blacks, and to a lesser extent, Hispanics and Jews. (Hispanics include a widely diverse group from different national backgrounds—Mexican, Cuban, Puerto Rican, and the numerous countries of Central and South America—whose party affiliation varies widely.) In 1984, blacks comprised 17 percent of Democratic voters and only 2 percent of the Republicans. The Republicans' principal advantage continued to be among northern white Protestants who made up 36 percent of their affiliated voters, compared to only 15 percent for the Democrats.

Racial and ethnic partisanship is linked in part to socioeconomic status, which also continues to be an important determinant of party affiliation. Blacks and Hispanics on average are more likely to be in the middle-to-lower socioeconomic groups, which are also more heavily Democratic. Whites in the same groups are also more likely to identify themselves as Democrats.

Following the 1988 election, the Republican party leadership announced that it would aggressively recruit black voters. Some analysts saw this as a ploy to force the Democrats to actively protect their black political constituency and thereby drive more white voters toward the Republicans. Whether that is the intent, or whether the strategy reflects a sincere attempt to increase Republican votes among blacks—or whether it is pursued as a no-lose strategy that would benefit the Republican party in either case—is less important than its effect. Republican success in attracting a reasonable proportion of black voters could have the salutary effect of dampening the force of racial politics. However, if the Democratic reaction to the Republican initiative drives more whites out of the Democratic party, the consequences could be to further polarize the two parties along racial lines.

RELIGION

Religion, like region, appears to have diminished as a factor in determining party affiliation. Catholics are nearly evenly split in party allegiance. White Protestants continue to identify closely with the Republican party, although this may be rooted more in socioeconomic status than in religion. Blacks, who are also overwhelmingly Protestant, are also overwhelmingly Democratic. Jews are still predominantly Democratic, but an increasing number have been identifying themselves as Republicans. The one salient exception to the fading of religion as a partisan factor has been the increased tendency for the evangelical Christian orders to identify, or to be identified, with the Republican party.

AGE

Age historically has not been an important factor in party affiliation, but it is more of an imponderable today. Between 1982 and 1984 both of the two youngest cohorts of voters shifted their party preference toward the Republicans by about 12 percentage points. This was in keeping with the widely noted appeal of Ronald Reagan for younger voters.[59] Older voters (those who entered the electorate prior to 1949) shifted their party preference toward the Republicans by nearly 20 percentage points between 1982 and 1984.[60] But there have also been shifts by the elderly in favor of the Democrats before and since the 1986 election. Pollster Richard Wirthlin reported that identification with the Republicans by voters 65 and over dropped sharply from 45 percent in 1986 to 31 in the first part of 1987.[61]

Conclusion

The nation's changing social and political demography reflects a population in the American pluralistic tradition. The assertion of individual effort and group identification has yielded benefits for Americans across the spectrum. But it has also placed stress on political institutions, as they attempt both to deal with the consequences of change and to achieve a synthesis of widely differing values and diverse power bases.

These forces are in play not only at the national level, but also at the state, regional, and local levels, where changing demographic characteristics add to the complexity.

CHAPTER 12

Regional Variations

MIGRATION AND settlement patterns within the United States are having a significant impact on the distribution of social costs and capacities, but not in ways that are commonly recognized. Most national attention has focused on the regional shifts between the Sun Belt and the Frost Belt, and the emergence of a "bicoastal economy." More important are the demographic and economic shifts occurring *within* the traditionally defined regions. Areas whose economies have been based on the availability of natural resources such as coal, iron, gas, and oil suffered economically during the mid-eighties, and many have been losing population. But urban areas have expanded and been transformed from the "city-suburb" configuration of common imagery into complex, multinodal agglomerations that are becoming the primary units of economic geography in the new global economy.

Meanwhile, national demographic trends mask wide variations from region to region. For example, school enrollment patterns vary widely in different parts of the country. Children under the age of 15 are projected to *decrease* in the Northeast by 9 percent between 1980 and 1990, while they will *increase* by nearly 25 percent in the West.[1] The 5–14 age group is projected to grow by 55.5 percent in Nevada between 1990 and 2000, while falling 6.5 percent in New York. In 1984, 34.5 percent of Alabama's public school children were black, compared with 1.4 percent in Alaska. In the same year, nearly 28 percent of Texas schoolchildren were Hispanic, compared with less than 1 percent in Georgia.[2] The non-Hispanic white pupil enrollment is now a small minority—only 26 percent—in California's public schools.[3]

Regional Population and Political Strength

The census provides the basis for the distribution of congressional districts and votes in the presidential electoral college. As table 10

TABLE 10
Regional Population in the United States, 1970–1987
(in millions)

	1970		1980		Change in % Share	1987	
	Pop.	% of Total	Pop.	% of Total		Pop.	% of Total
Total	203.3	100.0	226.5	100.0	—	243.3	100.0
Northeast	49.1	24.2	49.1	21.7	−2.5	50.2	20.6
North-Central	56.6	27.8	58.9	26.0	−1.8	59.5	24.5
South	62.8	30.9	75.3	33.2	+2.3	83.9	34.5
West	34.8	17.1	43.2	19.1	+2.0	49.7	20.4

Source: U.S. Dept. of Commerce, Bureau of the Census, *Population Profile of the United States, 1980,* Current Population Reports, ser. P-20, no. 363 (Washington, D.C.: GPO, January 1981); ibid., *Geographical Mobility, 1985,* Current Population Reports, ser. P-20, no. 420 (Washington, D.C.: GPO, December 1987).

shows, the relative population ranking of the four major regions did not change between 1970 and 1980. The South remained the most populous region, followed by the North-Central region, the Northeast, and the West. The U.S. population continued its historic shift from east to west, and its more recent trend from north to south.[4]

The 1990 census is likely to confirm a continuation of the long-term trend shifting national population and political strength from the North and the North-Central region to the South and the West.[5] California, whose 45 seats in the U.S. House of Representatives is already the largest number of any state, may pick up six more seats. A likely gain of four seats would give Texas a delegation of 31, possibly equaling New York which could lose three of its 34 seats. States which may lose two House seats include Illinois, Pennsylvania, Michigan, and Ohio, while those likely to lose one seat each include Iowa, Kansas, Massachusetts, and West Virginia.[6]

The 1988 elections produced some realignments in state political control that are significant both for state policy and because the incumbent state officials will redraw congressional districts on the basis of the 1990 census. Republicans controlled 22 governorships, a loss of one, while there were 28 Democratic governors. The Democrats increased their majorities in state senate and house chambers from 67 to 68, leaving the Republicans with 29. (The Indiana senate was split evenly between the Democrats and Republicans.) The Democrats controlled the governorship, the senate, and the house in

14 states. The Republicans had complete control in four states, down from their previous total of six.[7]

Shaping Regional Character

Changes in regional population are determined by a combination of fertility, mortality, and migration.

Fertility generally has been falling in all regions of the United States over the past two decades, but it still varies widely from place to place. Regions with large Hispanic populations and substantial immigration, such as California and Texas, have high birth rates compared to most of the rest of the country. Mortality is not a major factor in comparative regional population changes, since life expectancy has been generally increasing at comparable rates throughout the United States. Migration includes both domestic migration among regions within the United States, and immigration from abroad (emigration out of the United States is insignificant by comparison).

These forces can have strikingly different demographic consequences for different regions. California has been adjusting to the massive inflow of Mexican immigrants and Florida to the steady growth in the number of elderly persons moving to the state. Both states have had to accommodate enormous pressures of population and economic growth in general. Meanwhile, Minnesota, like many states, is dealing simultaneously with growth in its major metropolitan area and declines in its rural and nonurban population. Five states lost population between 1980 and 1985 (Pennsylvania, Ohio, Michigan, Iowa, and West Virginia). According to projections by the Bureau of the Census, the populations of nine states—eight of them in the South or West—are expected to grow at twice the national rate between 1990 and 2000. During the same period, 13 states—principally in the Midwest—are projected to lose population.[8]

The recessions of the early 1980s tended to accelerate the migration from the Northeast and North-Central regions to the South and the West, which were still enjoying the benefits of strong agricultural and natural resource markets. The recovery of the mid-1980s, however, boosted the economies of the Northeast, and to a lesser extent the North-Central region. Meanwhile, the agricultural and natural resource industries of the South and West suffered significant setbacks. As a consequence, the force of western and southern migration slowed.[9] In fact, between 1983 and 1984, the West, historically the prime recipient of migrants from the East, actually had a net negative—although statistically insignificant—inter-regional migration relative to the rest of the country. The West resumed its net in-migration between 1984 and 1986, however. The Midwest, meanwhile, registered a small (and statistically insignificant) net in-migration of 15,000 in 1985–86.

To the extent that fertility and mortality become less important determinants of inter-regional population variations, migration could become relatively more important. But this will depend largely on the relative success among regions in developing their economies, since economic factors continue to be the principal motivation for migration today, as they have been historically.

Two other demographic changes could have mixed consequences for inter-regional migration in the future. One is the aging of the population. The older people become, the less likely they are to move. Even among the retired, only a relatively small proportion change their residence to a different region. However, given the growing numbers of elderly, that small proportion is likely to represent an increasing number of elderly migrants. In addition, increasing numbers of retirees have the pensions or asset income that enable them to live where they like. Between 1975 and 1979, for example, the South (principally Florida) received 132,000 people aged 65 and older from the Northeast and 96,000 from the North-Central region.[10]

Changing family structure might also affect migration patterns. In two-worker families, the inconvenience of one spouse changing job locations can be more than doubled by the fact that the other spouse must give up a secure job for uncertain employment in a new location. By the same token, an unemployed person may be less inclined to seek work in another location if a spouse provides a source of income support where she or he is currently living. The increased incidence of single-adult households may facilitate migration, if those households are truly mobile. However, many single-adult households are comprised of single parents, widows, and widowers, many of whom may be even less inclined to move from locations where they have established support systems of relatives, friends, neighbors, and familiar surroundings.

Since most people now live in urban areas, the principal source of migrants to any given urban region is no longer rural areas, as it has been historically, but other urban regions. Thus, the demographic profile of regions in the United States is increasingly a story of migration among the major urban agglomerations, augmented by

immigration from abroad (which still includes a significant proportion of people from rural areas).[11]

In today's economy, key economic factors such as capital, knowledge, technology, labor, and goods move more and more freely from
one place to another, not just within the United States but also
throughout the world. Improvements in technology and in the costs
of transportation and communication permit even cheaper and faster
movement. Improved highways now permit high-speed and high-
volume transport. Air travel puts the entire world within easy and
economical reach. People can communicate as easily and almost as
cheaply with someone on another continent as with someone in the
building across the street. Consequently, regions in the United States
and throughout the world find themselves in ever greater competition in their ability to produce goods and services that can compete
in international markets, and in their ability to attract and retain the
resources that are key to competitive production.

For regional economies geared toward high value-added goods
and services, highly trained people are a priority. People with professional, managerial, and technical skills who can command high sala-
ries no matter where they go are more likely to be able to choose
where they would like to live. Thus, the quality of life is becoming
more important as a competitive factor among various regions of the
country. The growing importance of such mobile economic factors as
human resources, capital, and technology have increased the economic policy role of state and local government. Since the 1970s,
states have initiated numerous new programs to strengthen their
economies internally, as well as to attract investment from outside
the state.[12]

The New Urban Region

The changes occurring *within* the nation's major regions may be
more important than the shifts occurring among them. Most significant is the transformation of urban regions in both their contour and
composition.

Urban areas today rarely conform to the conventional model of a
core city with a suburban periphery of residential areas surrounded
by rural countryside. The suburbs not only have outpaced the central
city as places of residence, but also have been transformed into primary employment centers. Today, multiple nodes of high-density

office, retail, and industrial activity constitute "outer cities" scattered in a sea of residential and lower-density economic activity throughout the urban region. Increasingly, people not only live in the suburbs, but also work there, shop there, and spend leisure time there. A study of the Philadelphia regional economy, for example, found that "daily interaction between the suburban counties and Philadelphia has decreased" in recent years.[13]

The character of these new urban agglomerations has not been widely recognized, partly because they evolved both simultaneously with and as a consequence of several more familiar demographic and economic changes.

Until the twentieth century, most Americans lived on farms. The rural population continued to grow even as ever greater numbers of people moved to the city. As late as the 1930s, during the Great Depression, more than half the population lived outside metropolitan areas and nearly one-third of the population still lived on farms.[14]

But throughout the twentieth century, cities expanded as a consequence of rural migration, immigration from abroad (much of which was from rural areas), and births among city dwellers, many of whom were fertile rural migrants. At the same time, city dwellers spread out from the center into the suburbs, expanding the metropolitan area.

By the 1950s, the migration of rural populations to the central cities was already insufficient to replace the city dwellers who continued to move to the suburbs in large numbers. As a consequence, between 1950 and 1980, the older central cities of the Northeast and North-Central region lost as much as one-third of their populations. Boston's population declined by 29.8 percent; Cleveland, 37.3; Detroit, 34.9; Pittsburgh, 37.4; and St. Louis, 47.1—nearly half its population.[15] The losses were only somewhat less dramatic in Chicago (17.0 percent), Philadelphia (18.5 percent) and New York (10.4 percent).[16] These losses essentially reflected the expansion of the urban population beyond the central city boundaries into the suburbs. Between 1980 and 1984, however, the nation's central cities as a whole gained population at an average annual rate of 0.6 percent, faster than in the 1970s but still below the 1.3 average annual increase of the suburbs (inside Metropolitan Statistical Areas but outside the central cities).[17]

By 1960, 128.8 million Americans, or about 71 percent of the total population, lived in metropolitan areas. That number grew to 169.4

million, or 75 percent, in 1980. The nonmetropolitan population also grew during this period, and, in fact, technically outpaced metropolitan growth in the 1970s. But a substantial part of that "nonmetropolitan" growth took place on the fringe of metropolitan areas, representing simply a continued expansion of the urban area. This growing population was not counted as "metropolitan" because the U.S. Bureau of the Census and the federal Office of Management and Budget did not include the larger de facto urban area in its official definition of Standard Metropolitan Statistical Area, or SMSA.

But, as Alonso notes, part of the nonmetropolitan growth in the seventies was real in the sense that, for the first time in modern times, counties far from metropolitan areas were attracting migrants. The draw of these outlying areas included employment opportunities in forestry, mineral extraction, and manufacturing, and the appeal of resort and retirement communities. The turnaround in metro to nonmetro growth was short-lived, however. By the early 1980s, metropolitan growth had resumed its advantage over nonmetropolitan areas.[18]

Meanwhile, the expanding urban agglomerations were also changing form. The definition of *metropolitan area* has always been less than fully descriptive. Some of the 261 officially designated metropolitan areas in 1986 contained far fewer than 100,000 people (50,000 is the minimum definitional requirement) while others now exceed 10 million. Less than 10 percent of the territory of all metropolitan areas taken together is urban, while they also encompass two-fifths of the nation's rural population. Meanwhile, 40 percent of the nonmetropolitan population in 1986 was defined as urban (that is, living in places of more than 2,500 inhabitants).[19]

By the mid-1980s, some metropolitan areas had urban fields that extended as far as 100 miles.[20] These and others had expanded to the extent that their outer orbits overlapped those of other metro areas. New York and Philadelphia, for example, now constitute a fused urban agglomeration. Washington, D.C., and Baltimore, Maryland, now overlap to the point that business leaders in the two jurisdictions have created a Washington/Baltimore Regional Association to mutually promote the "Baltimore-Washington Common Market." The entire eastern seaboard, from Washington, D.C., to Boston—indeed, from Richmond to Portland, Maine—has been steadily moving toward the "megalopolis" of a single, continuous urban corridor that had been proclaimed by urban analysts decades ago. Similar fusions have occurred in other parts of the nation, including southeastern Florida,

Dallas–Fort Worth, Austin–San Antonio, southeastern Michigan, the Lake Michigan urban crescent, Colorado's Front Range, south Puget Sound, the San Francisco Bay area, and Southern California.

The Challenge to Regional Governance

The new urban regions pose a major challenge to government in the United States. In the past, this challenge has been viewed principally as a matter of improving the provision of urban services, such as transportation, water supply, and waste management in expanded metropolitan areas. It is more important today because the new urban regions constitute primary units of world economic geography. Global competition is not just a matter of the United States versus Japan, but of Southern California, Silicon Valley, the Greater Boston area, and southwestern Michigan, in competition with other urban regions throughout the world. And yet, the institutions of regional governance in the United States as currently constituted are ill-suited for this task.

For 200 years, the classic local, state, and federal divisions of government have served reasonably well, in large measure because they could accommodate the principal concentrations and flows of people and economic factors. However, the strains have been building as the demographic and economic patterns of geographical concentration and population movement have grown ever more sharply at odds with the political jurisdictions and their associated governmental powers and responsibilities.

With rare exceptions, government in metropolitan areas is highly fragmented. The political boundaries of most original central cities have remained essentially unchanged as urban areas have expanded far beyond them. Today, a far greater share of metropolitan population resides outside the traditional central city than within it. For example, Washington, D.C., with a 1986 population of 623,000, had less than 20 percent of the total population of the Washington metropolitan area. Three suburban counties—Montgomery, Fairfax, and Prince George's—each exceeded the population of the nation's capital.

A few metropolitan areas have radically restructured local government in an effort to provide comprehensive coverage of these greatly expanded urban areas. Some have annexed growing suburban areas to the original central city (most notably cities in Texas, which has liberal annexation laws). A few have consolidated the city with the principal county in which it was located: Nashville–Davidson

County, Tennessee; Jacksonville–Duvall County and Miami–Dade County, Florida; Indianapolis–Marion County, Indiana. A few have established metropolitan area–wide governing bodies, while retaining local governments, such as St. Paul–Minneapolis, Minnesota, with its metropolitan council, and Toronto with its two-tier government structure.

For the most part, however, major government restructuring in metropolitan areas has proved to be politically unfeasible. Suburban whites have resisted consolidation for fear of losing local control and out of a desire not to be entangled with the problems of the central city that many of them had left. Blacks in the central city have resisted consolidation for fear of losing actual or imminent political control of the city government through the addition of white voters from the suburbs. Central-city whites, businesses, and government reform groups that typically support metropolitan consolidation generally have been no match for the two powerful constituencies that oppose it.

Three principal schools of thought dominate the debate over how to restructure metropolitan government.

- Consolidationists, or those who advocate a unitary government, call for a single all-encompassing government providing all services to the metropolitan area.
- Federationists advocate two or three tiers of government along the models of Miami-Dade or Toronto.
- Polycentrists, confederationists, and public-choice advocates argue that smaller, even fragmented units are best.

Proponents of each of these schools can find evidence to support their theories from among a wide variety of metropolitan governments. As a practical matter, however, no single theory has had much impact. Lacking a more systematic vision with the political backing necessary to implement it, governments in metropolitan areas have made do with a series of pragmatic approaches to specific pressures as they have arisen.

Many urban regions have created special districts to handle specific services areawide, such as mass transit, sewerage, and water supply. Many also have joint planning bodies, such as councils of governments. And there are numerous formal and informal agreements among local governments for providing specific services. Many local governments in metropolitan areas resist the notion of comprehensive metropolitan government not just out of contrariness or to protect their jurisdictional integrity, but in the sincere belief that they can provide higher-level, better-quality, and more efficient service than could a larger more "comprehensive" government entity.[21]

Even in those few metropolitan areas that have expanded the central city's political boundaries by consolidating with their surrounding county government, urban growth has spread far beyond the consolidated city-county boundary. Consolidated Nashville–Davidson County, Tennessee, is a case in point.

General Motors' decision to locate its new Saturn plant in Spring Hill was, given the threshold decision to build in Tennessee, based principally on GM's desire to be on the outer orbit of the Nashville metropolitan area. There it could find relatively inexpensive land in an uncluttered environment, and still be close to the labor and supply markets, transportation networks, and the social amenities of the greater Nashville area. GM planners reasoned that while the plant would be located in rural Maury County about 30 miles from Nashville, many of their salaried employees would live in suburban Williamson County. This would afford them good public services, such as schools for their children, and enable working spouses of GM employees to be employed in Nashville. Thus, Williamson County may be a fiscal loser in the deal if it gets none of the Saturn plant's tax revenue but bears the burden of providing services to many of GM's employees.

Whatever their form of government, most growing metropolitan areas are showing signs of severe strain: unprecedented traffic congestion, labor force imbalances, housing shortages, environmental pollution, and crowded schools in parts of jurisdictions that are closing schools elsewhere. Few metropolitan areas have the institutional capacity to provide comprehensive administration of services such as transportation, water supply, and sewage disposal that are more efficiently provided on a metropolitan area–wide basis, to account for labor imbalances between areas of high unemployment in the central city and labor shortages in the "outer city," to address the new economic need for strong regional educational and technological capability, and to provide comprehensive land-use planning.[22]

Southern California

The Greater Los Angeles area offers an example of the variation in urban demographic and economic patterns, one that may foretell conditions that other areas will face in the future.[23]

The population of the five-county metropolitan area was 13.4 million people in 1988, and is projected to grow to 18.1 million by 2010, a 35 percent increase likely to be twice the national population growth rate.[24] Anglos (non-Hispanic whites, who are themselves a heterogeneous ethnic mix) are projected to decline from the 70 percent of the population they represented in 1970 to less than a majority by the turn of the century. By 1985, slightly over half of the population under 20 years of age already was comprised of minorities. While Hispanics (principally Mexicans, but including other Latin American nationalities) accounted for only 14 percent of the region's population in 1970, they are projected to grow to over 40 percent by 2010, replacing Anglos as the largest minority group. The Asian population (itself a heterogeneous mix of Japanese, Chinese, Vietnamese, Filipinos, and representatives of other Asian nationalities) is gaining in proportional share, although not as quickly and not coming anywhere near the magnitude of the Latinos. Asians made up 6 percent of the population in 1970 and are projected to claim 9 percent in 2010. Meanwhile, the black population is expected to retain its proportional share of about 10 percent of the region's population through 2010.

Between 1975 and 1980, net foreign immigration accounted for about 60 percent of the region's population increase. This proportion is expected to decline in the future as a consequence of high fertility among Hispanics already in the region, and presumed enforcement of tighter restrictions on immigration. The proportion of the population 65 and over is projected to increase from 10 percent in 1988 to 13 percent in 2010. Elderly people will be predominantly Anglo, while the younger population will be increasingly Hispanic, Asian, and black.

There is immense cultural and vocational diversity among immigrant groups in the Los Angeles area. Asian immigrants are often highly educated, while Mexican immigrants are generally low-skilled workers. However, there is also wide variation within these groups. For example, Asians include the Vietnamese, who tend to be highly educated and middle-class, as well as Cambodians and Laotians, who tend to have less education.

Some research has found that recent Mexican immigrants have followed a course similar to that of European immigrants in the past.[25] They work hard at low-paying jobs, improve their education or promote the education of their children, and, over successive generations, move up in level of skill, income, and vocational and social status. The second generation is likely to be bilingual, and the third generation monolingual in English. The recent surge in immigration from Mexico—in the early 1980s about 60 percent of the Hispanic population in California was foreign-born—may have obscured that pattern of behavior by causing observers to equate the language, employment, and cultural status of recent Mexican immigrants with those of the Hispanic population as a whole, and to ignore the changes that occur in the status of immigrant families over time.

For all its demographic and economic variety, the Los Angeles area functions as an integrated regional economy. Its 13 million people constitute both a huge labor market and a consumer market, and its industries and firms interact with one another to produce the innovations and synergy that make the Los Angeles area one of the most dynamic economies in the world. Security Pacific Bank estimates that the economy bounded within a 60-mile radius of downtown Los Angeles (the "60-mile circle") is equivalent to the seventh largest national economy in the world.

But there is concern that the rapid growth of recent years has strained the region's capacity to accommodate further economic expansion. Traffic congestion has reached epidemic proportions; the high cost of housing has forced medium- and low-wage employees to look for homes further and further from their places of employment; environmental pollution is raising health threats; and primary and secondary education is strained by growing numbers of disadvantaged children and inadequate resources. Meanwhile, fiscal constraints on government resulting from a series of citizen-initiated tax and expenditure constraints (such as the Proposition 13 restrictions on property taxes and Gann limits on state government spending) have limited the government's ability to respond to these problems with new highways, mass transit, pollution control, and disposal mechanisms, more effective housing programs, and better schools.[26]

One of the few regional institutions is the South Coast Air Quality Management District (AQMD), which in March 1989 adopted Southern California's controversial air quality management plan. The AQMD has some significant powers, especially in regulating land use, but it still must rely on other governments to implement the plan.

The Southern California Association of Governments (SCAG), comprised of the region's local governments, also adopted the air quality plan. SCAG also recognizes the interdependence of regional issues—human resource, workforce training, growth management, transportation, job creation, and air quality—and it attempts to integrate those regional features in its planning. However, SCAG is only a planning body, with no formal implementation powers.

Some suggest that the state of California should assert greater responsibility for these issues. Others feel that the pressing need is for the Los Angeles area to create regional institutions to deal with problems in an integrated fashion. The Los Angeles 2000 Committee, for example, recommended the creation of a regional growth management agency that would cover the five-county Greater Los Angeles area. But there are powerful political barriers that stand in the way of creating such institutions, or otherwise taking actions to address regional needs.

Demographic forces can further complicate the political challenge. For example, while there is widespread agreement that education should be improved, demographic forces appear to have eroded the traditional political base of support for public education. While Anglos still represent a majority of the population, they comprise only 26 percent of the public school population. Minorities comprise 73 percent of the enrollment of the Los Angeles public school system: 51 percent Hispanic, 12 percent black, 7 percent Asian, and 3 percent other. There are also fewer adults whose children are in public school, because of the aging of the population, the tendency to have fewer children, and the large proportion of children attending private school. As a consequence, support for public education has declined since the peak of the baby boom, when it was a top political priority.

There is also a demographic split on the issue of growth, with a far higher proportion of the Hispanic, Asian, and black minorities supporting steady or faster growth for the area because of the jobs and income it is expected to generate. The Anglo population, meanwhile, is more inclined to support slow-growth policies that are thought to protect environmental and aesthetic values.[27]

The diversity of the Southern California population offers a rich cultural heritage that has always been associated with America's underlying strength. In today's global economy, the polyglot Los Angeles economy has an enormous practical potential for marketing its goods and services to the rest of the world by building on a cultural and linguistic intimacy with foreign markets that few countries can match. But taking advantage of that potential while dealing effectively with the numerous challenges posed by the same diversity will require the development of a core of common civic values and institutions through which a multicultural society can address its common interests.

National Implications of Regional Change

Federal government policy rarely has accounted for the economic dynamics among and within regions in the United States. Occasionally, federal policy has addressed special regional needs, as it did in the creation of the Tennessee Valley Authority and the Appalachian Regional Commission. It has also occasionally attempted to promote multistate organizations, such as for water resources management and economic development. For the most part, however, the federal government has tended to treat the United States as a single, closed economy, to be governed by national macroeconomic policy, common program standards, and traditional pork-barrel politics. Ironically, the federal policies that have had the greatest impact on regional patterns of development have done so inadvertently. The interstate highway system and federal support of home mortgages through tax exemptions, for example, reinforced the depopulation of central cities. And defense manufacturing has been an engine of economic growth in some regions.

Today, the regional impacts of federal policy are further complicated by international forces. Economic or political upheaval in a foreign country caused by any one or a combination of factors (the debt problem, economic mismanagement, environmental depletion, political or military conflict) can substantially increase pressure to emigrate to the United States. U.S. policy with respect to Cuba and Southeast Asia, for example, resulted in major waves of immigration from those areas into the United States, and the immigrants in turn have concentrated in certain locations, with economic, social, and political consequences for those areas and their respective state and local governments. Federal protectionist actions to curb imports have widely varying effects on regional employment and residential location, favoring some locales (at least temporarily) while harming others. Washington State, for example, is keenly aware that protectionist legislation that would invite retaliation and close down foreign markets to U.S. products would be especially damaging to the Washington economy, which relies heavily on exports.

In these circumstances, the failure of federal policy to account for regional demographic and economic dynamics could be damaging to the national economy as a whole.

CHAPTER 13

Institutional Stress and Opportunity

It would be impossible to calculate with any precision the net impact of the many demographic forces that are reshaping U.S. society. But it is possible to see an emerging pattern of forces that will create both stress and opportunity.

Some points of stress are obvious. Chronic federal budget deficits, for example, are driven in part by both worldwide and domestic demographic forces that will, if anything, exert even greater pressure in the future.

But many points of stress are not so obvious—and are even less predictable—because they involve the cumulative consequences of numerous demographic changes as they interact with one another and with other forces. For example, how will an increasing number of elderly people combined with a shrinking number of workforce entrants affect government benefit levels, tax payments, the nation's economic performance, and political alignments? Will a shrinking pool of new workers attract immigrants, and will immigration alleviate the growing ratio of nonworkers to workers? Will the exploding number of young people in the developing world, unable to find work in their stagnant home economies, result in more immigration than even a labor-squeezed American economy can handle? What effect would such a surge in immigration have on relations between various ethnic groups within the United States? And how could all of these factors be affected by an economic downturn?

Numerous options are available to head off or dampen the negative consequences of demographic forces, and to take fuller advantage of the many positive forces that tend to be obscured. In some instances, what may be perceived as negative trends could have positive effects. Most demographic forces are essentially neutral in their potential impact, subject as they are to social action that will determine whether, on balance, they will be beneficial or detrimental. In some instances, the demographic trends themselves can be altered through social action.

237

The point is that there is wide room for choice and action in confronting the nation's demographic future. But an effective response will be complicated by the fact that the same demographic forces are also placing stress on political institutions whose function it is to make the choices and take appropriate action. Let us summarize the principal demographic forces and the choices they pose.

The United States' Role in the World

The United States' international role is a growing challenge for numerous reasons, but demographic factors contribute in several ways:

- To the extent that the productivity of some other nations converges with American productivity, relative American economic strength could decline in the direction of its share of world population.

- No longer is economic and military power concentrated in the industrial nations; holders of such power now include the populous nations in the Third World.

- No single nation other than the United States appears to have the combined population, economic, and military weight to exercise the leadership role upon which the international economic system has depended, and which the United States has played until recently.

- Rapid population growth contributes to or exacerbates sluggish economic performance in some Third World nations, creating social and political tensions and pressure for migration.

- The world's large population and continued rapid increase in absolute size, in combination with economic and technological factors, is causing environmental effects of potentially serious magnitude.

- Rapid growth in the Third World's workforce is likely to create more competition for the United States, as well as new market opportunities.

- Economic and technological forces are creating unprecedented interdependence among the world's massive and heterogeneous population.

- Differences in age structures among nations could have multiple effects on capital flows, national economic priorities, political perspectives, and migration patterns.

The sum of these forces suggests a world that is significantly different from the one that U.S. foreign policy is currently designed to deal with. The mismatches are of three principal types.

First, the United States does not currently possess the relative economic strength it had when it defined its international goals following the Second World War. The United States might compensate for that lost advantage by allocating a greater share of resources to its military and foreign policy program and investing more of the resources it now consumes in order to strengthen its economy. The more pressing strategic question, however, is how the resources already allocated to the military and other aspects of foreign policy can be most effectively adapted to new circumstances.

The kinds of threats posed today are more varied and complex than they were 40 years ago. The Soviet Union continues to be regarded as the principal military threat to the United States, even if the nature of the U.S.-Soviet strategic relationship is changing. But there are other threats and potential challenges to American interests in numerous other regions of the world, in both large and small, wealthy and poor countries. The type of military, economic, and diplomatic action called for in these circumstances is likely to be quite different from those appropriate to dealing with the Soviet Union.

Second, because the United States' relative economic strength has declined, and because no other country appears to have the combined population and economic weight to take its place, the international economic system is not likely to have a single, dominant national power to provide stability and direction. This is of consequence to the United States in three respects. The nation's economic independence is further constrained; it must learn to function in an international economic system that has lost its traditional source of stability; and, as still the largest economic power in the world, the United States is in the most influential position to reassert its leadership or to find an alternative means of promoting international economic stability. Alternative forms that the international economic order might take include greater cooperation among major economic powers, stronger international organizations, more flexible national economic policy, the creation of regional economic blocs, or a greater tolerance for turbulence. Which of these evolves could depend in part on what the United States chooses to promote or acquiesce in.

Third, the increasing interdependence among the world's peoples, and between the human population and environmental forces, poses technically complex and politically challenging problems of policy coordination. This issue is really inseparable from that of economic interdependence. It speaks to the need to deal with forces that flow easily over national borders—information, communications, capital, people, goods (including drugs), pollution, and weapons—and with increasing volume, speed, complexity of interaction, and uncertainty of consequence. It is increasingly clear that the nation-state is inadequate to deal with these forces, but the necessary and politically feasible alternatives to that institution are not clear. Treaties and other forms of agreement among nations, political bargaining, unilateral adjustment, and relatively weak international organizations continue to be the principal institutional means of coping with the higher degree of interdependence among nations. Here again, the United States, as the world's most powerful country, has a major role to play in determining how the world's nations respond to these new institutional challenges.

National Priorities

By the mid-1980s, the inclination to beef up defense as one way of compensating for a relative decline in the United States' world influence had begun to clash with powerful demographic forces in the domestic sphere. This dynamic is reflected in the federal budget.

From 1970 to 1980, defense spending declined as a proportion of GNP from 8.3 to 5.0 percent, while federal payments for individuals rose from 6.5 percent to 10.4 percent. By 1987, defense spending had grown to 6.4 percent of GNP, while payments to individuals stayed nearly constant at 10.6 percent. However, the portion of payments to elderly individuals increased from 6.8 percent in 1980 to 7.6 percent in 1987. Meanwhile, interest payments on the national debt rose steadily between 1970 and 1987, more than doubling as a proportion of GNP from 1.5 to 3.1 percent.[1]

In sum, from 1980 to 1987, the big gainers in the budget were defense, the elderly, and debt payments, which together increased from 13.8 to 17.1 percent of GNP. During the same period, spending for everything else—basic government functions, grants to state and local governments, assistance to the poor, and remaining programs—dropped from 8.4 percent to 5.6 percent of GNP.

Virtually all of the growth in the federal budget as a proportion of GNP was financed by borrowing. From 1980 to 1987, total federal outlays increased from 22.1 percent to 22.8 percent of GNP, while revenues remained essentially unchanged at a little below 20 percent of GNP (although the source of revenues shifted from the income tax to the Social Security payroll tax). By 1985, the mounting U.S. budget deficit and the trade deficit had begun to generate sufficient political concern to force a tradeoff between the two principal sources of budget growth: programs for defense and for the elderly. (The third principal source of budget growth, payment of interest on the debt, was accepted as a given). Elderly programs prevailed. Defense spending essentially stopped growing in real terms, and then once again started to decline as a proportion of GNP.

The significance of this dynamic is that the demographics of aging are driving the budget and forcing decisions on the allocation of national resources. Social Security and Medicare entitlements are established in law, so each year, as the number of elderly people increases, the budget cost for these items, inflation aside, is driven upward.

Today, nearly 29 percent of the U.S. federal budget is allocated to programs for the elderly (including but not limited to Social Security and Medicare), 28 percent to defense and international affairs, and nearly 15 percent to payment of interest on the debt. The remaining 28 percent covers all nondefense and nonelderly domestic programs.

Given established eligibility and benefit standards, the rising number of elderly people is projected to increase the proportion of the budget allocated to programs for the elderly to 36 percent by 2010. New programs covering long-term care, catastrophic health insurance, and expanded medical coverage could increase that proportion even more. With that magnitude of budget growth already built into public policy, future budget options will be defined by the question of how to deal with the strong upward trajectory of spending for elderly programs.

There are five options.

The first is to reduce other areas of the budget commensurately. If one assumes that defaulting on debt payments is not an alternative, that means reducing either the share of the budget allocated to defense or the share allocated to nonelderly domestic programs.

Defense outlays, which as noted have already fallen as a proportion of GNP (from 6.5 percent of GNP in 1986 to 6.4 percent in 1987), are projected to continue declining under the Gramm-Rudman-Hollings baseline to 5.3 percent in 1993.[2] Equally important, the defense budget is likely to decline in real-dollar terms. Reducing the defense budget at a time when the United States' influence in the world appears to be declining would suggest the possibility of accelerating that loss of influence. This need not be the case, of course, if a smaller military establishment could be more effectively designed and deployed, or if strategic, diplomatic, and economic resources could be more effectively used to compensate for a smaller military capability. Clearly, there are options here for rethinking the United States' global strategy and making better use of the substantial resources at the nation's disposal.

Maintaining an effective military establishment also requires a productive economy. With the defense budget falling below 7 percent of GNP, the concern is not so much that total defense expenditures are a drag on investment, but rather that the composition of defense spending may be squeezing civilian research and development. Between 1980 and 1987, federal spending for civilian research and development grew by only 20 percent, from $14.7 billion in 1980 to $17.6 billion, while military R&D expenditures soared by over 150 percent, rising from $15.5 to $38.4 billion.[3] Consequently, a large segment of the United States' scientific and technological talent today is consumed in producing high-quality military technology, while their intellectual counterparts in Japan, Germany, and other economic competitor nations are dedicated to producing high-quality commercial products. This allocation of technical talent may contribute to a stronger military capabilty, but it also diverts talent that could boost American competitiveness, and thereby in the long run may weaken the economic base on which an effective military capacity depends.

There is no pat formula by which this question can be answered. High levels of both military spending (including R&D) and civilian R&D could be sustained simultaneously without impeding investment if the difference were made up by reducing national consumption. The Soviet Union maintains a competitive military capacity on an economic base far weaker than the United States' by allocating an estimated 15 to 20 percent of GNP to the military, while sacrificing both consumption and civilian R&D. The Soviet Union, of course, is feeling the economic strain of this burden, no doubt a key force driving Mikhail Gorbachev's program of perestroika. The point is not that the United States should emulate the Soviet Union, but that U.S. policy has wide latitude to adjust its mix of defense, nondefense, consumption, and investment spending to achieve the multiple objectives of a strong defense, support for domestic programs, and a strong economy.

There are ways in which U.S. military spending could be reduced without impairing the nation's defense capability, and it is arguable that resources now allocated directly to the defense budget could more effectively contribute to U.S. military strength if they were invested in economic growth. Still, there should be no illusion as to how difficult it will be to pursue America's security interests in an increasingly challenging international environment while at the same time reducing defense spending. "Burden-sharing" with the United States' allies is gaining popularity as one option, but to the extent the United States shifts the burden of military spending to its allies, it also loses that degree of direct control over allied military operations.

The opportunities for reductions in the 28 percent of the budget that goes for nondefense and nonelderly programs pose similarly difficult choices. About one-third of that total goes for nonelderly entitlements, including payments to the poor and farm subsidies. The remaining two-thirds includes such programs as civilian research and development, education and training, and infrastructure, all of which could be important investments in future economic vitality. Here again, other demographic trends will squeeze the budget; for example, providing adequate early childhood programs, education, and training for the large and growing proportion of disadvantaged children will entail substantial government investment. Failure to make this investment not only could undermine American competitiveness, but also is likely to increase the proportion of the budget in the future devoted to welfare and other programs associated with a poorly prepared workforce and expanding underclass.

The second option for dealing with the rising proportion of GNP consumed by programs for the elderly is to increase the total federal budget as a proportion of GNP so that the additional cost could be absorbed without commensurate reductions elsewhere in the budget. Federal budget outlays as a proportion of GNP declined from their peak of 24.0 percent in 1985 to 22.8 percent in 1987. These expenditures are projected to continue declining, falling to 21.3 percent of GNP by 1993.[4] Consequently, it would be possible to expand the budget marginally without exceeding the proportional levels of GNP reached earlier in this decade. However, to do so without a tax increase would expand the budget deficit, reverse its recent decline as a proportion of GNP, require additional borrowing, and place upward pressure on interest rates.

The third option is to strengthen the economy sufficiently to accommodate the growth in programs for the elderly without reducing other expenditures, expanding the federal budget share of GNP, or increasing taxes. There is, of course, much debate as to whether or how this might be done. Part of the dilemma, as already noted, is that

long-term economic growth may require federally supported investment in research and development, physical infrastructure, and human resources.

The fourth option is to restrain the growth in the cost of programs
for the elderly, by redefining eligibility or benefit levels, applying
means tests, or taxing a larger share of benefits. But even restraint in
the growth of current elderly programs could be offset by rising costs
associated with new programs for long-term care, catastrophic health,
and expanded medical care. Significant leverage could be achieved in
dealing with those rising costs if more elderly people were to remain
employed longer, which would simultaneously postpone their dependency on government programs and retain them as taxpayers, contributing to the support of programs for the less productive members of
their own age cohort. It would also ease the labor squeeze. The intent
of the 1983 Social Security reforms to increase the retirement age to 67
by the year 2022 is a step in that direction.

A fifth option is, of course, some combination of the first four.
One approach is a "share the pain" strategy that would make marginal cuts in numerous programs while increasing taxes, and thereby
minimize the burden on any one group, establish a sense of fairness,
and promise a stronger capacity to meet critical social needs in the
future. Another approach is to subject more entitlement programs to
means testing, or otherwise to be more precise in distinguishing
genuine needs and investment opportunities from those that reflect
conventional wisdom, demographic stereotypes, or narrow political
interests. For example, a 70-year-old person in good health and with
abundant personal wealth has far less need for government assistance than an 85-year-old who is incapacitated and has no financial
assets, yet current eligibility standards tend to treat both people
alike.

All of these options have major implications for the security and
economic health of the nation, and for the protection and well-being
of vulnerable groups within our population. All will involve political pain.

But the pain involved in these choices for the next decade or so
will be relatively light compared to what is in store for the next
century. Then, by some estimates, programs for the elderly may grow
to absorb as much as 50 percent of the federal budget. While such
projections are highly speculative, they nonetheless suggest the general magnitude of difficulty in the policy choices the United States is
likely to confront in the future.

It should be understood that these federal policy tradeoffs are not just between programs for the elderly and all other national pursuits. The point is that elderly programs, which already constitute one of the largest segments of the federal budget, are being driven by powerful demographic trends, and therefore are forcing the choices.

The Role of State and Local Governments

One consequence of the expanding proportion of the federal budget consumed by defense, entitlement programs, and debt payments is that responsibilities for other domestic governmental functions have tended to shift to the state and local level. About 85 percent of all nondefense government purchases of goods and services in the United States—that is, everything but defense, personal transfer payments, and debt payment—are made by state and local governments. States and localities have responded to this growing responsibility with innovation and energy. The states have initiated imaginative programs to improve their economies, and in many ways now lead the federal government in their understanding and capacity for effective economic strategy.[5]

The federal system as a whole, however, also has a responsibility to deal with the strikingly different variations that national demographic trends can manifest at the regional and local levels, and with the growth and changing composition of regions. Local and regional government institutions vary widely in their forms and effectiveness, but in general are straining to meet the task of regional governance. State governments in recent years have begun to recognize the economic importance of urban regions that are wholly or partially within their borders. But state efforts to improve the institutions and governance of regions are still rudimentary.

As the United States has become increasingly integrated with the world economy, the global reach and vulnerability of the nation's regional economies have become more pronounced. Effective regional governance is no longer just a matter of improving public services, but is now a concern of growing national economic consequence. The flexibility and traditions of its federal system provide the United States with a unique opportunity, if the three levels of government can work in reasonable harmony so that the domestic problems of the country—with their interdependent local, regional, national, and international dimensions—can be addressed in a more coordinated fashion.

The Workforce

Demographic forces in combination with economic and technological changes are transforming the U.S. workforce. Workers are increasingly black, Hispanic, Asian, and female. Non-Hispanic white males are now a minority of the workforce and are projected to comprise no more than 10 percent of net new workforce entrants between now and the year 2000.

A larger percentage of the total population is employed than ever before, more than in any other country. (The one conspicuous exception to this trend is the elderly population which, because of extended life and earlier retirement, has a smaller proportion of its members in the workforce than ever before.) But despite an increasing proportion of the population that is employed, and an unemployment rate of below 6 percent (plus substantial underemployment), labor shortages have appeared in numerous industries and regions of the country. This trend is likely to continue (barring an economic downturn) due to a slowdown in the number of entry-level workers, and will require more effective training (especially for the disadvantaged), greater flexibility in accommodating workers with special needs (such as working parents), and higher productivity through more imaginative uses of workers' skills, creativity, and energy.

Immigration will be a key element in the equation. Pressures for migration to the United States will continue to build abroad, especially in the Caribbean Basin. There will be pressures within the United States from employers to loosen the legislative constraints on immigration, in order to compensate for the declining number of new entrants into the workforce. Those likely to oppose looser restrictions will include state and local jurisdictions that have the greatest concentration of immigrants, and segments of the population who are concerned that immigrants will undermine their cultural values or take jobs from indigenous Americans.

The principal responsibility for accommodating the changing dynamics of the workforce will fall to the private sector. The market system has created 27 million new jobs over the past 15 years to accommodate the maturing baby boom generation and the increasing proportion of women seeking work. In the future, corporations confronted by a shortage of adequately prepared labor are likely to become even more involved in training, child care, and helping employees to care for elderly parents, even as they seek ways to reduce their dependence on labor.

Education

Educational institutions are being heavily affected by demographic change in several ways: their enrollments have fluctuated dramatically, they often bear responsibilities sloughed off by other social institutions, and their primary mission of generating and imparting knowledge is challenged by the sweep and complexity of social change.

Many schools and colleges have confronted shrinking enrollments that entail layoffs, program cutbacks, school closings, redrawing of boundaries, and for colleges, the loss of tuition. Pressure is building on state legislatures and Congress to compensate for the loss of tuition revenue with increased direct financial support and student loans.

While declining enrollment places stress on individual colleges and universities, it also affords the opportunity to concentrate resources on fewer students. If public support and private endowments and contributions remain at current levels, the cutbacks required by some colleges and universities could be held to the tuition lost through declining enrollment; that is, financial resources may not fall as quickly as the reduction in the number of students, so that there will be more educational resources per student.

Declining enrollment also challenges many institutions of higher education to rethink their mission, their universe of potential students, and their mode of operation. In particular, the drop in traditional entry-level students affords a special opportunity to expand the role of higher education toward lifelong learning. Community colleges, in particular, have already moved in this direction, substantially increasing the number and proportion of their adult students.

But while some educational institutions are experiencing a decline in pupils, others are struggling to accommodate a resurgence in enrollments. Some public school jurisdictions whose child populations are growing through both migration and higher birth rates are facing enrollment increases that recall the 1950s and 1960s. This growth creates fiscal and administrative stress, but it also provides an opportunity to build renewed educational support and vigor.

In many jurisdictions, families with children comprise a minority of all households, and thus do not have the numerical political potential of earlier generations of parents with school-age children. An increasing proportion are also minority parents who in the past have not had the political clout required to assure high-quality education for their children. There is some compensation for this numerical disadvantage in the intensity of interest displayed by some new parents in their children's education. Many business leaders have also come to recognize that they must become a more or less permanent constituency for the public schools in order to compensate for the decline in parents' political clout, and to assure an educated pool of new workers. There is also hope in the heightened public awareness of the importance of education to a community's own strength and to the United States' world competitiveness.

Today's schools are expected to provide a wide range of services that were once the responsibility of other social institutions, especially the family. They provide all-day child care for families with no parent at home, counseling centers for troubled children, early childhood and remedial programs for the disadvantaged, special education for the handicapped and learning-disabled, value instruction for the religiously and ethically untutored, drug and alcohol counseling for substance abusers, recreational programs, and life-skills training.

Their responsibility can be expected to increase even further, given the rapidly increasing proportion of students who require special programs to overcome the disadvantages associated with higher-than-average rates of poverty and family dislocation. Since a majority of net workforce entrants between now and the year 2000 will come from minority groups, the effectiveness of public schools in educating minority children will be a major determinant of the nation's economic performance and world competitiveness.

Civic Culture

U.S. civic culture has been buffeted by numerous forces in recent years, including important demographic changes. Civic culture is rooted in the rights, responsibilities, and habits of citizenship. But the traditional concept of citizenship for many has become a cliché. Barely half the voting-age population bothers to exercise even the most rudimentary right and responsibility of democratic citizenship: voting. Voter turnout in presidential elections declined from 63 percent in 1960 to 53 percent in 1984.

People today are more likely to define themselves in a public context according to their job, profession, avocation, or some other personal interest, rather than as a citizen of the jurisdiction in which they live. Involvement in public affairs tends to be confined to membership in a group that represents those interests and lobbies on behalf of them.

The civic culture is also undermined when the distribution of income and wealth becomes excessively skewed. Today, a growing underclass appears to be trapped in poverty and a world of constant threat and hopelessness. In these circumstances, the underclass becomes self-perpetuating and produces a disproportionately high number of disadvantaged children unprepared not only for employment, but also for the rudimentary tasks of citizenship. The growing perception by many people that the distribution of income and wealth is unfair tends to undermine the fundamental legitimacy of social institutions.

Civic institutions, including government, are more complex because society is more urban, and the urban economy is increasingly specialized and interdependent. The citizen's task has been further complicated by the expansion and changing nature of urban regions and the paucity or absence of effective civic institutions—government or otherwise—that are coterminous with that broader region. People living in the Chicago suburbs, for example, may say they are from Chicago, when in fact they do not live in the city of Chicago and are unlikely to have great interest in the affairs of Chicago or even of the Chicago metropolitan area.

The paradox of civic paralysis in many communities today is not that power is concentrated in the hands of a few, but that it is widely dispersed among many groups that do not recognize their own strength, or else use that strength solely to pursue their narrowly defined interests. Few groups, it seems, regularly identify their own interests with the broader interests of the community as a whole. Nor are there adequate mechanisms to build coalitions among fragmented power bases. The challenge to civic leadership is for leaders of numerous small groups—many of whom have considered themselves outside the traditional "power structure"—to build the coalitions that can transform them from mere advocates of narrow constituent interests into promoters of broader community goals that also serve their constituents. Increasing demographic diversity will complicate this task, and yet make it all the more important.

Demographic changes will create opportunities as well as impediments for civic leadership. At the state, regional, and local levels, new definitions of community are being formulated. There is a growing pool of blacks, Hispanics, Asians, women, and other groups who generally have not formed the core of civic leadership in the past, but who could provide vigorous and effective leadership in the future. There is already evidence at the state and local levels of new civic energy experimenting with ways of recasting the definition of community to fit a more complex multicultural society.

The baby boom generation has an especially great opportunity—and responsibility—for several reasons. Because of its size, it will continue to have a major influence on the future course of events in the United States, as it has since its birth. For the next generation, it essentially will constitute the bulk of the adult American population. It is also now the "in-between" generation, the potential bridge between those whose formative years were dominated by the Great Depression and ascendant U.S. world power, and those whose formative years have been characterized by domestic affluence but diminishing American influence abroad.

The baby boomers are steeped in the culture of assertive diversity that will characterize United States and world politics for the next generation. Their ability to synthesize and live harmoniously with multiple, complex, and politically powerful claims within their own generation will in many ways be a test of whether far more complex and volatile political conflicts on the national and world scene can be resolved.

The baby boom generation still has time to define the character of the aging society America is becoming before they themselves become the aged. But their time is short: a little more than one decade. When they retire, the sheer size of their generation will place an unprecedented burden on the remaining workforce. In the narrowest sense, the question will be whether the baby boom generation, in looking out for their own interests, will have prepared the emerging workforce for the burden of supporting them in their old age. But the broader question is what legacy the baby boom generation will leave by the course they chart for U.S. institutions in the years immediately ahead.

Personal Responsibility and Adaptation

The capacity of social institutions to meet their responsibilities will depend in large part on people taking greater personal responsibility for themselves and their dependents, for those who are most important to them.

Important demographic changes are associated with stress in private lives: divorce, separation, single-parent families, unmarried couples, single working parents, unwed mothers, two-worker marriages, and absent parents. One consequence is that other institutions must either assume the functions once borne by the traditional family or deal with the consequences of those functions not being performed at all. Old role models, sources of identity, and personal points of reference have been disoriented. The toll in mental health, drug and alcohol addiction, and emotional pain has been great. For many, however, the stress also gives rise to new understanding and creative forms of behavior.

It is in this personal crucible that the new social tissue is being formed: new relationships between men and women, parents and children, employees and employers, business associates, and citizens and their public institutions. The experiments are both constructive and destructive, and the outcomes are uncertain. Furthermore, many of these experiments in social adjustment are intensely personal. Those undertaking them therefore yearn for privacy, even as their very number and social importance make them matters of public concern.

Providing the proper balance of support and incentive for people to make adjustments and take greater responsibility for themselves poses one of the most formidable challenges, and perhaps one of the greatest opportunities, for dealing with the consequences of demographic change.

A National Window of Opportunity: The 1990s

The next decade offers what in historical perspective is likely to be a narrow window of opportunity for Americans to address the implications of both international and domestic demographic forces. Partly by coincidence and partly because they are closely related, forces in both spheres are traveling a similar time path that offers a limited period of fading opportunity. In both the international and domestic spheres, the pressures are likely to mount slowly for the remainder of the century, and then accelerate in the early part of the next century.

The United States will continue to be a major and influential international force, and may well remain the single most powerful country in the world into the indefinite future. But the extraordinary relative power it has enjoyed over the past several decades is not likely to endure, at least not in its conventional form. The United States continues to enjoy a remnant of that special advantage, in part because its relative economic strength is still superior to most other countries, and in part because the inertia of America's past image of superiority carries into the present. The question is whether the United States will use its passing special advantage in a timely fashion to renew its vigor and to shape a world that in the future will be safer and more prosperous for democratic countries with limited individual influence—like the United States itself.

In the meantime, America's elderly population will be growing only slowly until the early years of the next century. However, by the time the baby boomers begin to join the ranks of the elderly (and recall that they will reach the early retirement age of 55 beginning in the year 2000), the opportunity for advance preparation to deal with a rapidly expanding elderly population will have been lost. While the baby boomers were young, they retarded the long-term aging trend in the United States; now, as they begin to enter middle age, they will accelerate it. For the next decade, the United States will have a larger proportion of its population in their prime working years than it ever had in the past, and larger than it is likely ever to have again. After 2010, however, the proportion of workers to elderly people will shrink rapidly as the elderly population explodes.

Because these trends are occurring gradually over a long period of time, their power and direction tends to be ignored. The tendency is to make small, incremental adjustments in reaction to immediate pressures, rather than to rethink the conceptual and strategic implications of these trends. Nor is the close relationship among them generally recognized.

As a consequence, political constituencies that are focused intensely on their own narrowly defined priorities frame the policy debate and define the action. One can see this dynamic at work with unusual clarity in the federal budget process. Because growing deficits and tax increases are considered to be politically unacceptable ways to finance the budget, and because Social Security and Medicare spending continue to expand, the defense budget has proved to be the biggest and politically most vulnerable source of compensating budget reduction. But military and international affairs programs are being reduced incrementally, without the reconceptualization that might permit a smaller defense structure to cope with changing strategic demands.

Continued incremental adjustments in response to narrowly focused political clashes may relieve budget pressure in the short run, but by themselves will not produce the conceptual and strategic adjustment that is needed—and ultimately will be forced one way or another—in the long run. When pressure becomes too great for incremental adjustments, then major structural changes in international and domestic programs will be forced without adequate preparation.

The alternative is a prompt reconceptualization of America's strategic interests and domestic priorities, including a recognition of the integral relationship between the two, to permit adjustment during the period of slowly mounting pressure in the 1990s. Goals could be redefined and responsibilities reassigned so as to reduce or better distribute costs. Strategy could be recast to invest in new capacity for the long run. Within a broader strategic framework, politically negotiated incremental adjustments would be more likely to avoid destructive consequences.

Confronting these mounting pressures could well constitute a test of the nation's political character equal to any it has confronted in its history, in part because the stresses are not concentrated into a clear crisis, but are broadly dispersed and are being stretched out over many years. It is worth recalling, therefore, how quickly a decade can pass. The traumas of the sixties—the political assassinations, the Vietnam War, the racial clashes—are still fresh in the minds of most adult Americans, but they are now two decades in the past. In half that time again, the high school class of 2000—which entered the first grade in 1988—will graduate, and the first baby boomers will begin to take early retirement. Soon thereafter, the remainder of the baby boom generation will be retiring and settling in to watch the United States journey into the twenty-first century. What they observe and what Americans of all ages will be forced to live with then, will be largely a consequence of policy choices that are made in the next few years.

Notes

About the Authors

Notes

CHAPTER 2
THE CONNECTEDNESS AND THE LIMITS OF DEMOGRAPHY

1. Japan, as it often does, provides a curious twist to this universal dilemma of the prosperous societies. It has recently toyed with a national program to export its elderly to retirement communities in low-wage countries. This is, to a large degree, reciprocal to the U.S. and European experiments with importing cheap labor. Adverse reactions from the prospective hosts of these enclaves have caused the Japanese government to back down on this policy, at least for the moment.

2. For the moment, only a few of these countries (Germany, Austria, Belgium, Denmark, and Britain) are flirting with zero population growth, at times going into actual population decline as deaths exceed births. But this is only because all of these countries experienced a baby boom to some degree in the 1960s, and the echo of this boom temporarily raised their birth rate in spite of low fertility. The U.S. baby boom was more peaked and more sustained than that of the European countries, and American total fertility is higher than that of most European nations. For this reason, under existing demographic regimes actual decline of the U.S. population will be forestalled for some fifty years, while many European countries face this prospect in the near future.

3. The first modern broadside on this subject in the United States is Ben J. Wattenberg's The Birth Dearth: What Happens When People in Free Countries Don't Have Enough Babies? (New York: Pharos Books, 1987).

CHAPTER 3
HOW MANY PEOPLE? POPULATION PROJECTIONS

1. U.S. Dept. of Commerce, Bureau of the Census, Current Population Reports, ser. P-25, no. 952, Projections of the Population of the United States, by Age, Sex, and Race: 1983 to 2080 (Washington, D.C.: GPO, 1984).

2. U.S. Bureau of the Census, Statistical Abstract of the United States, 1987 (Washington, D.C.: GPO, 1986), table 6.

CHAPTER 4
MIGRATION AND GEOGRAPHIC DISTRIBUTION

1. Several theories have been advanced for the quite unexpected happening of the baby boom, but none are in my opinion quite convincing. For instance, the best known of these theories address the increase of births in the white middle class; but the baby boom was even more peaked for the poor urbanizing blacks: how to explain this?

2. Information is not systematically available for this period as to the degree to which international Third World immigrants replaced earlier domestic rural-to-urban migrants in sustaining the demand for low-rent central city housing. The magnitude of this replacement of effective demand at the low end of the housing market is visibly different from one area to another: the experience of Miami or Los Angeles is undoubtedly different from that of Minneapolis–St. Paul or Chicago.

3. A middle-class family with children might find the price of central city housing attractive, but they would then be faced with the nearly impossible dilemma of sending their children to poor public schools or of paying for their private schooling. Thus the effective cost of central city housing would be high for such families. This, of course, was one of the main reasons for the departure from central cities of middle-class families of every race.

4. There is, of course, an image of a racial as well as a class implication in the process of gentrification. Simply put, yuppie (middle-class) whites displace poor people of color, blacks, Hispanics, etc. But the evidence thus far seems to favor a class explanation. For instance, in Washington, D.C., where there is a large black middle class, there is considerable gentrification by blacks.

5. The working-age population is here that between 20 and 64 years of age.

CHAPTER 5
THE AGING OF THE POPULATION

1. U.S. Dept. of Commerce, Bureau of the Census, *U.S. Population Estimates by Age, Sex, and Race, 1980–1987*, ser. P-25, no. 1022 (Washington, D.C.: GPO: July 1987).

2. Thomas J. Espenshade and Tracy Ann Goodis, "Demographic Trends Shaping the American Family and Work Force" (Washington, D.C.: Urban Institute, 1986).

3. U.S. Congress, House Ways and Means Committee, *Background Materials and Data on Programs Within the Jurisdiction of the Committee on Ways and Means*, 101st Cong., 1st sess., March 15, 1989, pp. 40–65.

4. Ibid., p. 127.

5. William C. Birdsall and John L. Hankins, "The Future of Social Security," *Annals, AAPSS* 479 (May 1985).

6. Kenneth McLennan, "Global Competition and the Special Challenges of Developing Countries: A U.S. Perspective," presented at the National Science Foundation Conference on Cooperation and Competition in the Global Economy, April 27–29, 1986.

7. Alicia Munnell, "The Current Status of Social Security Financing," presented at the Forum on the Future of Social Security, November 19, 1984.

8. Ibid.

9. U.S. Congress, House Ways and Means Committee, *Background Materials and Data on Programs Within the Jurisdiction of the Committee on Ways and Means* (Washington, D.C.: GPO, March 6, 1987), p. 60.

10. Munnell, "The Current Status of Social Security."

11. Martin Feldstein, "The Social Security Explosion," *The Public Interest*, Fall 1985.

12. Employee Benefit Research Institute (EBRI), *America in Transition: Benefits for the Future* (Washington, D.C.: EBRI, 1987), p. 171.

13. U.S. Congress, House Ways and Means Committee, *Background Materials*, 1987, p. 163.

14. EBRI, *The Changing Profile of Pensions in America* (Washington, D.C.: EBRI, 1985), pp. 33–34.

15. U.S. Congress, Senate Committee on the Budget, "Issues in Civil Service Retirement System," *Financing Work Related Entitlement Programs*, Committee Print (Washington, D.C.: GPO, 1983).

16. U.S. Department of Health and Human Services, *Databook on the Elderly: A Statistical Portrait* (Washington, D.C.: GPO, June 1987).

17. Barbara Torrey, "Guns vs. Canes: The Fiscal Implications of an Aging Population," *American Economic Review* 72 (1982).

18. EBRI, *The Changing Profile of Pensions; America in Transition*, pp. 1–4.

19. EBRI, *The Changing Profile of Pensions*, pp. 15–16.

20. Ibid., p. 26.

21. U.S. Office of Management and Budget, *Budget of the United States Government, Fiscal Year 1987*, pp. 5–125.

22. EBRI, *America in Transition*, p. 32.

23. Ibid.

24. John C. Weicher, "Wealth and Poverty Among the Elderly," in *The Care of Tomorrow's Elderly*, ed. Marion Ein Lewin and Sean Sullivan (Washington, D.C.: American Enterprise Institute, 1989), pp. 11–27.

25. EBRI, *America in Transition*, p. 39.

26. U.S. Congress, House Ways and Means Committee, *Background Materials*, 1987, p. 199.

27. Alan S. Blinder and Rebecca M. Blank, "Macroeconomics, Income Distribution, and Poverty," in *Fighting Poverty: What Works and What*

Doesn't, ed. Sheldon H. Danziger and Daniel J. Weinberg (Cambridge, Mass.: Harvard University Press, 1986), pp. 180–208; Sheldon H. Danziger, Robert H. Haveman, and Robert Plotnick, "Anti-Poverty Policy: Effects on the Poor and the Nonpoor," in ibid., pp. 50–77.

28. Wayne Vroman and Susan Vroman, "The Increase in Early Retirement Since 1969," in *The Care of Tomorrow's Elderly*, ed. Marion Ein Lewin and Sean Sullivan (Washington, D.C.: American Enterprise Institute, 1989), pp. 81–102.

29. Committee for Economic Development, *Work and Change* (New York: 1987); William J. Baumol and Kenneth McLennan, *Productivity Growth and U.S. Competitiveness* (New York: Oxford University Press, 1985); Committee for Economic Development, *Strategy for U.S. Industrial Competitiveness* (New York: 1984).

30. Committee for Economic Development, *Investing in Our Children: Business and the Public Schools* (New York: 1985); Committee for Economic Development, *Children in Need: Investment Strategies for the Educationally Disadvantaged* (New York: 1987).

31. Samuel S. Peng, "High School Dropouts, A National Concern," National Center for Education Statistics, U.S. Department of Education; presented at a meeting of the Business Advisory Commission, Education Commission of the States, Denver, March 1985.

32. Wayne Manhood, "Born Losers: School Dropouts," *NAASP Bulletin* 65, no. 441 (January 1981); Institute for Educational Leadership, "Draft Report of the July 1985 Institute of Educational Leadership Conference on Dropouts" (Washington, D.C.: IEL, December 1985).

33. U.S. Department of Education, "Update on Adult Illiteracy," internal report, April 1986, p. 1.

CHAPTER 6

CHANGES IN THE COMPOSITION OF FAMILIES

1. U.S. Department of Commerce, Bureau of the Census, *Household and Family Characteristics*, ser. P-20 (Washington, D.C.: GPO, 1986).

2. Ibid.

3. Ibid.

4. Dana Friedman, "Eldercare: The Employee Benefit of the 1990's," *Across the Board*, June 1986, pp. 45–51.

5. Urban Institute, *Annual Report* (Washington, D.C.: Urban Institute, 1986), p. 15.

6. Frank F. Furstenberg, J. Brooks-Gunn, and S. Philip Morgan, *Adolescent Mothers in Later Life* (Cambridge: Cambridge University Press, 1987).

7. Ibid.

8. Public/Private Ventures, *Summer Training and Educational Program* (Philadelphia: Public/Private Ventures, 1987).

9. Sandra Danziger, "Breaking the Chains: From Teenage Girls to Welfare Mothers, Or, Can Social Policy Increase Options?" in *Ladders Out of Poverty,* ed. Jack A. Mayer (Washington, D.C.: American Horizons, December 1986), pp. 63–84.

10. U.S. Congress, Congressional Budget Office, *Work-Related Programs for Welfare Recipients* (Washington, D.C.: GPO, April 1987).

11. U.S. Congress, House Ways and Means Committee, *Background Materials and Data on Programs Within the Jurisdiction of the Committee on Ways and Means* (Washington, D.C.: GPO, March 3, 1986).

12. Judith Gueron, *Work Incentives for Welfare Recipients* (New York: Manpower Demonstration Research Corporation, 1986).

13. Ibid.

14. Danziger, "Breaking the Chains."

CHAPTER 7
IMMIGRATION

1. Thomas J. Espenshade and Tracy Ann Goodis, "Demographic Trends Shaping the American Family and Work Force," Washington, D.C.: American Enterprise Institute, 1986.

2. Kingsley Davis, "The Migrations of Human Populations," *Scientific American* 231, no. 3 (September 1974), 105.

3. Thomas Muller and Thomas Espenshade, *The Fourth Wave: California's Newest Immigrants* (Washington, D.C.: Urban Institute, 1985).

4. Kevin F. McCarthy and R. B. Valdez, *Current and Future Effects of Mexican Immigration in California* (Santa Monica, Calif.: Rand Corporation, 1985).

5. Vernon M. Briggs, "Employment Trends and Contemporary Immigration Policy," in *Clamor at the Gates,* ed. Nathan Glazer (San Francisco: Institute for Contemporary Studies, 1985).

6. Muller and Espenshade, *The Fourth Wave.*

7. Bruce Kelley, in U.S. Congress, House Select Committee on Children, Youth, and Families, *Hearings,* 100th Cong., 1st sess., March 27, 1987.

CHAPTER 8
GLOBAL INTERDEPENDENCE

1. Paul Ehrlich, *The Population Bomb* (New York: Random House, 1968).

2. World population reached approximately 1 billion people by 1800, and doubled over the next 130 years to 2 billion. From 1930 to 1975, it doubled again to 4 billion, this time in only 45 years. But it appears that world population growth reached its peak of over 2 percent per year in the 1960s. The annual growth rate has since fallen to 1.65 percent in 1985. If the

growth rate were to continue its drop and stay in the 0.5 percent range, world population would still climb to the 10 billion range by the end of the twenty-first century. At the current growth rate of 1.65 percent, world population would exceed 25 billion by the 2090s, a result no one expects. (Paul Demeny, "The World Demographic Situation," in *World Population and U.S. Policy: The Choices Ahead,* American Assembly, ed. Jane Menken [New York: W. W. Norton & Co., 1986]).

3. Carl Haub and Mary Kent, *1987 World Population Data Sheet* (Washington, D.C.: Population Reference Bureau, April 1987).

4. Notestein's classification has since been applied to world population change. See Regina McNamara, "Demographic Transition Theory," *International Encyclopedia of Population,* vol. 1 (New York: Macmillan Publishing Co., 1982).

5. Lester R. Brown and Jodi L. Jacobson, *Our Demographically Divided World,* Worldwatch Paper no. 74 (Washington, D.C.: Worldwatch Institute, 1986).

6. David Hale, "The Twilight of Anglo-American Power, or The Historical Significance of the Venice Summit Conference," Kemper Financial Services, June 1987.

7. Daniel Bell, "The World and the United States in 2013," *Daedalus* 116, no. 3 (Summer 1987), 16.

8. In their 1958 book, *Population Growth and Economic Development in Low Income Countries* (Princeton, N.J.: Princeton University Press, 1958), Ansley J. Coale and Edgar M. Hoover presented models showing that high fertility in such countries as Mexico and India would impede per capita income growth by reducing investment per worker. This view was instrumental in the expansion of efforts by the United States and other industrial countries to try to limit population growth in developing countries. It was sharply challenged by the leaders of Third World countries at the 1974 World Population Conference in Bucharest, Romania.

In 1984, the World Bank reaffirmed the view that rapid population growth could inhibit economic development, concluding in their annual report, "For the poorest countries, development may not be possible at all, unless slower population growth can be achieved soon" (World Bank, *World Development Report 1984* [New York: Oxford University Press, 1984], p. 185). At the 1984 world population conference in Mexico City, many of the developing countries seemed to have come to the same conclusion. Ironically, while far more developing countries supported limiting population growth as part of a strategy for economic development than before, the United States reversed its position and argued that free market economies would resolve any economic problem associated with population growth ("Policy Statement of the United States of United Nations International Conference on Population," rpt. in *Population and Development Review* 10, no. 3 [September 1984], 574–79).

9. National Research Council, Committee on Population, Working Group on Population and Development, *Population Growth and Economic Development: Policy Questions* (Washington, D.C.: National Academy Press, 1986).

10. Ibid., p. 90.

11. These arguments and the history of the debate regarding population growth and economic development are summarized in Thomas W. Merrick, *World Population in Transition*, Population Bulletin 41, no. 2 (Washington, D.C.: Population Reference Bureau, April 1986).

12. Herbert R. Block, *The Planetary Product in 1980: A Creative Pause?* (Washington, D.C.: U.S. Department of State, 1981).

13. Based on data provided by the Inter-American Development Bank compiled in James L. Rowe, Jr., "The Latin American Debt Morass," *Washington Post*, August 16, 1987, pp. H4–H5.

14. Michael S. Teitelbaum, "Intersections: Immigration and Demographic Change and Their Impact on the United States," in *World Population and U.S. Policy*, ed. Jane Menken, p. 138.

15. Donella H. Meadows, Dennis L. Meadows, Jorgen Randers, and William W. Behrens III, *The Limits to Growth: A Report for the Club of Rome's Project on the Predicament of Mankind*, 2d ed. (New York: New American Library, 1975), p. 29.

16. U.S. Council on Environmental Quality, *The Global Report to the President of the United States: Entering the 21st Century* (New York: Pergamon Press, 1980).

17. Julian L. Simon, *The Ultimate Resource* (Princeton, N.J.: Princeton University Press, 1981). Simon also published a further refutation of the limits to growth thesis in *The Resourceful Earth: A Response to Global 2000*, ed. Julian L. Simon and Herman Kahn (New York: Basil Blackwell, 1984).

18. "Buying Debt, Saving Nature," *Newsweek*, August 31, 1987, p. 46.

19. A study by Donald R. Blake and F. Sherwood Rowland, reported in an article in *Science* (March 1988), suggests another form of integration between population growth and ozone depletion. In this formulation, ozone over Antarctica is destroyed by an increasing amount of methane in the atmosphere. Methane is the main component of natural gas produced chiefly by bacterial composition of organic materials. It is generated at the bottom of rice paddies and in the digestive process of plant-eating animals, such as cows and termites. The researchers hypothesize that growing populations in Asia have caused more rice to be planted, while the destruction of forests in the Amazon have increased the termite population, which feeds on fallen trees. Meanwhile the cattle population has increased to serve growing populations throughout the Third World. All of these are sources of increased methane production.

20. Brown and Jacobson, *Our Demographically Divided World*, pp. 14–15. A recent World Bank study of seven West African countries illuminates the dynamics of population change and the carrying capacity of the environ-

mental resource base. (World Bank, *Desertification in the Sahelian and Sudranian Zones of West Africa* [Washington, D.C.: World Bank, 1985].) A similar interplay of forces can be seen throughout much of Africa, and in the Indian subcontinent, Central America, the Andean countries, and Brazil (Brown and Jacobson, *Our Demographically Divided World*).

Successful economic development in the Third World can also place stress on the world's forests and other natural resources (ibid., p. 46). Some U.S. environmental groups have proposed to address this problem by paying off part of the debt of Third World countries in exchange for their creating preservation areas, an idea originated by Thomas Lovejoy of the World Wildlife Fund. For example, Conservation International will buy $650,000 of Bolivia's $4 billion external debt at a discounted price of $100,000 in exchange for the setting aside of 3.7 million acres of Amazon River country around the Beni Biosphere Reserve, the habitat of endangered species of cats and monkeys.

Brazil is making major investments in highways, railroads, farming, and iron production in the Amazon in hopes of boosting its debt-ridden economy. One such project, a 900-mile road from Cuiaba to Porto Velho opened in 1984, permitted 200,000 settlers to move into the region and led to the clearing of 10,000 square miles of forests in a region inhabited by 10,000 Indians. (Richard House, "Brazil Faces Fund Cutoff Over Failure to Protect Rain Forests," *Washington Post*, August 18, 1987, p. E1.)

21. House, "Brazil Faces Fund Cutoff." Philip Fearnside, a University of Michigan ecologist working in the Amazon, argues that highway projects financed by the World Bank and IDB are producing rapid migration into the Amazon and the devastation of forests. Fearnside also claims that if pig iron plants approved for the eastern Amazon were to use charcoal, they would require an area of forest 35 times the size of the Jari Project, which covers an area half the size of Belgium.

In April 1985, the World Bank stopped payment on a $425 million development project in the Amazon frontier states of Rondonia and Malto Grasso when the Brazilian government (then military) failed to use $26 million to protect Indian and forest resources (ibid.).

22. James K. Hammit, *Timing Regulations to Prevent Strastopheric-Ozone Depletion* (Santa Monica, Calif.: Rand Corporation, April 1987), p. vii.

23. Ibid.

24. Robert T. Watson, F. Sherwood Rowland, and John Gile, *Ozone Trends Panel* (Washington, D.C.: Report of the National Aeronautics and Space Administration, March 1988).

25. Steven Weisman, "India's Drought Is Worst in Decades," *New York Times*, August 16, 1987. The drought in much of India in the summer of 1987 was expected to require the use of India's 23 million tons of buffer grain to compensate for failed crops.

26. According to the World Food Council, most of those described as hungry are not starving, but are "chronically deprived of the food needed to enjoy an active, healthy life." (Paul Lewis, "World Hunger Found Still Growing," *New York Times*, June 28, 1987.)

27. Ibid. According to the World Bank, the lower range describes people with a calorie intake below what is necessary "to prevent serious health risks and stunted children," while the higher number was based on a calorie intake permitting "an active working life."

28. James P. Grant, *The State of the World's Children*, UNICEF (New York: Oxford University Press, April 1987).

29. UNICEF, "Adjustment with a Human Face," 1987, report summarized in ibid.

30. Brown and Jacobson, *Our Demographically Divided World*, p. 17.

31. The World Commission on Environment and Development, *Our Common Future* (Oxford: Oxford University Press, 1987), p. 16.

32. Bell, "The World and the United States in 2013," p. 15.

33. Sergio Díaz-Briquets, *Conflict in Central America: The Demographic Dimension*, Population Trends and Public Policy no. 10 (Washington, D.C.: Population Reference Bureau, 1986).

34. Brown and Jacobson, *Our Demographically Divided World*.

35. Jorge Castañeda, "Mexico's Coming Challenges," *Foreign Policy*, Fall 1986.

36. Demeny, "The World Demographic Situation."

37. The Caribbean Basin includes Mexico, Central America, the island states, and the littoral nations of Colombia, Venezuela, and Guyana.

38. Leon Bouvier and David Simcox, *Many Hands, Few Jobs: Population, Unemployment and Emigration in Mexico and the Caribbean* (Washington, D.C.: Center for Immigration Studies, 1986), pp. 8–9.

CHAPTER 9
THE UNITED STATES' INTERNATIONAL STANDING

1. K. C. Zachariah and My T. Vu, *World Population Projections 1987–88 Edition, Short- and Long-term Estimates* (Baltimore, Md.: Johns Hopkins University Press, 1988). Richard Easterlin is one of the few demographers who believes that U.S. fertility is likely to begin rising soon, due to the inclination of smaller generations to have relatively more children.

2. Manufacturing and Allied Products Institute, "Progress and Prospects for U.S. Manufacturing," Policy Review no. 107 (Washington, D.C.: MAPI, 1989).

3. Directorate of Intelligence, U.S. Central Intelligence Agency, *Handbook of Economic Statistics, 1987*, CPAS 87-10001 (Washington, D.C.: GPO, September 1987), p. 34.

4. David Hale, "The Twilight of Anglo-American Power, or The Histori-cal Significance of the Venice Summit Conference," Kemper Financial Ser-vices, June 1987, chart 3. In 1950, the United States' Gross National Product was 61 percent of the GNPs of all the industrial countries. In 1985, despite a threefold increase in real U.S. GNP, its share had dropped to 52 percent. During the same 1950–85 period, by contrast, Japan's GNP increased from 5 to 17 percent of the industrial world's total.

5. Paul Kennedy, *The Rise and Fall of the Great Powers: Economic Change and Military Conflict from 1500 to 2000* (New York: Random House, 1987).

6. Paul Kennedy, "The Relative Decline of America," *Atlantic* 260, no. 2 (August 1987), 34.

7. Samuel P. Huntington, "The U.S.—Decline or Renewal?" *Foreign Af-fairs* 67, no. 2 (Winter 1988–89), 82–83, citing data from World Bank, *World Development Report, 1988* (New York: Oxford University Press, 1988), table 2, pp. 224–25.

8. Charles P. Kindleberger, *The World Depression, 1929–1939* (Berkeley and Los Angeles: University of California Press, 1986), p. 289.

9. Robert Gilpin, *The Political Economy of International Relations* (Princeton, N.J.: Princeton University Press, 1987).

10. Presidential Commission on Integrated Long-term Strategy, *Discrimi-nate Deterrence* (Washington, D.C.: GPO, 1988).

11. The Western industrial democracies, in addition to the United States, include Canada, Australia, New Zealand, Japan, Austria, Belgium, Denmark, Finland, France, West Germany, Iceland, Italy, Luxembourg, the Nether-lands, Norway, Spain, Sweden, Switzerland, and the United Kingdom (United Nations, *World Population Prospects, 1985*).

12. Ben J. Wattenberg, *The Birth Dearth* (New York: Pharos Books, 1987), p. 81.

13. Zachariah and Vu, *World Population Projections 1987–88.*

14. Ibid., p. 175. The Eastern European communist countries include Albania, Bulgaria, Czechoslovakia, East Germany, Hungary, Poland, and Ro-mania.

15. Michael S. Teitelbaum and Jay M. Winter, *The Fear of Population Decline* (New York: Academic Press, 1985), p. 99, using data from M. Fesbach, "The Soviet Union: Population Trends and Dilemmas," *Population Bulletin* 37, no. 3 (1982).

16. Wattenberg, *The Birth Dearth*, p. 175.

17. Zachariah and Vu, *World Population Projections, 1987–88.*

18. Kennedy, *The Rise and Fall of the Great Powers*, p. 415.

19. Ibid., p. 436.

20. The variations among countries are so great that the shorthand label of "Third World" is vastly distorting. It will soon become an historical arti-fact, reflecting a time when the focus of world events was on Europe and its

progeny, which comprise the "First" (democratic) and "Second" (socialist) worlds.

21. George P. Shultz, "A Time of Transformation," *Washington Post*, December 1987.

22. Daniel Bell, "The World and the United States in 2013," *Dedalus* 116, no. 3 (Summer 1987), 171.

23. Wattenberg, *The Birth Dearth*.

24. Teitelbaum and Winter, *The Fear of Population Decline*, p. 129.

25. "The Birth Dearth: An AEI Symposium," *Public Opinion*, Dec. 1985–Jan. 1986, p. 19.

26. Data provided by Wattenberg in *The Birth Dearth* offer a useful "worst case scenario" for considering some of the propositions regarding the dangers of low U.S. fertility.

27. Ibid., p. 55.

28. *Current Population Reports*, as presented in the *Washington Post*, August 30, 1987.

29. U.S. Central Intelligence Agency, *Handbook of Economic Statistics*, *1987*, p. 35.

CHAPTER 10

AN AGING WORLD POWER

1. U.S. Dept. of Commerce, Bureau of the Census, ser. P-25, no. 995.

2. Thomas J. Espenshade and Tracy Ann Goodis, "Demographic Trends Shaping the American Family and Work Force," presented to the Employee Benefit Research Institute (EBRI) and ERF Policy Forum, "America in Transition: Benefits for the Future," n.d., p. 8.

3. American Association of Retired Persons (AARP) and the Administration on Aging, U.S. Department of Health and Human Services (HHS), "A Profile of Older Americans: 1986," p. 2.

4. Ibid., p. 19.

5. Ibid., pp. 18–19.

6. Barbara Boyle Torrey, "Guns vs. Canes: The Fiscal Implications of an Aging Population," *American Economic Review* 72, no. 2 (May 1982), 309.

7. Ibid., p. 312.

8. Espenshade and Goodis, "Demographic Trends," p. 19.

9. AARP and HHS, "A Profile of Older Americans: 1986," p. 1.

10. Beth J. Soldo and Kenneth G. Manton, "Demographic Challenges for Socioeconomic Planning," *Socio-Economic Planning Science* 19, no. 4 (1985), 229. Soldo and Manton note the dramatic though still speculative projected increase in the number of centenarians from 32,000 in 1982 to 597,000 in 2040.

11. AARP and HHS, "A Profile of Older Americans: 1986," p. 4.

12. Espenshade and Goodis, "Demographic Trends," p. 20.

13. Alice M. Rivlin and Joshua M. Wiener, *Caring for the Disabled Elderly: Who Will Pay?* (Washington, D.C.: Brookings Institution, May 1988), reported in Robert Pear, "Broader Medicare Is Urged to Cover Long-Term Cases," *New York Times*, February 7, 1988.

14. Samuel H. Preston, "Children and the Elderly in the U.S.," *Scientific American* 251, no. 6 (December 1984), 45, as cited in Phillip Longman, *Born to Pay: The New Politics of Aging in America* (Boston: Houghton Mifflin, 1987), p. 9.

15. Robert L. Clark and J. J. Spengler, "Changing Demography and Dependency Costs: The Implications of Future Dependency Ratios," in *Aging and Income: Essays on Policy Prospects*, ed. Barbara R. Herzog (New York: Human Sciences Press, 1977), pp. 55–89. This is cited in Phillip Longman, *Born to Pay*, who also estimates that "the disparity is no doubt much larger today. Social Security pensions and Medicare pensions have become much more generous, while welfare and educational programs for the young have been cut" (p. 9). This does not account, however, for increased educational expenditures at the state and local levels.

16. Irwin S. Kirsch and Ann Jungeblut, *Literacy: Profiles of America's Young Adults*, National Assessment of Education Progress, 1986; and "Study Links Poor Writing Ability to Lack of Higher-order Skills," *Education Week* 6, no. 14 (December 10, 1986), 1.

17. Population Reference Bureau, "Work Trends in the U.S.: Looking to the Future."

18. Sidney L. Jones, "Demographic Trends in America: Squaring the Population Pyramid" (Washington, D.C.: Washington Forum, 1987).

19. Nathaniel Semple, "The Urgent Business Role in School Reform," *Bell Atlantic Monthly*, August 1986, pp. 1–3.

20. Before 1950, fewer than one-half of Americans graduated from high school. See Committee for Economic Development, *Children in Need: Investment Strategies for the Educationally Disadvantaged* (New York: CED, 1987).

21. Ibid.

22. AARP and HHS, "A Profile of Older Americans: 1986," p. 12.

23. Torrey, "Guns vs. Canes," p. 312.

24. *New York Times/CBS News Poll*, *New York Times*, March 10, 1988, p. A23.

25. AARP and HHS, "A Profile of Older Americans: 1986," p. 10.

26. Should there be price deflation in the future, the political problem would be all the greater since nominal benefit levels would have to be *reduced* to keep real benefit levels from escalating. Nothing short of dire economic conditions is likely to persuade Congress to actually *cut* nominal Social Security benefit levels for current recipients, even though reductions

in nominal levels at rates less than deflation would leave recipients with greater real income than upward nominal adjustments that failed to keep up with inflation. The monetary illusion and political symbolism associated with actually reducing nominal benefit levels would make such an act highly unlikely, certainly, at least, in the early years of price deflation.

During the Great Depression of the 1930s, the French government attempted to reduce payments to pensioners, veterans, and government employees to keep their real payments in line with declining prices. Charles Kindleberger records that "Pensioners, veterans, and functionaries experienced money illusion and regarded their incomes as determined by the money amounts received, taking no account of the decline in prices. Or those who understood that they had gained in real income through falling prices despite fixed incomes in francs were unwilling to share with their less fortunate compatriots" (Charles P. Kindleberger, *The World Depression, 1929–1939* [Berkeley and Los Angeles: University of California Press, 1986], pp. 247–48).

27. Jack A. Meyer and Rosemary Kern, "Economic and Social Implications of Demographic Changes in the U.S.," prepared for the Committee for Economic Development Project on Policy Implications of Demographic Change, October 1987, pp. 10–17.

28. Alan L. Otten, "Warning of Generational Fighting Draws Critics—Led by the Elderly," *Wall Street Journal*, Jan. 13, 1987.

29. Ibid.

30. Eric R. Kingson, Barbara A. Hirshorn, and John M. Cornman, *Ties That Bind, An Interdependence of Generations*, A Report of the Gerontological Society of America (Washington, D.C.: Seven Locks Press, 1986).

31. Otten, "Warning of Generational Fighting."

32. Ibid.

33. Ibid.

34. The presidential election of 1984 reflected that lack of political definition. In the Democratic primary, Gary Hart appealed directly to baby boomers on what were perceived to be generational themes. One Hart television commercial had a voiceover saying: "We acted as a generation against racial hatred . . . to stop the war in Vietnam . . . to demand a halt to pollution in our land," as pictures of civil rights marches, Vietnam War dead, and antinuclear rallies were shown. (Paul Taylor, "A Theme for 1988: Baby Boom Politics," *Washington Post*, June 11, 1987.) Hart hotly contested the Democratic frontrunner, former Vice-President Walter Mondale, winning by up to 20 points over Mondale in some state primaries on the strength of younger voters. After Mondale had won the nomination, however, about one-third of Hart's voters switched to Ronald Reagan in the general election, apparently attracted by the president's appeal to "strength, prosperity, and entrepreneurship" (ibid.).

CHAPTER 11
ASSERTIVE DIVERSITY

1. Frank Levy, *Dollars and Dreams: The Changing American Income Distribution* (New York: Russell Sage Foundation, 1987), p. 2.

2. U.S. Dept. of Commerce, Bureau of the Census, *Measuring the Effects of Benefits and Taxes on Income and Poverty: 1986*, Current Population Reports, ser. P-60, no. 164-RD-1 (Washington, D.C.: GPO, 1988).

3. Levy, *Dollars and Dreams*, p. 6.

4. Congressional Budget Office, *Trends in Family Income: 1970–1986* (Washington, D.C.: GPO, 1988).

5. Phillip Longman, *Born to Pay: The New Politics of Aging in America* (Boston: Houghton Mifflin, 1987), p. 12.

6. Conference Board, *Baby Boomers in Midpassage* (New York: Conference Board, 1987).

7. John Weicher and Susan Wachter, "The Distribution of Wealth Among Families: Increasing Inequality?" presented at the Working Seminar on the Family and American Welfare Policy, American Enterprise Institute, November 10, 1986, as cited in Longman, *Born to Pay*, p. 14.

8. Conference Board, *Baby Boomers in Midpassage*.

9. Daniel Patrick Moynihan, *Family and Nation* (New York: Harcourt, Brace, Jovanovich, 1986), p. 93.

10. Ibid., pp. 52, 95–97.

11. Ravi Battra, in *The Great Depression of 1990*, argues that the principal difference between a recession and more severe depression has to do with the distribution of income and wealth. Recessions occur, he argues, when overall demand slackens. They become depressions when the financial system is weakened by the consequences of an uneven distribution of wealth and income. People with relatively lower incomes borrow beyond their means in an effort to maintain their standard of living; banks compete to make increasingly risky loans to such people; and the wealthy invest in increasingly speculative and unproductive ventures.

12. Thomas J. Espenshade, "Marriage Trends in America: Estimates, Implications, and Underlying Causes," *Population and Development Review* 2, no. 2 (June 1985), 239.

13. Ibid., p. 194.

14. Ibid., p. 236.

15. Ibid., p. 238.

16. In 1986, children lived in one-parent households because of divorce (42 percent), because of separation (24 percent), because their mothers never married (27 percent), or because one parent had died (7 percent) (Bureau of the Census, Current Population Reports, ser. P-20, no. 418, *Marital Status and Living Arrangements: March 1986* [Washington, D.C.: GPO, 1986]).

17. Ibid.

18. Moynihan, *Family and Nation*, p. 93.

19. U.S. Bureau of the Census, *Statistical Abstract of the United States, 1986*, 106th ed. (Washington, D.C.: GPO, 1985).

20. Espenshade, "Marriage Trends in America," pp. 193–245.

21. Beth J. Soldo and Kenneth G. Manton, "Demographic Challenges for Socioeconomic Planning," *Socio-Economic Planning Science* 10, no. 4 (1985), 229.

22. Barbara Boyle Torrey, "The Demographics of Aging: Implications for Pension Policy," a study paper, for *National Journal Issues Book*, p. 24.

23. Soldo and Manton, "Demographic Challenges," p. 228.

24. Ibid., p. 233.

25. American Association of Retired Persons (AARP) and the Administration on Aging, U.S. Department of Health and Human Services (HHS), "A Profile of Older Americans: 1986," p. 3.

26. Soldo and Manton, "Demographic Challenges," p. 237.

27. AARP and HHS, "A Profile of Older Americans," p. 4.

28. Michael Hurd, "The Poverty of Widows: Future Prospects," in David A. Wise, *The Economics of Aging*, National Bureau of Economic Research Project Report (Chicago: University of Chicago Press, 1989).

29. Conversation with Betty Friedan, Mt. Sinai School of Medicine Conference, "Who Is Responsible for My Old Age," New York City, November 28–30, 1988. Ms. Friedan is writing a book tentatively titled "The Fountain of Age."

30. U.S. Bureau of the Census, *Statistical Abstract of the United States, 1987*, 107th ed. (Washington, D.C.: GPO, 1986).

31. U.S. Bureau of the Census, Current Population Reports, ser. P-25, no. 952, *Projections of the Population of the United States: 1983 to 2050* (Washington, D.C.: GPO, 1984), Middle Series Projection.

32. Harold L. Hodgkinson, *All One System: Demographics of Education, Kindergarten through Graduate School* (Washington, D.C.: Institute for Educational Leadership, Inc. 1985), p. 5.

33. These figures are based on census data presented in George Sternlieb and James W. Hughes, "The Demographic Long Wave: Population Trends and Economic Growth," *Economic Development Quarterly* 1, no. 4 (November 1987), 307–22.

34. Hodgkinson, *All One System*.

35. Karl Zinsmeister, "Black Demographics," *Public Opinion*, January/February 1988, p. 41.

36. Bureau of the Census, Current Population Reports, ser. P-20, no. 416, *The Hispanic Population in the United States: March 1986 and 1987* (Washington, D.C.: GPO, August 1987); Bureau of the Census, Current Population Reports, ser. P-25, no. 995, *Projections of the Hispanic Population: 1983 to 2080* (Washington, D.C.: GPO, 1986).

37. Hodgkinson, *All One System*.

38. Ibid., pp. 5–9.

39. Jean G. McDonald, "Readiness for the New Educational Standards," National Governors' Association Task Force on Readiness, National Governor's Association Center for Policy Research and Analysis, August 1986. While a higher proportion of black and Hispanic children than white children live in poverty, nearly two-thirds of poor children are white.

40. Minneapolis Community Business Employment Alliance, "Preventing Unemployment: A Case for Early Childhood Education," December 1985, pp. 7, 19–22.

41. American Council of Life Insurance, DataTrack 14: Children, December 1984, p. 13.

42. "Single Parents Head 25% of Families in U.S.," New York Times, November 6, 1986.

43. Arch Parsons, "Racial, Other 'Hate Violence' Has Become 'Epidemic' in U.S., 7 Year Study Says," Baltimore Sun, January 14, 1988. The report by the Center for Democratic Renewal in Atlanta cited a total of 2,919 incidents of violence, principally against blacks and other racial minorities, Jews, and homosexuals.

44. Zinsmeister, "Black Demographics," p. 44.

45. U.S. Bureau of the Census, The Hispanic Population of the United States: March 1986 and 1987.

46. Hodgkinson, All One System.

47. Michael S. Teitelbaum, "Intersections: Immigration and Demographic Change and Their Impact on the United States," in World Population and U.S. Policy: The Choices Ahead, ed. Jane Menken (New York: W.W. Norton, 1986), p. 138.

48. Ibid., p. 145.

49. Rita J. Simon, "Immigration and American Attitudes," Public Opinion, July/August 1987, p. 49.

50. Leon F. Bouvier and Robert W. Gardner, Immigration to the United States: The Unfinished Story, Population Bulletin vol. 41, no. 4 (Washington, D.C.: Population Reference Bureau, November 1986), p. 3.

51. Simon, "Immigration and American Attitudes," p. 48.

52. Jack A. Meyer and Rosemary Kern, "Economic and Social Implications of Demographic Changes in the U.S.," prepared for the Committee for Economic Development Project Policy Implications of Demographic Change, October 1987, pp. 10–17.

53. Joel Kotkin and Yoriko Kishimoto, The Third Century: America's Resurgence in the Asian Era (New York: Crown Publishers, Inc., 1988).

54. Kevin F. McCarthy and R. Burciaga Valdez, Current and Future Effects of Mexican Immigration in California (Santa Monica, Calif.: Rand Corporation and the California Roundtable, 1985), p. viii.

55. Ibid.

56. Rushworth M. Kidder, "Pluribus Doesn't Fuse into Unum." Baltimore Sun, September 22, 1987.

57. Warren E. Miller and John R. Petrocik, *Where's the Party? An Assessment of Changes in Party Loyalty and Party Coalitions in the 1980s* (Washington, D.C.: Center for National Policy, 1987), p. 27.

58. Thomas B. Edsall, *The New Politics of Inequality* (New York: W.W. Norton, 1984).

59. Helmut Norpoth, "Change in Party Identification: Evidence of a Republican Majority," presented at the 1985 annual meeting of the American Political Science Association, New Orleans, 1985.

60. Miller and Petrocik, *Where's the Party?* p. 42.

61. David S. Broder, "GOP Pins '88 Hopes on Democrats' Youth," *Washington Post,* June 28, 1987.

CHAPTER 12
REGIONAL VARIATIONS

1. U.S. Dept. of Commerce, Bureau of the Census, Current Population Reports, ser. P-25, no. 937 (Washington, D.C.: GPO, n.d.).

2. U.S. Dept. of Education, Office for Civil Rights, 1984 State Summaries of Elementary and Secondary School Civil Rights Survey (Washington, D.C.: GPO, 1984).

3. Leon F. Bouvier and Philip L. Martin, *Population Change and California's Education System* (Washington, D.C.: Population Reference Bureau, 1987).

4. By 1970, the South was already the largest of the nation's four major regions, with 62.8 million people, or 30.9 percent of the national total. During the 1970s, it dramatically increased that lead, adding 12.5 million to its population (a growth of 20.0 percent) and increasing its share of the national population total to 33.2 percent.

The second most populous region, the North-Central, increased its population by a mere 4.0 percent in the seventies. Its 58.9 million people in 1980 constituted 26.0 percent of the national total, down from its 27.8 percent share in 1970.

The third largest region, the Northeast, had essentially no change in population during the seventies. While the New England region gained 501,000 people, the Middle Atlantic region actually lost 425,000, for a slight net gain of 76,000 for the Northeast region as a whole. The Northeast's 49.1 million people in 1980 constituted 21.7 percent of the nation's population.

Throughout American history, the population has moved steadily westward. The 1970s were no exception, although the dramatic shift southward was even more prominent. Moreover, for the first time the Mountain states had a larger percentage gain in population, a massive 37.1, than the Pacific states, which still grew by a robust 19.8 percent. But the Pacific states' population of 31.8 million (predominantly in California) still overshadowed the Mountain states' 11.4 million. While the West's growth rate of 23.9

percent was the greatest of the four regions, by 1980, with 43.2 million people, it was still the smallest, although greatly gaining on the Northeast.

5. A major issue in the census figures is whether illegal aliens are to be counted, as they have been in past censuses. Since estimates of the number of illegal residents run as high as 8 million, the consequences of including them are significant, the more so given their concentration in certain states such as California (where estimates run as high as 1 million).

The techniques used by the census also matter. The conventional "head count"—that is, actually contacting and establishing the existence of every person included in the official count—is generally recognized to undercount the population in general and certain groups in particular. The Census Bureau estimates that the 1980 census underestimated the total population by 1 percent, while blacks may have been undercounted by as much as 7.2 percent and Hispanics by as much as 5.9 percent. (See U.S. Bureau of the Census, as reported in "The Mayors Say: Yes, 'Adjust' the Census," Washington Post, September 2, 1987.) Undercounting not only reduces the political representation of certain jurisdictions, but also reduces their share of government funds that are distributed on the basis of population.

6. These projections were made by Election Data Services based on population estimates released by the U.S. Bureau of the Census early in 1988.

In 1983, the Census Bureau projected that New York would lose five of its current 34 House seats; Pennsylvania would lose three; Illinois, Michigan, and Ohio would lose two; and Massachusetts, Connecticut, New Jersey, Iowa, and Kansas would lose one each. Predicted gains include Florida and Texas with four new House seats; California with three, Arizona with two, and Georgia, Arkansas, Colorado, Utah, Washington, and Oregon with one. Under these projections, California would increase its first place electoral vote total from 47 to 50, and Texas with 33 votes would take over second place from New York, which would drop to third place with 31 votes. Florida's 25 votes would move it from seventh to fourth place, passing Illinois, Ohio, and Pennsylvania. (Warren Weaver, Jr., "East and Midwest Expected to Continue Political Lag," New York Times, June 28, 1987).

In 1985, the Bureau of Economic Analysis of the Department of Commerce projected that only 13 House seats would change states, rather than the 19 projected earlier by the Census Bureau, although these would involve shifts in the same general direction. (New York would lose two, and Pennsylvania, Illinois, Michigan, and Ohio, one; California and Texas would gain four and Florida three). The National Planning Association, using 1983 population estimates, has projected that only nine House seats would change states. (New York would lose three and California and Texas would gain two).

7. Congressional Quarterly, November 12, 1988; and National Journal, November 12, 1988.

8. U.S. Bureau of the Census, Current Population Reports, ser. P-25, no.

1017, *Projections of the Population of States, by Age, Sex, and Race: 1988 to 2010* (Washington, D.C.: GPO, 1988).

9. The National Planning Association recently revised its projections for regional population change to account for changing patterns of economic growth. It now predicts that for the 15-year period, 1985–2000, the largest gainers in population will be California (5.7 million), Florida (3.7 million), Texas (2.4 million), Arizona (1.3 million), and Massachusetts (1.1. million). NPA's population estimates are presented in *State Policy Reports* 4, no. 9 (May 14, 1986), 18.

NPA predicts that five states will now lose population: Iowa, North Dakota, Nebraska, South Dakota, and West Virginia. Percentage changes in population are projected to range widely from significant increases in Arizona (41.1), Nevada (34.8), New Hampshire (33.0), and Florida (32.6) to losses of up to 4.6 for North Dakota.

The influence of migration is expected to remain strong. Florida, for example, is one of the biggest projected gainers in both absolute and percentage increases, and yet in 1985 was 40th among the states in birth rate (14.4 births per 1,000 population). North Dakota, meanwhile, with the fifth highest natural birth rate in 1985 (18.6) is projected to have the largest percentage loss of all the states through the end of the century (ibid., p. 19).

10. George Sternlieb, James W. Hughes, and Connie O. Hughes, *Demographic Trends and Economic Reality: Planning and Markets in the '80s* (New Brunswick, N.J.: Center for Urban Policy Research/Rutgers University, 1982), p. 106.

11. For example, during the five-year period 1950–55, the South lost 1.6 million people through net out-migration, but more than compensated for that loss with a natural population increase (births minus deaths) of 4.5 million (ibid., p. 133).

Thus the South had a net population gain of 2.9 million people for the five-year period. From 1975–79, by contrast, the South's natural population increase had slowed to only 1.9 million (even with a larger base than in the earlier period), but it had a net in-migration of 1.5 million, mostly from urban areas in the Northeast and North-Central regions. Thus, while its natural population growth slowed dramatically (from 9.5 percent between 1950 and 1955, to 2.8 percent between 1975 and 1979), its total population increased by an even larger number, 3.4 million, in the later five-year period.

During the same two five-year periods, the Northeast's natural population growth also slowed, but the region was not able to compensate for that slower growth through in-migration. In fact, because it lost 1.0 million people through out-migration from 1975 to 1979, but added only 0.7 million through natural growth, the Northeast suffered a net population loss of 300,000 people.

12. R. Scott Fosler, ed., *The New Economic Role of American States* (New York: Oxford University Press, 1988).

13. Anita A. Summers and Thomas F. Luce, *Economic Development within the Philadelphia Metropolitan Area* (Philadelphia: University of Pennsylvania Press, 1987), p. 2.

14. During the Depression, many families were able to subsist on their own farm products and to support unemployed relatives who returned from the city. This buffer or safety valve would be far less significant in a future major economic downturn.

15. Sternlieb et al., *Demographic Trends and Economic Reality*, p. 133.

16. Ibid., p. 133.

17. Bureau of the Census, Special Studies, ser. P-23, no. 150, *Population Profile of the United States, 1984–85* (Washington, D.C.: GPO, 1987), p. 2.

18. William Alonso, "Migration and Population Distribution in the United States," prepared for the Committee for Economic Development Project on Policy Implications of Demographic Change, July 1987, p. 8.

19. Ibid., p. 6.

20. Ibid., p. 7.

21. See David B. Walker, "Metropolitan Cooperation and Governance: The Governmental Dimensions," prepared for the 92nd annual meeting of the National Municipal League, Kansas City, Nov. 8, 1986, p. 24. Walker has identified 17 approaches to regional service delivery:

1. Informal cooperation
2. Extraterritorial powers
3. Interlocal service contracts
4. Joint powers agreements
5. Regional councils
6. Federally encouraged substate districts
7. State planning and development districts
8. Contracting out
9. Local special districts
10. Transfer of functions
11. Annexation
12. Regional special districts and authorities
13. Metropolitan multipurpose district
14. Reformed urban county
15. One-tier consolidations
16. Two-tier restructurings
17. Three-tier reforms

22. Timothy J. Bartik, Charles Becker, Steve Lake, and John Bush, "Saturn: Implications for State Economic Development Policies"; Anthony Borden, "Saturn: Union and Community Issues"; and William F. Fox and C. Warren Neel, "Saturn: The Tennessee Lessons," in the *Forum for Applied Research and Public Policy* 2, no. 1 (Spring 1987).

23. Parts of this section are taken from R. Scott Fosler, "Demography and Jobs in Southern California" (Washington, D.C.: Committee for Economic Development, 1989).

24. Figures for the Los Angeles region are for the five counties of Los Angeles, San Bernadino, Riverside, Ventura, and Orange, based on data in *Los Angeles 2000: A City for the Future,* published by the Los Angeles 2000 Committee, 1988. Data for California as a whole are based on Peter A. Morrison and Judith Payne, "Ethnic and Racial Profile of California," excerpted from Judith Payne, *Public Libraries Face California's Ethnic and Racial Diversity,* R-3635-Jul. (Santa Monica, Calif.: Rand Corporation, May 1988).

25. Kevin F. McCarthy and R. Burciaga Valdez, *Current and Future Effects of Mexican Immigration in California,* Executive Summary (Santa Monica, Calif.: Rand Corporation, November 1985).

26. For a description of some of these forces in geographical context, see E. W. Soja and A. J. Scott, "Los Angeles: Capital of the Twentieth Century," *Society and Space* 4 (1986), 249–54.

27. Sandra H. Berry, *Los Angeles Today and Tomorrow: Results of the Los Angeles 2000 Community Survey,* R-3705-LA2000 (Santa Monica, Calif.: Rand Corporation, October 1988), p. 20.

CHAPTER 13
INSTITUTIONAL STRESS AND OPPORTUNITY

1. Executive Office of the President, Office of Management and Budget, *Budget of the United States Government 1989* (Washington, D.C.: GPO, 1988), pp. 2a–3.

2. Ibid., historical tables; and projections of the Congressional Budget Office.

3. Executive Office of the President, Office of Management and Budget, *Special Analyses: Budget of the United States Government 1989,* p. J33.

4. Ibid.

5. R. Scott Fosler, ed., *The New Economic Role of American States* (New York: Oxford University Press, 1988).

About the Authors

R. Scott Fosler, M.P.A., is vice-president and director of government studies for the Committee for Economic Development in Washington, D.C. He is also a senior fellow at the Institute for Policy Studies, Johns Hopkins University. Mr. Fosler served as co-director of CED's project on demographic trends, whose research resulted in the papers in this volume; as co-director of CED's project on demographics and jobs; as director of CED's project on state economic progress; and as advisor to CED's projects on fiscal, trade, and competitiveness, risk management, education, and tax policy. He has served as a consultant to government, business, and private organizations at all levels in the United States and abroad. Mr. Fosler has authored numerous publications on state, local, and regional issues; productivity; economic development; and public-private partnership. He is the editor of *The New Economic Role of American States: Strategies in a Competitive World Economy* (Oxford University Press, 1988).

William Alonso, Ph.D., is Richard Saltonstall Professor of Population Policy at Harvard University. He has served as an advisor to many private and public institutions, including the World Bank, the United Nations, the National Academy of Sciences, the Ford Foundation, the Urban Institute, the U.S. Department of Commerce, Department of Agriculture, and Department of Housing and Urban Development. In addition to his work in the United States, Dr. Alonso has consulted in Australia, Canada, Europe, the Far East, the Middle East, and South America. Dr. Alonso is the editor of *Population in an Interacting World* (Harvard University Press, 1988), and is co-editor, with Paul Starr, of *The Politics of Numbers* (Russell Sage Foundation, 1988).

Jack A. Meyer, Ph.D., is president and founder of New Directions for Policy, a research and policy analysis organization in Washington, D.C., that studies social welfare and health care reform issues. He served as co-director of CED's project on demographic trends, which led to this volume; co-director of CED's project on demographics and jobs; counselor to CED's project on risk management; and co-director of CED's project on health policy. In addition to his work with CED, Dr. Meyer has prepared numerous studies of health policy alternatives for government, business, and the foundation community. He is the principal author of *The Common Good: Social Welfare and the American Future,* a comprehensive report on America's social policy published by the Ford Foundation in 1989. From 1981 to 1986, he was the director of the Center for Health Policy Research at the American Enterprise Institute.

ROSEMARY KERN, M.Sc., is vice-president of the Economic and Social Research Institute, a nonprofit research organization in Reston, Virginia, that provides public policy analysis of human resource and health care issues. She is also a consultant to New Directions for Policy in Washington, D.C. Recent studies conducted by Ms. Kern include an evaluation of programs for disadvantaged youth, an analysis of the dual impact of mandated health benefits and proposed increases in the minimum wage, a model for alternative health care delivery systems, and identification of strategies to contain health care costs.

Pitt Series in Policy and Institutional Studies

BERT A. ROCKMAN, EDITOR